INTRODUCTION

In the Spring of 2016 a small group of friends decided to have a Facebook Bible study through the book of **Psalms**. This study would be joined by people from all over the world. Over a period of 186 weeks we read through the entire book and focused on a verse or two each week. The most verses read in a day are 23. I believe each devotional can easily be read in 10 minutes or less.

We received some very encouraging feedback from those who were involved in our study. Some said that there were certain days that the devotional was exactly what they needed for that day. Others told of how they had seen things in the **Psalms** that they had never seen before. One lady, who had read through the **Psalms** many times, commented that it was as if she was reading them again for the first time.

It is my prayer that your time reading through the **Psalms** will give you comfort, encouragement, blessing and insight into how much our LORD loves you. Be blessed as you make your ways through the **Psalms**!

The *King James Version* (**KJV**) version is used in this study unless otherwise noted. Other translations used include:

CJB – *Complete Jewish Bible*
NASB – *New American Standard Bible*
NIV – *New International Version*
NLT – *New Living Translation*

DAY #1

READ Psalm 1 (*6 verses*)

*1 Blessed is the man that walketh not in the counsel of the
ungodly, nor standeth in the way of sinners, nor sitteth in the seat
of the scornful. 2 But his delight is in the law of the LORD;
and in his law doth he meditate day and night. 3 And he shall be
like a tree planted by the rivers of water, that bringeth forth his
fruit in his season; his leaf also shall not wither; and whatsoever
he doeth shall prosper. 4 The ungodly are not so: but are like the
chaff which the wind driveth away. 5 Therefore the ungodly shall
not stand in the judgment, nor sinners in the congregation of the
righteous. 6 For the LORD knoweth the way of the righteous:
but the way of the ungodly shall perish.*

VERSES OF THE DAY: Psalm 1:1-2
'Blessed is the man that walketh not in the counsel of the ungodly, nor standeth in the way of sinners, nor sitteth in the seat of the scornful. But his delight is in the law of the LORD; and in his law doth he meditate day and night.'

These verses state the practice of the blessed man. We see 3 positions: walking, standing and sitting. There is a procession: first you walk, then you stand (*stopping to check something out*), finally you sit (*participating comfortably*). The blessed man walks NOT, stands NOT, sits NOT with the godless (**Proverbs 14:12, Proverbs 16:2**). Instead he finds his delight, his joy, in the Lord and His Word. The word '*meditate*' is a very figurative word picturing a cow chewing its cud. May our study in **Psalms** draw you to '*chew on the Word*' throughout your day!

# # # # #

Saturdays in Psalms
Matthew Eckel

TTGOG

DAY #2

READ Psalm 2 (*12 verses*)

1 *Why do the heathen rage, and the people imagine a vain*
thing? **2** *The kings of the earth set themselves, and the rulers take*
counsel together, against the LORD, and against his
anointed, saying, **3** *Let us break their bands asunder, and cast*
away their cords from us. **4** *He that sitteth in the heavens shall*
laugh: the Lord shall have them in derision. **5** *Then shall he*
speak unto them in his wrath, and vex them in his sore
displeasure. **6** *Yet have I set my king upon my holy hill of Zion.*
7 *I will declare the decree: the LORD hath said unto me,*
Thou art my Son; this day have I begotten thee. **8** *Ask of me, and*
I shall give thee the heathen for thine inheritance, and the
uttermost parts of the earth for thy possession. **9** *Thou shalt*
break them with a rod of iron; thou shalt dash them in pieces like
a potter's vessel. **10** *Be wise now therefore, O ye kings:*
be instructed, ye judges of the earth. **11** *Serve the LORD with*
fear, and rejoice with trembling. **12** *Kiss the Son, lest he be*
angry, and ye perish from the way, when his wrath is kindled but
a little. Blessed are all they that put their trust in him.

VERSE OF THE DAY: Psalm 2:11
'Serve the LORD with fear, and rejoice with trembling.'

'*Fear*' in this verse means '*a holy reverence.*' '*Trembling*' has to do with an anxiety to strive for success. It is our duty to have a deep respect and awe for our LORD and desire to live for Him daily. Rejoice my friend, we serve the one true God! Strive every day to live for Him!

# # # # #

DAY #3

READ Psalm 3 (*8 verses*)

1 LORD, how are they increased that trouble me! many are they
that rise up against me. 2 Many there be which say of my
soul, There is no help for him in God. Selah. 3 But thou,
O LORD, art a shield for me; my glory, and the lifter up of mine
head. 4 I cried unto the LORD with my voice, and he heard me
out of his holy hill. Selah. 5 I laid me down and slept; I awaked;
for the LORD sustained me. 6 I will not be afraid of ten thousands
of people, that have set themselves against me round
about. 7 Arise, O LORD; save me, O my God: for thou hast
smitten all mine enemies upon the cheek bone; thou hast broken
the teeth of the ungodly. 8 Salvation belongeth unto the LORD:
thy blessing is upon thy people. Selah.

VERSE OF THE DAY: Psalm 3:5
'I laid me down and slept; I awaked; for the LORD sustained me.'

After time in battle David laid himself down to sleep. In the midst of strife he was able to sleep well for he knew who was watching over him. His sustainer was the LORD! When you go to bed tonight know that He cares for you (**I Peter 5:7**). Give your troubles and trials to Him and sleep well tonight. The LORD will sustain you, too!

# # # # #

DAY #4

READ Psalm 4 (*8 verses*)

1 Hear me when I call, O God of my righteousness: thou hast
enlarged me when I was in distress; have mercy upon me, and
hear my prayer. 2 O ye sons of men, how long will ye turn my
glory into shame? how long will ye love vanity, and seek after
leasing? Selah. 3 But know that the LORD hath set apart him that
is godly for himself: the LORD will hear when I call unto
him. 4 Stand in awe, and sin not: commune with your own heart
upon your bed, and be still. Selah. 5 Offer the sacrifices of
righteousness, and put your trust in the LORD. 6 There be many
that say, Who will shew us any good? LORD, lift thou up the light
of thy countenance upon us. 7 Thou hast put gladness in my heart,
more than in the time that their corn and their wine
increased. 8 I will both lay me down in peace, and sleep:
for thou, LORD, only makest me dwell in safety.

VERSE OF THE DAY: Psalm 4:3
'But know that the LORD hath set apart him that is godly for himself: the LORD will hear when I call unto him.'

There is comfort to be had in the knowledge that the LORD has set aside His people. He desires to hear from us! He loves to hear your praise, your worship, your thanks as well as your petitions. We are told to pray without ceasing (**I Thessalonians 5:17**). Take the LORD with you throughout your day – He will hear you whenever you call on Him!

# # # # #

DAY #5

READ Psalm 5 (*12 verses*)

*1 Give ear to my words, O LORD, consider my
meditation. 2 Hearken unto the voice of my cry, my King, and my
God: for unto thee will I pray. 3 My voice shalt thou hear in the
morning, O LORD; in the morning will I direct my prayer unto
thee, and will look up. 4 For thou art not a God that hath
pleasure in wickedness: neither shall evil dwell with
thee. 5 The foolish shall not stand in thy sight: thou hatest all
workers of iniquity. 6 Thou shalt destroy them that speak leasing:
the LORD will abhor the bloody and deceitful man. 7 But as for
me, I will come into thy house in the multitude of thy
mercy: and in thy fear will I worship toward thy holy
temple. 8 Lead me, O LORD, in thy righteousness because of
mine enemies; make thy way straight before my face. 9 For there
is no faithfulness in their mouth; their inward part is very
wickedness; their throat is an open sepulchre; they flatter with
their tongue. 10 Destroy thou them, O God; let them fall by their
own counsels; cast them out in the multitude of their
transgressions; for they have rebelled against thee. 11 But let all
those that put their trust in thee rejoice: let them ever shout for
joy, because thou defendest them: let them also that love thy name
be joyful in thee. 12 For thou, LORD, wilt bless the righteous;
with favour wilt thou compass him as with a shield.*

VERSE OF THE DAY: Psalm 5:8

'Lead me, O LORD, in thy righteousness because of mine enemies; make thy way straight before my face.'

Who are your enemies? Are there those that make your life difficult? How do you react to them? Jesus told us to love our enemies (**Matthew 5:44, Luke 6:27**). That is a tough thing to do. That is possible only if you are being led by our LORD. Follow Jesus – He will guide you amongst those who hate you. He will make a way!

# # # # #

DAY #6

READ Psalm 6 (*10 verses*)

*1 O LORD, rebuke me not in thine anger, neither chasten me in
thy hot displeasure. 2 Have mercy upon me, O LORD; for
I am weak: O LORD, heal me; for my bones are vexed. 3 My soul
is also sore vexed: but thou, O LORD, how long? 4 Return,
O LORD, deliver my soul: oh save me for thy mercies'
sake. 5 For in death there is no remembrance of thee: in the
grave who shall give thee thanks? 6 I am weary with my
groaning; all the night make I my bed to swim; I water my couch
with my tears. 7 Mine eye is consumed because of grief; it waxeth
old because of all mine enemies. 8 Depart from me, all ye workers
of iniquity; for the LORD hath heard the voice of my weeping.
9 The LORD hath heard my supplication; the LORD will receive
my prayer. 10 Let all mine enemies be ashamed and sore vexed:
let them return and be ashamed suddenly.*

VERSE OF THE DAY: Psalm 6:9
'The LORD hath heard my supplication; the LORD will receive my prayer.'

'*Supplication*' is to humbly petition the LORD. When we come to Him with a humble spirit, He will hear our prayer. A great example of a humble prayer is Jesus' prayer in the garden of Gethsemane on that first Good Friday, found in **Mark 14:36**: '*Abba, Father, all things are possible unto thee; take away this* *cup from me: nevertheless not what I will, but what thou wilt.*' As always, Jesus is our example.

What a humbling matter to know that the LORD of all creation hears our prayers. Take joy in knowing that your prayers are heard in the highest heaven!

# # # # #

DAY #7

READ Psalm 7 (*17 verses*)

1 O LORD my God, in thee do I put my trust: save me from all
them that persecute me, and deliver me:2 Lest he tear my soul
like a lion, rending it in pieces, while there is none to
deliver. 3 O LORD my God, if I have done this; if there be iniquity
in my hands; 4 If I have rewarded evil unto him that was at peace
with me; (yea, I have delivered him that without cause is mine
enemy:) 5 Let the enemy persecute my soul, and take it; yea, let
him tread down my life upon the earth, and lay mine honour in
the dust. Selah. 6 Arise, O LORD, in thine anger, lift up thyself
because of the rage of mine enemies: and awake for me to the
judgment that thou hast commanded. 7 So shall the congregation
of the people compass thee about: for their sakes therefore return
thou on high. 8 The LORD shall judge the people: judge me,
O LORD, according to my righteousness, and according to mine
integrity that is in me. 9 Oh let the wickedness of the wicked come
to an end; but establish the just: for the righteous God trieth the
hearts and reins. 10 My defence is of God, which saveth the
upright in heart. 11 God judgeth the righteous, and God is
angry with the wicked every day. 12 If he turn not, he will whet
his sword; he hath bent his bow, and made it ready. 13 He hath
also prepared for him the instruments of death; he ordaineth his
arrows against the persecutors. 14 Behold, he travaileth with
iniquity, and hath conceived mischief, and brought forth
falsehood. 15 He made a pit, and digged it, and is fallen into the
ditch which he made. 16 His mischief shall return upon his own

head, and his violent dealing shall come down upon his own pate. 17 *I will praise the LORD according to his righteousness: and will sing praise to the name of the LORD most high.*

VERSE OF THE DAY: Psalm 7:11

'God judgeth the righteous, and God is angry with the wicked every day.'

If we continue in sin we can be sure that God will discipline us. He has promised that He will chasten His own (**Hebrews 12:6**). If one can sin and not be corrected by the LORD, that person should consider whether or not they are of the faith. Have you ever wondered why nonbelievers seem to prosper while believers struggle? It is better to be corrected by a loving Heavenly Father today than judged by a righteous God as all nonbelievers will one day be judged. They will one day feel His wrath. It is a fearful thing to fall into the hands of the living God (**Hebrews 10:31**).

# # # # #

DAY #8

READ Psalm 8 (*9 verses*)

*1 O LORD our Lord, how excellent is thy name in all the earth!
who hast set thy glory above the heavens. 2 Out of the mouth of
babes and sucklings hast thou ordained strength because of thine
enemies, that thou mightest still the enemy and the avenger.
3 When I consider thy heavens, the work of thy fingers, the moon
and the stars, which thou hast ordained; 4 What is man, that thou
art mindful of him? and the son of man, that thou visitest
him? 5 For thou hast made him a little lower than the angels, and
hast crowned him with glory and honour. 6 Thou madest him to
have dominion over the works of thy hands; thou hast put
all things under his feet: 7 All sheep and oxen, yea, and the
beasts of the field; 8 The fowl of the air, and the fish of the
sea, and whatsoever passeth through the paths of the
seas. 9 O LORD our Lord, how excellent is thy name in all the
earth!*

VERSES OF THE DAY: Psalm 8:3-4

'When I consider thy heavens, the work of thy fingers, the moon and the stars, which thou hast ordained; What is man, that thou art mindful of him? and the son of man, that thou visitest him?'

We should be in awe when we look at the stars in the heavens. I saw online that the estimated number of stars in the universe is 1,000,000,000,000,000,000,000,000 – that's a septillion stars! We are told in Scripture that '*He breathed the word, and all the stars were born'* (**Psalm 33:6 NLT**). Our great Creator calls them all by name (**Psalm 147:4**). With that said how amazing it is that our Almighty God cares about us personally! WOW! The very hairs of our head are numbered – not counted! (**Luke 12:7**). To think that the Creator of the stars would come to earth to die for mankind – it is beyond our comprehension. I will never understand it, but I am forever grateful. May our contemplation on our personal God draw us to serve Him every day of our lives!

'He counts the stars and calls them all by name.'

(Psalm 147:4 NLT)

# # # # #

DAY #9

READ Psalm 9 (*20 verses*)

1 *I will praise thee, O LORD, with my whole heart; I will shew*
forth all thy marvellous works. ***2*** *I will be glad and rejoice in*
thee: I will sing praise to thy name, O thou most High. ***3*** *When*
mine enemies are turned back, they shall fall and perish at thy
presence. ***4*** *For thou hast maintained my right and my cause;*
thou satest in the throne judging right. ***5*** *Thou hast rebuked the*
heathen, thou hast destroyed the wicked, thou hast put out their
name for ever and ever. ***6*** *O thou enemy, destructions are come*
to a perpetual end: and thou hast destroyed cities; their memorial
is perished with them. ***7*** *But the LORD shall endure for ever:*
he hath prepared his throne for judgment. ***8*** *And he shall judge*
the world in righteousness, he shall minister judgment to the
people in uprightness. ***9*** *The LORD also will be a refuge for the*
oppressed, a refuge in times of trouble. ***10*** *And they that know thy*
name will put their trust in thee: for thou, LORD, hast not
forsaken them that seek thee. ***11*** *Sing praises to the LORD,*
which dwelleth in Zion: declare among the people his
doings. ***12*** *When he maketh inquisition for blood, he*
remembereth them: he forgetteth not the cry of the
humble. ***13*** *Have mercy upon me, O LORD; consider my*
trouble which I suffer of them that hate me, thou that liftest me up
from the gates of death: ***14*** *That I may shew forth all thy praise*
in the gates of the daughter of Zion: I will rejoice in thy
salvation. ***15*** *The heathen are sunk down in the pit that they*
made: in the net which they hid is their own foot
taken. ***16*** *The LORD is known by the judgment which he*
executeth: the wicked is snared in the work of his own hands.
Higgaion. Selah. ***17*** *The wicked shall be turned into hell, and all*
the nations that forget God. ***18*** *For the needy shall not alway be*

forgotten: the expectation of the poor shall not perish for
ever. **19** *Arise, O LORD; let not man prevail: let the heathen be*
judged in thy sight. **20** *Put them in fear, O LORD: that the*
nations may know themselves to be but men. Selah.

VERSES OF THE DAY: Psalm 9:7-8

'But the LORD shall endure for ever: he hath prepared his throne for judgment. And he shall judge the world in righteousness, he shall minister judgment to the people in uprightness.'

We live in a world that wants a warm and fuzzy God, one who loves everyone in spite of their violation of His commands. God is love, but he is also just. To not understand that He is just is to not know the God of Scripture. He is the ultimate Judge who will judge justly (**Genesis 18:25; Exodus 5:21; Judges 11:27; I Samuel 2:10; I Samuel 24:12, 15; I Chronicles 16:33; II Chronicles 20:12; Psalm 7:11; Psalm 9:8; Psalm 35:24; Psalm 50:1, 4, 6; Psalm 51:4, Psalm 67:4; Psalm 75:7; Psalm 82:8; Psalm 94:2; Psalm 96:1, 10, 13; Psalm 98:9; Psalm 110:6; Psalm 135:14; Ecclesiastes 3:17; Isaiah 2:4; Isaiah 3:3; Isaiah 11:4; Isaiah 33:22; Lamentations 3:59; Ezekiel 7:3, 8, 27; Ezekiel 11:10, 11; Ezekiel 16:38; Ezekiel 18:30; Ezekiel 21:30; Ezekiel 24:14; Ezekiel 33:20; Ezekiel 34:17, 20, 22; Ezekiel 35:11; Micah 4:3; Micah 5:1; Acts 7:7; Acts 10:42; Acts 17:31; Romans 2:6; Romans 3:6; II Timothy 4:1,8; Hebrews 10:30; Hebrews 12:23; Hebrews 13:4; James 4:12; I Peter 4:5**).

How wonderful to be forgiven through the blood of Jesus, knowing that we will not have to face the wrath of a just God! He shall endure forever!

# # # # #

DAY #10

READ Psalm 10 (*18 verses*)

1 *Why standest thou afar off, O LORD? why hidest thou thyself in*
times of trouble? **2** *The wicked in his pride doth persecute the*
poor: let them be taken in the devices that they have
imagined. **3** *For the wicked boasteth of his heart's desire, and*
blesseth the covetous, whom the LORD abhorreth. **4** *The wicked,*
through the pride of his countenance, will not seek after God:
God is not in all his thoughts. **5** *His ways are always grievous;*
thy judgments are far above out of his sight: as for all his
enemies, he puffeth at them. **6** *He hath said in his heart, I shall not*
be moved: for I shall never be in adversity. **7** *His mouth is full of*
cursing and deceit and fraud: under his tongue is mischief and
vanity. **8** *He sitteth in the lurking places of the villages: in the*
secret places doth he murder the innocent: his eyes are privily set
against the poor. **9** *He lieth in wait secretly as a lion in his den:*
he lieth in wait to catch the poor: he doth catch the poor, when
he draweth him into his net. **10** *He croucheth, and humbleth*
himself, that the poor may fall by his strong ones. **11** *He hath said*
in his heart, God hath forgotten: he hideth his face; he will never
see it. **12** *Arise, O LORD; O God, lift up thine hand: forget not*
the humble. **13** *Wherefore doth the wicked contemn God? he hath*
said in his heart, Thou wilt not require it. **14** *Thou hast seen it;*
for thou beholdest mischief and spite, to requite it with thy hand:
the poor committeth himself unto thee; thou art the helper of the
fatherless. **15** *Break thou the arm of the wicked and the evil man:*
seek out his wickedness till thou find none. **16** *The LORD is King*

for ever and ever: the heathen are perished out of his land. **17** *LORD, thou hast heard the desire of the humble: thou wilt prepare their heart, thou wilt cause thine ear to hear:* **18** *To judge the fatherless and the oppressed, that the man of the earth may no more oppress.*

VERSE OF THE DAY: Psalm 10:17
'LORD, thou hast heard the desire of the humble: thou wilt prepare their heart, thou wilt cause thine ear to hear.'

I Peter 5:5 tells us that we are to be clothed in humility; He gives grace to the humble while resisting the proud. **James 4:6** reinforces this truth. When we clothe ourselves in humility it will be evident in every part of our life. He will lift us up! (**James 4:10, I Peter 5:6**). We will definitely have a more powerful prayer life. May we be humble before our loving God!

# # # # #

DAY #11

READ Psalm 11 (*7 verses*)

1 In the LORD put I my trust: how say ye to my soul, Flee as a
bird to your mountain? 2 For, lo, the wicked bend their bow,
they make ready their arrow upon the string, that they may privily
shoot at the upright in heart. 3 If the foundations be destroyed,
what can the righteous do? 4 The LORD is in his holy temple,
the LORD'S throne is in heaven: his eyes behold, his eyelids try,
the children of men. 5 The LORD trieth the righteous: but the
wicked and him that loveth violence his soul hateth. 6 Upon the
wicked he shall rain snares, fire and brimstone, and an horrible
tempest: this shall be the portion of their cup. 7 For the righteous
LORD loveth righteousness; his countenance doth behold the
upright.

VERSE OF THE DAY: Psalm 11:6
'Upon the wicked he shall rain snares, fire and brimstone, and an horrible tempest: this shall be the portion of their cup.'

The future for the wicked is dreadful. They will get what they deserve for rejecting Christ. In fact the default for every man today is that they are condemned already (**John 3:18**). That is the bad news. But there is good news: Jesus has made a way to be redeemed. For those of us who have found forgiveness and salvation in Christ, may we realize that our unsaved family members, coworkers, neighbors and friends are in store for a violent and Godless future. May we show compassion and share the love of Jesus so they may not have to face this horrible tempest! Lord, give us boldness to share Your gospel!

# # # # #

DAY #12

READ Psalm 12 (*8 verses*)

1 Help, LORD; for the godly man ceaseth; for the faithful fail
from among the children of men. 2 They speak vanity every one
with his neighbor: with flattering lips and with a double heart do
they speak. 3 The LORD shall cut off all flattering lips, and the
tongue that speaketh proud things: 4 Who have said, With our
tongue will we prevail; our lips are our own: who is lord over
us? 5 For the oppression of the poor, for the sighing of the needy,
now will I arise, saith the LORD; I will set him in safety from him
that puffeth at him. 6 The words of the LORD are pure
words: as silver tried in a furnace of earth, purified seven
times. 7 Thou shalt keep them, O LORD, thou shalt preserve them
from this generation for ever. 8 The wicked walk on every side,
when the vilest men are exalted.

VERSE OF THE DAY: Psalm 12:3
'The LORD shall cut off all flattering lips, and the tongue that speaketh proud things.'

Do you know anyone who constantly talks about how great they are? I am reminded of Muhammad Ali, who always voiced that he was the '*greatest of all time!*' God's Word tells us not to brag about ourselves (**Proverbs 27:1**). If there is any bragging to do, let someone else brag about you (**Proverbs 27:2**). God's Word also encourages us to brag on others when they are deserving (**Proverbs 3:27**). May we be like the Apostle Paul, who stated '*may it never be that I would boast, except in the cross of the Lord Jesus*' (**Galatians 6:14 NASB**).

# # # # #

DAY #13

READ Psalm 13 (*6 verses*)

*1 How long wilt thou forget me, O LORD? for ever? how long
wilt thou hide thy face from me? 2 How long shall I take counsel
in my soul, having sorrow in my heart daily? how long shall mine
enemy be exalted over me? 3 Consider and hear me, O LORD my
God: lighten mine eyes, lest I sleep the sleep of death; 4 Lest mine
enemy say, I have prevailed against him; and those that trouble
me rejoice when I am moved. 5 But I have trusted in thy mercy;
my heart shall rejoice in thy salvation. 6 I will sing unto the
LORD, because he hath dealt bountifully with me.*

VERSE OF THE DAY: Psalm 13:5
'But I have trusted in thy mercy; my heart shall rejoice in thy salvation.'

'*Mercy*' is defined as '*compassionate or kindly forbearance shown toward an offender, an enemy, or other person in one's power.*' How merciful was Jesus that he would die for sinners like us! (**Romans 5:8**). When we realize how sinful we are and how merciful He is toward us we must be caused to rejoice in His great salvation. In our original study we looked at this passage the day after Good Friday, the day that we remember our Lord's sacrificial death. But tomorrow is coming; Easter Sunday, Resurrection Day, is tomorrow! We serve a risen Savior indeed! Thank You, Lord Jesus, for the great salvation You purchased with Your blood. Thank You, Lord Jesus, for being merciful unto a sinner like me. Rejoice, my friend. Tomorrow the grave will be empty!

# # # # #

DAY #14

READ Psalm 14 (*7 verses*)

*1 The fool hath said in his heart, There is no God. They are
corrupt, they have done abominable works, there is none that
doeth good. 2 The LORD looked down from heaven upon the
children of men, to see if there were any that did
understand, and seek God. 3 They are all gone aside, they
are all together become filthy: there is none that doeth good,
no, not one. 4 Have all the workers of iniquity no knowledge?
who eat up my people as they eat bread, and call not upon the
LORD. 5 There were they in great fear: for God is in the
generation of the righteous. 6 Ye have shamed the counsel of the
poor, because the LORD is his refuge. 7 Oh that the salvation of
Israel were come out of Zion! when the LORD bringeth back the
captivity of his people, Jacob shall rejoice, and Israel shall be
glad.*

VERSE OF THE DAY: Psalm 14:1

'The fool hath said in his heart, There is no God. They are corrupt, they have done abominable works, there is none that doeth good.'

I've heard it said many times that April 1st - APRIL FOOL's DAY - is NATIONAL ATHEISTS DAY because of this verse. How sad that some people do not recognize the existence of God. I love how Easter this year was on April 1st. The fool says that there is no God, yet on Easter morning He rose from the grave!

Psalm 19:1 states that '*the heavens declare the glory of God; and the firmament sheweth his handywork.*' All of creation screams the existence of our awesome Creator God! Think of those today who would deny the existence of God and pray that they may come to know Him and the love, peace, mercy, joy, forgiveness and salvation that is provided in Jesus Christ alone!

# # # # #

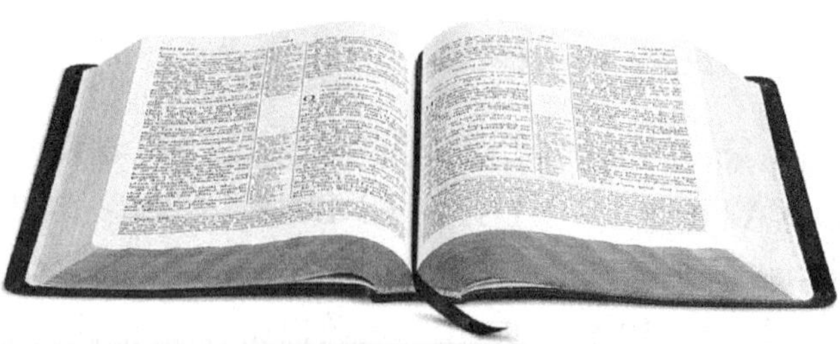

DAY #15

READ Psalm 15 (*5 verses*)

1 *LORD, who shall abide in thy tabernacle? who shall dwell in*
thy holy hill? 2 *He that walketh uprightly, and worketh*
righteousness, and speaketh the truth in his
heart. 3 *He that backbiteth not with his tongue, nor doeth evil to*
his neighbour, nor taketh up a reproach against his
neighbour. 4 *In whose eyes a vile person is contemned; but he*
honoureth them that fear the LORD. He that sweareth to his
own hurt, and changeth not. 5 *He that putteth not out his money*
to usury, nor taketh reward against the innocent. He that doeth
these things shall never be moved.

VERSES OF THE DAY: Psalm 15:1-2
'LORD, who shall abide in thy tabernacle? who shall dwell in thy holy hill? He that walketh uprightly, and worketh righteousness, and speaketh the truth in his heart.'

Three words are used in these verses to describe our spiritual activity: **walketh**, **worketh** and **speaketh**. As we walk through our daily lives we must be cognizant of our testimony before a lost world. As we go about our work we must realize that we need to work as unto the Lord (**Colossians 3:23**). Our conversation must be encouraging rather than condemning. As we live in a world that desperately needs Jesus, may they see our good works (*by our walk, our work and our speech*), and glorify our Father who is in heaven (**Matthew 5:16**).

# # # # #

DAY #16

READ Psalm 16 (*11 verses*)

1 *Preserve me, O God: for in thee do I put my trust.* ***2*** *O my soul,*
thou hast said unto the LORD, Thou art my Lord: my
goodness extendeth not to thee; ***3*** *But to the saints that are in the*
earth, and to the excellent, in whom is all my
delight. ***4*** *Their sorrows shall be multiplied that hasten after*
another god: their drink offerings of blood will I not offer, nor
take up their names into my lips. ***5*** *The LORD is the portion of*
mine inheritance and of my cup: thou maintainest my
lot. ***6*** *The lines are fallen unto me in pleasant places; yea, I have*
a goodly heritage. ***7*** *I will bless the LORD, who hath given me*
counsel: my reins also instruct me in the night seasons. ***8*** *I have*
set the LORD always before me: because he is at my right hand,
I shall not be moved. ***9*** *Therefore my heart is glad, and my glory*
rejoiceth: my flesh also shall rest in hope. ***10*** *For thou wilt not*
leave my soul in hell; neither wilt thou suffer thine Holy One to
see corruption. ***11*** *Thou wilt shew me the path of life: in thy*
presence is fulness of joy; at thy right hand there are pleasures
for evermore.

VERSE OF THE DAY: Psalm 16:1
'Preserve me, O God: for in thee do I put my trust.'

I'm sure you've heard people pray that God would put a hedge of protection around someone. The word '*preserve*' in this verse is the Hebrew word **shamar**, meaning *'to hedge about, to protect.'* When we trust in Him, He will be our protector. The **NLT** translates this verse as follows: '*Keep me safe, O God, for I have come to you for refuge.*' We can feel safe with the Lord God as our refuge!

# # # # #

DAY #17

READ Psalm 17 (*15 verses*)

*1 Hear the right, O LORD, attend unto my cry, give ear unto my
prayer, that goeth not out of feigned lips. 2 Let my sentence come
forth from thy presence; let thine eyes behold the things that are
equal. 3 Thou hast proved mine heart; thou hast visited me in the
night; thou hast tried me, and shalt find nothing; I am
purposed that my mouth shall not transgress. 4 Concerning the
works of men, by the word of thy lips I have kept me from the
paths of the destroyer. 5 Hold up my goings in thy paths, that my
footsteps slip not. 6 I have called upon thee, for thou wilt hear me,
O God: incline thine ear unto me, and hear my speech.
7 Shew thy marvellous lovingkindness, O thou that savest by thy
right hand them which put their trust in thee from those that rise
up against them. 8 Keep me as the apple of the eye, hide me under
the shadow of thy wings, 9 From the wicked that oppress
me, from my deadly enemies, who compass me
about. 10 They are inclosed in their own fat: with their mouth
they speak proudly. 11 They have now compassed us in our steps:
they have set their eyes bowing down to the earth; 12 Like as a
lion that is greedy of his prey, and as it were a young lion lurking
in secret places. 13 Arise, O LORD, disappoint him, cast him
down: deliver my soul from the wicked, which is thy
sword: 14 From men which are thy hand, O LORD, from men of
the world, which have their portion in this life, and whose belly
thou fillest with thy hid treasure: they are full of children, and
leave the rest of their substance to their babes. 15 As for me,*

I will behold thy face in righteousness: I shall be satisfied, when I awake, with thy likeness.

VERSE OF THE DAY: Psalm 17:5
'Hold up my goings in thy paths, that my footsteps slip not.'

Life can be a rocky road. Satan will do everything he can to put detours and temptations in your path. It is vital that we are on HIS path, not Satan's. To stay on HIS path we must spend time daily with HIM. How vital to spend time daily in HIS Word, our owner's manual for life, as well as time daily in prayer. We must follow HIM with all our heart. '*Trust in the LORD with all thine heart, and lean not unto thine own understanding. In all thy ways acknowledge him, and he shall direct thy paths.*' (**Proverbs 3:5-6**). If we follow HIM, HE will keep our footsteps firm.

# # # # #

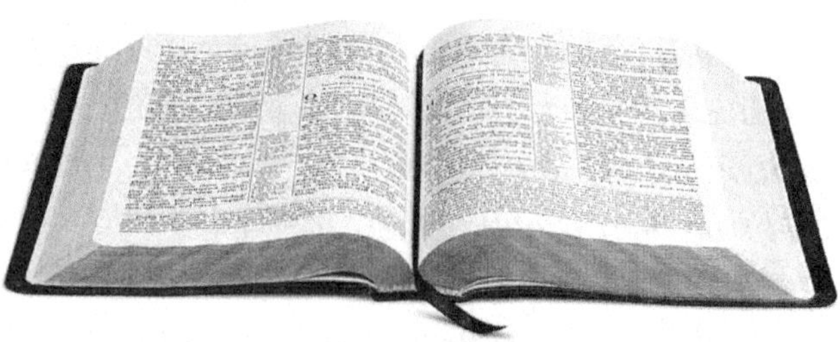

DAY #18

READ Psalm 18:1-14 (*14 verses*)

*1 I will love thee, O LORD, my strength. 2 The LORD is my rock,
and my fortress, and my deliverer; my God, my strength, in whom
I will trust; my buckler, and the horn of my salvation, and my
high tower. 3 I will call upon the LORD, who is worthy to be
praised: so shall I be saved from mine enemies. 4 The sorrows of
death compassed me, and the floods of ungodly men made me
afraid. 5 The sorrows of hell compassed me about: the snares of
death prevented me. 6 In my distress I called upon the LORD, and
cried unto my God: he heard my voice out of his temple, and my
cry came before him, even into his ears. 7 Then the earth shook
and trembled; the foundations also of the hills moved and were
shaken, because he was wroth. 8 There went up a smoke out of his
nostrils, and fire out of his mouth devoured: coals were kindled
by it. 9 He bowed the heavens also, and came down: and
darkness was under his feet. 10 And he rode upon a cherub, and
did fly: yea, he did fly upon the wings of the wind. 11 He made
darkness his secret place; his pavilion round about
him were dark waters and thick clouds of the skies. 12 At the
brightness that was before him his thick clouds passed,
hail stones and coals of fire. 13 The LORD also thundered in the
heavens, and the Highest gave his voice; hail stones and coals of
fire. 14 Yea, he sent out his arrows, and scattered them; and he
shot out lightnings, and discomfited them.*

VERSE OF THE DAY: Psalm 18:2
'The LORD is my rock, and my fortress, and my deliverer; my God, my strength, in whom I will trust; my buckler, and the horn of my salvation, and my high tower.'

It is hard to find a verse in Scripture that better describes how mighty our LORD is as our protector. Rock, fortress, deliverer, strength, buckler, horn and high tower. Do you ever worry? Do you ever wonder if God hears your prayers? Take heart, my friend. Our God is more than able to provide all your needs. Lean on Him, He is always there for you!

David's LORD is the **deliverer (II Samuel 22:2; Psalm 18:2; Psalm 34:1; Psalm 40:17; Psalm 70:5; Psalm 144:2**). He is our deliverer as well! May that encourage you today!

# # # # #

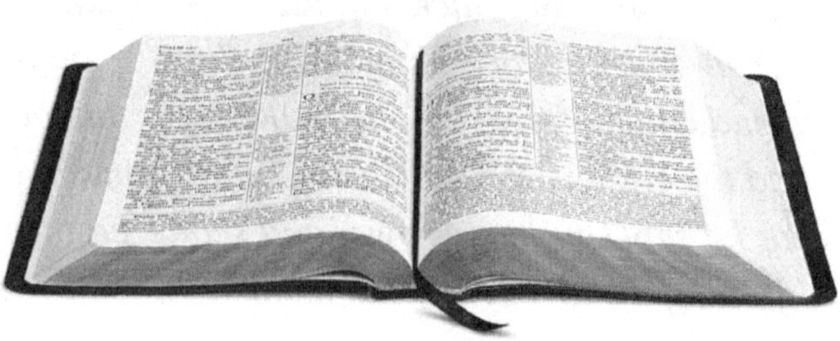

DAY #19

READ Psalm 18:15-32 (*18 verses*)

15 *Then the channels of waters were seen, and the foundations of*
the world were discovered at thy rebuke, O LORD, at the blast of
the breath of thy nostrils. **16** *He sent from above, he took me,*
he drew me out of many waters. **17** *He delivered me from my*
strong enemy, and from them which hated me: for they were too
strong for me. **18** *They prevented me in the day of my calamity:*
but the LORD was my stay. **19** *He brought me forth also into a*
large place; he delivered me, because he delighted in me.
20 *The LORD rewarded me according to my righteousness;*
according to the cleanness of my hands hath he recompensed
me. **21** *For I have kept the ways of the LORD, and have not*
wickedly departed from my God. **22** *For all his*
judgments were before me, and I did not put away his statutes
from me. **23** *I was also upright before him, and I kept myself from*
mine iniquity. **24** *Therefore hath the LORD recompensed me*
according to my righteousness, according to the cleanness of my
hands in his eyesight. **25** *With the merciful thou wilt shew thyself*
merciful; with an upright man thou wilt shew thyself
upright; **26** *With the pure thou wilt shew thyself pure; and with*
the froward thou wilt shew thyself froward. **27** *For thou wilt save*
the afflicted people; but wilt bring down high looks. **28** *For thou*
wilt light my candle: the LORD my God will enlighten my
darkness. **29** *For by thee I have run through a troop; and by my*
God have I leaped over a wall. **30** *As for God, his way is perfect:*
the word of the LORD is tried: he is a buckler to all those that

trust in him. 31 For who is God save the LORD? or who is a rock
save our God? 32 It is God that girdeth me with strength, and
maketh my way perfect.

VERSE OF THE DAY: Psalm 18:30
'As for God, his way is perfect: the word of the LORD is tried: he is a buckler to all those that trust in him.'

This is one of my favorite verses in the **Psalms**. When times are hard I rest on this verse knowing that God knows what I am going through. He has a plan for my life. His way for me is perfect. It is my obligation to be obedient and follow His way for my life. I can trust His Word because it has been tried and found to be faithful and true. He is a buckler, a shield, to all those who trust in Him. The Lord takes care of His own. Follow His path for you. Trust Him in all your ways and His perfect way will be made known in your life (**Proverbs 3:5-6**).

# # # # #

DAY #20

READ Psalm 18:33-50 (*18 verses*)

33 *He maketh my feet like hinds' feet, and setteth me upon my*
high places. **34** *He teacheth my hands to war, so that a bow of*
steel is broken by mine arms. **35** *Thou hast also given me the*
shield of thy salvation: and thy right hand hath holden me up, and
thy gentleness hath made me great. **36** *Thou hast enlarged my*
steps under me, that my feet did not slip. **37** *I have pursued mine*
enemies, and overtaken them: neither did I turn again till they
were consumed. **38** *I have wounded them that they were not able*
to rise: they are fallen under my feet. **39** *For thou hast girded me*
with strength unto the battle: thou hast subdued under me those
that rose up against me. **40** *Thou hast also given me the necks*
of mine enemies; that I might destroy them that hate
me. **41** *They cried, but there was none to save them: even unto*
the LORD, but he answered them not. **42** *Then did I beat them*
small as the dust before the wind: I did cast them out as the dirt
in the streets. **43** *Thou hast delivered me from the strivings of the*
people; and thou hast made me the head of the heathen:
a people whom I have not known shall serve me. **44** *As soon as*
they hear of me, they shall obey me: the strangers shall submit
themselves unto me. **45** *The strangers shall fade away, and be*
afraid out of their close places. **46** *The LORD liveth;*
and blessed be my rock; and let the God of my salvation be
exalted. **47** *It is God that avengeth me, and subdueth the people*
under me. **48** *He delivereth me from mine enemies: yea, thou*
liftest me up above those that rise up against me: thou hast
delivered me from the violent man. **49** *Therefore will I give*
thanks unto thee, O LORD, among the heathen, and sing praises
unto thy name. **50** *Great deliverance giveth he to his king;*

and sheweth mercy to his anointed, to David, and to his seed for evermore.

VERSE OF THE DAY: Psalm 18:46
'The LORD liveth; and blessed be my rock; and let the God of my salvation be exalted.'

In **Joshua 24:15**, Joshua admonished the Israelites to choose between the LORD God of Israel or the gods of the Amorites. The Amorites had many gods: El Elyon, their '*God Most High,*' was married to the mother goddess Athirat, the '*walker of the sea.*' Dagon was the god of crops, fertility and grain. He had a son (*Baal Hadad, master of thunder, god of the storm*) and a daughter (*Anat, virgin goddess of war and strife*) who were married to each. Incest among the gods? Anat killed Attar, the god of the morning star. They also had a god of all energies (*Baal Hammon*), god of plagues (*Resheph*), goddess of healing (*Eshmun*), goddess of love (*Qadeshtu*), goddess of marriage and pregnancy (*Kotharat*), god of craftsmanship (*Kothar-wa-Khasis*), god of the heavens (*Shamayim*), goddess of the sun (*Shapash*), god of the sea and the river (*Yaw*), god of righteousness and justice (*Sydyk*), god of fire (*Molech*) and god of death (*Mot*) just to name a handful. If El Elyon was their '*God Most High*' why is there a need for any of these other gods?

Today El Elyon is dead. Athirat is dead. Dagon is dead. Baal Hadad is dead. Anat is dead. Baal Hammon is dead. Resheph is dead. Eshmun is dead. Qadeshtu is dead. Kotharat is dead. Kothar-wa-Khasis is dead. Shamayim is dead. Shapash is dead. Yaw is dead. Sydyk is dead. Molech is dead. Attar has been dead for quite some time. Mot, the god of death, is dead. **Yet JESUS IS ALIVE!** We serve the one true living God! He is our rock and our strength! Joshua boldly exclaimed, '*As for me and my house we will serve the Lord.*' May we boldly do the same, exalting the God of our salvation today, every day for all our days! Amen and amen!

# # # # #

DAY #21

READ Psalm 19 (*14 verses*)

*1 The heavens declare the glory of God; and the firmament
sheweth his handywork. 2 Day unto day uttereth speech, and
night unto night sheweth knowledge. 3 There is no speech nor
language, where their voice is not heard. 4 Their line is gone out
through all the earth, and their words to the end of the world.
In them hath he set a tabernacle for the sun, 5 Which is as a
bridegroom coming out of his chamber, and rejoiceth as a strong
man to run a race. 6 His going forth is from the end of the
heaven, and his circuit unto the ends of it: and there is nothing
hid from the heat thereof. 7 The law of the LORD is perfect,
converting the soul: the testimony of the LORD is sure, making
wise the simple. 8 The statutes of the LORD are right, rejoicing
the heart: the commandment of the LORD is pure, enlightening
the eyes. 9 The fear of the LORD is clean, enduring for ever:
the judgments of the LORD are true and righteous
altogether. 10 More to be desired are they than gold, yea, than
much fine gold: sweeter also than honey and the
honeycomb. 11 Moreover by them is thy servant warned: and in
keeping of them there is great reward. 12 Who can
understand his errors? cleanse thou me from secret faults.
13 Keep back thy servant also from presumptuous sins; let them
not have dominion over me: then shall I be upright, and I shall
be innocent from the great transgression. 14 Let the words of my
mouth, and the meditation of my heart, be acceptable in thy sight,
O LORD, my strength, and my redeemer.*

VERSE OF THE DAY: Psalm 19:1
'The heavens declare the glory of God; and the firmament sheweth his handywork.'

The Bible begins with the great account of God's act of creation, yet the biblical account of creation does not stop there. The Old Testament supports the Genesis creation account in **Job 10:9; Job 38; Psalm 33:5-6; Psalm 104:24,30; Ecclesiastes 12:1** and **Jeremiah 31:35-36**. The New Testament is also full of passages that talk about the creation account: **Matthew 13:35; Matthew 24:21; Matthew 25:34; Mark 10:6; Mark 13:19; Luke 11:50; John 1:1-3; John 17:24; Acts 17:24; Romans 1:20; Romans 5:12-21; I Corinthians 11:8-9; I Corinthians 15:21,45,47; Ephesians 1:4; Ephesians 3:9; I Timothy 2:13; Hebrews 1:10; Hebrews 4:3; Hebrews 9:26; Hebrews 11:3; I Peter 1:20; II Peter 3:4; Revelation 3:14; Revelation 4:11; Revelation 13:8** and **Revelation 17:8**.

It is impossible to believe the Bible without believing in the Genesis creation account. Look around you – His handywork declares His glory! The heavens scream of the greatness of our Creator God! What an awesome God we serve!

# # # # #

DAY #22

READ Psalm 20 (*9 verses*)

1 The LORD hear thee in the day of trouble; the name of the God
of Jacob defend thee; 2 Send thee help from the sanctuary, and
strengthen thee out of Zion; 3 Remember all thy offerings, and
accept thy burnt sacrifice; Selah. 4 Grant thee according to thine
own heart, and fulfil all thy counsel. 5 We will rejoice in thy
salvation, and in the name of our God we will set up our banners:
the LORD fulfil all thy petitions. 6 Now know I that the LORD
saveth his anointed; he will hear him from his holy heaven with
the saving strength of his right hand. 7 Some trust in chariots,
and some in horses: but we will remember the name of the LORD
our God. 8 They are brought down and fallen: but we are risen,
and stand upright. 9 Save, LORD: let the king hear us when we
call.

VERSE OF THE DAY: Psalm 20:7
'Some trust in chariots, and some in horses: but we will remember the name of the LORD our God.'

We live in a world that measures success by the possessions you accumulate, whether that is the biggest house, the fastest car or the largest bank account. They say that he who dies with the most toys wins – but he still dies. The ungodly trust in worldly possessions, while the godly trust in the LORD! In what do you place your trust today?

'Lay not up for yourselves treasures upon earth, where moth and rust doth corrupt, and here thieves break through and steal. But lay yourselves treasures in heaven, where neither moth nor rust doth corrupt, and where thieves do not break through nor steal.' **(Matthew 6:19-20)**.

# # # # #

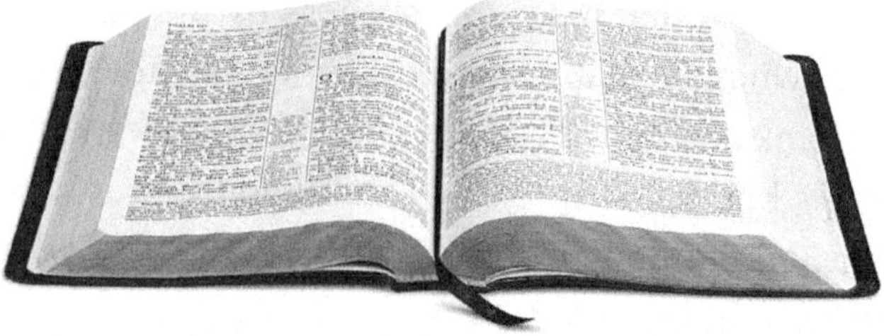

DAY #23

READ Psalm 21 (*13 verses*)

1 *The king shall joy in thy strength, O LORD; and in thy salvation*
how greatly shall he rejoice! **2** *Thou hast given him his heart's*
desire, and hast not withholden the request of his lips.
Selah. **3** *For thou preventest him with the blessings of goodness:*
thou settest a crown of pure gold on his head. **4** *He asked life of*
thee, and thou gavest it him, even length of days for ever and
ever. **5** *His glory is great in thy salvation: honour and majesty*
hast thou laid upon him. **6** *For thou hast made him most blessed*
for ever: thou hast made him exceeding glad with thy
countenance. **7** *For the king trusteth in the LORD, and through*
the mercy of the most High he shall not be moved. **8** *Thine hand*
shall find out all thine enemies: thy right hand shall find out those
that hate thee. **9** *Thou shalt make them as a fiery oven in the time*
of thine anger: the LORD shall swallow them up in his wrath,
and the fire shall devour them. **10** *Their fruit shalt thou destroy*
from the earth, and their seed from among the children of
men. **11** *For they intended evil against thee: they imagined a*
mischievous device, which they are not able to perform.
12 *Therefore shalt thou make them turn their back, when thou*
shalt make ready thine arrows upon thy strings against the face
of them. **13** *Be thou exalted, LORD, in thine own strength: so will*
we sing and praise thy power.

VERSE OF THE DAY: Psalm 21:13
'Be thou exalted, LORD, in thine own strength: so will we sing and praise thy power.'

Exodus 13:9 tells us that it was the strong hand of the LORD that brought His people out of Egypt. **Psalm 24:8** tells us that the LORD is strong and mighty (*we will look at that a little more this Friday*). We are instructed here to exalt Him, lift Him up, because of His strength and power. What a joy to sing to the mighty One! Praise Him today!

# # # # #

DAY #24

READ Psalm 22:1-22 (*22 verses*)

*1 My God, my God, why hast thou forsaken me? why art thou
so far from helping me, and from the words of my
roaring? 2 O my God, I cry in the daytime, but thou
hearest not; and in the night season, and am not
silent. 3 But thou art holy, O thou that inhabitest the praises of
Israel. 4 Our fathers trusted in thee: they trusted, and thou didst
deliver them. 5 They cried unto thee, and were delivered:
they trusted in thee, and were not confounded. 6 But I am a
worm, and no man; a reproach of men, and despised of the
people. 7 All they that see me laugh me to scorn: they shoot out
the lip, they shake the head, saying, 8 He trusted on the
LORD that he would deliver him: let him deliver him, seeing he
delighted in him. 9 But thou art he that took me out of the womb:
thou didst make me hope when I was upon my mother's
breasts. 10 I was cast upon thee from the womb: thou art my God
from my mother's belly. 11 Be not far from me;
for trouble is near; for there is none to help. 12 Many bulls have
compassed me: strong bulls of Bashan have beset me
round. 13 They gaped upon me with their mouths, as a ravening
and a roaring lion. 14 I am poured out like water, and all my
bones are out of joint: my heart is like wax; it is melted in the
midst of my bowels. 15 My strength is dried up like a potsherd;
and my tongue cleaveth to my jaws; and thou hast brought me
into the dust of death. 16 For dogs have compassed me:
the assembly of the wicked have inclosed me: they pierced my*

hands and my feet. **17** *I may tell all my bones: they look and stare*
upon me. **18** *They part my garments among them, and cast lots*
upon my vesture. **19** *But be not thou far from me, O LORD:*
O my strength, haste thee to help me. **20** *Deliver my soul from the*
sword; my darling from the power of the dog. **21** *Save me from*
the lion's mouth: for thou hast heard me from the horns of the
unicorns. **22** *I will declare thy name unto my brethren:*
in the midst of the congregation will I praise thee.

VERSE OF THE DAY: Psalm 22:11

'Be not far from me; for trouble is near; for there is none to help.'

Have you ever felt alone? Have you ever wondered if God was still there? We live in a world that is sinful; trouble lurks at every turn. We have no help other than the LORD. Trust Him, lean on Him, praise Him, thank Him. In times of trouble, He is our refuge.

'*God is our refuge and strength, a very present help in trouble.*' **(Psalm 46:1)**.

# # # # #

DAY #25

READ Psalm 22:23-31 (*9 verses*)

23 Ye that fear the LORD, praise him; all ye the seed of Jacob,
glorify him; and fear him, all ye the seed of Israel. 24 For he hath
not despised nor abhorred the affliction of the afflicted; neither
hath he hid his face from him; but when he cried unto him, he
heard. 25 My praise shall be of thee in the great congregation:
I will pay my vows before them that fear him. 26 The meek shall
eat and be satisfied: they shall praise the LORD that seek him:
your heart shall live for ever. 27 All the ends of the world shall
remember and turn unto the LORD: and all the kindreds of the
nations shall worship before thee. 28 For the kingdom is the
LORD'S: and he is the governor among the nations. 29 All they
that be fat upon earth shall eat and worship: all they that go down
to the dust shall bow before him: and none can keep alive his own
soul. 30 A seed shall serve him; it shall be accounted to the Lord
for a generation. 31 They shall come, and shall declare his
righteousness unto a people that shall be born, that he hath
done this.

VERSE OF THE DAY: Psalm 22:23
'Ye that fear the LORD, praise him; all ye the seed of Jacob, glorify him; and fear him, all ye the seed of Israel.'

To fear the LORD is to have a holy reverence. It is to show deep respect. When we have a holy reverence we will be led to give

Him glory. I am reminded of a great hymn written by Elisha Hoffman:

GLORY TO HIS NAME

Down at the cross where my Savior died
Down where for cleansing from sin I cried
There to my heart was the blood applied
Glory to His Name
I am so wondrously saved from sin
Jesus so sweetly abides within
There at the cross where He took me in
Glory to His Name

Oh, precious fountain that saves from sin
I am so glad I have entered in
There Jesus saves me and keeps me clean
Glory to His Name!

Come to this fountain so rich and sweet
Cast thy poor soul at the Savior's feet
Plunge in today, and be made complete
Glory to His Name!

# # # # #

DAY #26

READ Psalm 23 (*6 verses*)

1 The LORD is my shepherd; I shall not want. 2 He maketh me to
lie down in green pastures: he leadeth me beside the still
waters. 3 He restoreth my soul: he leadeth me in the paths of
righteousness for his name's sake. 4 Yea, though I walk through
the valley of the shadow of death, I will fear no evil:
for thou art with me; thy rod and thy staff they comfort
me. 5 Thou preparest a table before me in the presence of mine
enemies: thou anointest my head with oil; my cup runneth
over. 6 Surely goodness and mercy shall follow me all the days
of my life: and I will dwell in the house of the LORD for ever.

VERSE OF THE DAY: Psalm 23:6
'*Surely goodness and mercy shall follow me all the days of my life: and I will dwell in the house of the LORD for ever.*'

This is probably the most famous of all of the **Psalms**. It displays the LORD as the sovereign LORD; He is in complete control. He makes, leads, restores, prepares and anoints. **Verse 6** is the result of allowing the LORD to make, lead, restore, prepare and anoint: we will be blessed with goodness and mercy in this life and a blessed home in the next life. '*Surely*' is the Hebrew word **ak**, meaning '*a certainty*.' When we turn our life over to the Almighty God and allow Him to be the LORD of our life, goodness and mercy are certainties in this life and our eternal destination is sure forever. Have you yielded your life completely to Him?

# # # # #

DAY #27

READ Psalm 24 (*10 verses*)

*1 The earth is the LORD'S, and the fulness thereof; the world,
and they that dwell therein. 2 For he hath founded it upon the
seas, and established it upon the floods. 3 Who shall ascend into
the hill of the LORD? or who shall stand in his holy
place? 4 He that hath clean hands, and a pure heart; who hath
not lifted up his soul unto vanity, nor sworn deceitfully. 5 He shall
receive the blessing from the LORD, and righteousness from the
God of his salvation. 6 This is the generation of them that seek
him, that seek thy face, O Jacob. Selah. 7 Lift up your heads,
O ye gates; and be ye lift up, ye everlasting doors; and the King
of glory shall come in. 8 Who is this King of glory? The LORD
strong and mighty, the LORD mighty in battle. 9 Lift up your
heads, O ye gates; even lift them up, ye everlasting doors;
and the King of glory shall come in. 10 Who is this King of glory?
The LORD of hosts, he is the King of glory. Selah.*

VERSE OF THE DAY: Psalm 24:8
'Who is this King of glory? The LORD strong and mighty, the LORD mighty in battle.'

This verse asks us a question: Who is this King of glory? We are given a bold proclamation: it is the LORD who is strong and mighty! The title KING OF GLORY is seen in Scripture only three times – each time in the **24th Psalm (verses 8, 9 & 10)**. What a great title for our great God! He is the King that deserves honor and admiration. Who is this King of glory? **Verse 10** tells us: THE LORD OF HOSTS. The title '*LORD of hosts*'- first seen in **I Samuel 1:3** - occurs 261 times in the Old Testament, meaning the LORD of the armies of heaven. Of course He is mighty in battle!

DAY #28

READ Psalm 25 (*22 verses*)

1 *Unto thee, O LORD, do I lift up my soul.* **2** *O my God, I trust in*
thee: let me not be ashamed, let not mine enemies triumph over
me. **3** *Yea, let none that wait on thee be ashamed: let them be*
ashamed which transgress without cause. **4** *Shew me thy ways,*
O LORD; teach me thy paths. **5** *Lead me in thy truth, and teach*
me: for thou art the God of my salvation; on thee do I wait all the
day. **6** *Remember, O LORD, thy tender mercies and thy*
lovingkindnesses; for they have been ever of old. **7** *Remember*
not the sins of my youth, nor my transgressions: according to thy
mercy remember thou me for thy goodness' sake, O LORD.
8 *Good and upright is the LORD: therefore will he teach sinners*
in the way. **9** *The meek will he guide in judgment: and the meek*
will he teach his way. **10** *All the paths of the LORD are mercy*
and truth unto such as keep his covenant and his
testimonies. **11** *For thy name's sake, O LORD, pardon mine*
iniquity; for it is great. **12** *What man is he that feareth the*
LORD? him shall he teach in the way that he shall choose.
13 *His soul shall dwell at ease; and his seed shall inherit the*
earth. **14** *The secret of the LORD is with them that fear him;*
and he will shew them his covenant. **15** *Mine eyes are ever*
toward the LORD; for he shall pluck my feet out of the
net. **16** *Turn thee unto me, and have mercy upon me;*
for I am desolate and afflicted. **17** *The troubles of my heart are*
enlarged: O bring thou me out of my distresses. **18** *Look upon*
mine affliction and my pain; and forgive all my sins. **19** *Consider*

mine enemies; for they are many; and they hate me with cruel
hatred. **20** *O keep my soul, and deliver me: let me not be*
ashamed; for I put my trust in thee. **21** *Let integrity and*
uprightness preserve me; for I wait on thee. **22** *Redeem Israel,*
O God, out of all his troubles.

VERSE OF THE DAY: Psalm 25:7

'Remember not the sins of my youth, nor my transgressions: according to thy mercy remember thou me for thy goodness' sake, O LORD.'

Do you have anything in your past that you are embarrassed about? Did you have a godless youth? So many people have. What a blessing to know that when we humbly repent before a holy God, He is faithful and just to forgive us our sins and cleanse us from all unrighteousness (**I John 1:9**). He has removed our sin from us as far as the east is from the west (**Psalm 103:12**). **Micah 7:19** in the **NLT** says that our sins will be cast into the depths of the ocean. The deepest part of the ocean is approximately 36,200 feet deep – that's nearly 7 MILES! O, the LORD is good!

# # # # #

DAY #29

READ Psalm 26 (*12 verses*)

1 *Judge me, O LORD; for I have walked in mine integrity: I have*
trusted also in the LORD; therefore I shall not slide. 2 *Examine*
me, O LORD, and prove me; try my reins and my heart. 3 *For thy*
lovingkindness is before mine eyes: and I have walked in thy
truth. 4 *I have not sat with vain persons, neither will I go in with*
dissemblers. 5 *I have hated the congregation of evil doers;*
and will not sit with the wicked. 6 *I will wash mine hands in*
innocency: so will I compass thine altar, O LORD: 7 *That I may*
publish with the voice of thanksgiving, and tell of all thy
wondrous works. 8 *LORD, I have loved the habitation of thy*
house, and the place where thine honour dwelleth. 9 *Gather not*
my soul with sinners, nor my life with bloody men: 10 *In whose*
hands is mischief, and their right hand is full of bribes. 11 *But as*
for me, I will walk in mine integrity: redeem me, and be merciful
unto me. 12 *My foot standeth in an even place: in the*
congregations will I bless the LORD.

VERSE OF THE DAY: Psalm 26:7
'That I may publish with the voice of thanksgiving, and tell of all thy wondrous works.'

Do you have anything to be thankful for? I love the old hymn that Johnston Oatman, Jr. wrote in 1897: '*Count your blessings, name them one by one, and it will surprise you what the Lord hath done.*' Even with our perceived trials in life, we have so much to be thankful for. Have you ever shared with others what He has done for you? After all, He gave His life for you! Pray today and ask the LORD to allow you to share with someone today of the wondrous works the LORD has done for you!

DAY #30

READ Psalm 27 (*14 verses*)

*1 The LORD is my light and my salvation; whom shall I fear?
the LORD is the strength of my life; of whom shall I be
afraid? 2 When the wicked, even mine enemies and my foes,
came upon me to eat up my flesh, they stumbled and
fell. 3 Though an host should encamp against me, my heart shall
not fear: though war should rise against me, in this will I be
confident. 4 One thing have I desired of the LORD, that will I
seek after; that I may dwell in the house of the LORD all the days
of my life, to behold the beauty of the LORD, and to enquire in
his temple. 5 For in the time of trouble he shall hide me in his
pavilion: in the secret of his tabernacle shall he hide me; he shall
set me up upon a rock. 6 And now shall mine head be lifted up
above mine enemies round about me: therefore will I offer in his
tabernacle sacrifices of joy; I will sing, yea, I will sing praises
unto the LORD. 7 Hear, O LORD, when I cry with my voice:
have mercy also upon me, and answer me. 8 When thou saidst,
Seek ye my face; my heart said unto thee, Thy face, LORD,
will I seek. 9 Hide not thy face far from me; put not thy servant
away in anger: thou hast been my help; leave me not, neither
forsake me, O God of my salvation. 10 When my father and my
mother forsake me, then the LORD will take me up. 11 Teach me
thy way, O LORD, and lead me in a plain path, because of mine
enemies. 12 Deliver me not over unto the will of mine enemies:
for false witnesses are risen up against me, and such as breathe
out cruelty. 13 I had fainted, unless I had believed to see the*

goodness of the LORD in the land of the living. ***14*** *Wait on the LORD: be of good courage, and he shall strengthen thine heart: wait, I say, on the LORD.*

VERSE OF THE DAY: Psalm 27:14

'Wait on the LORD: be of good courage, and he shall strengthen thine heart: wait, I say, on the LORD.'

Have you ever had to wait for something? Have you ever prayed and wondered if God even heard your prayers? Sometimes He answers '**YES**', sometimes He answers '**NO**' and sometimes He answers '**WAIT**.' Each is an answer to prayer. Has the LORD had to teach you patience? I have been there! He will give you the courage and the strength to wait on Him. When you have to wait, remember **Psalm 18:30**: '*As for God, His way is perfect.*' He will make His perfect plan known to you in His perfect timing. Sometimes He desires that we wait on Him. Here He tells us TWICE to wait on Him. Take comfort: He knows, He is in control. He will do WHAT is best for you WHEN it is best for you. Wait on the LORD, wait on the LORD!

# # # # #

DAY #31

READ Psalm 28 (*9 verses*)

1 Unto thee will I cry, O LORD my rock; be not silent to me:
lest, if thou be silent to me, I become like them that go down into
the pit. 2 Hear the voice of my supplications, when I cry unto
thee, when I lift up my hands toward thy holy oracle. 3 Draw me
not away with the wicked, and with the workers of iniquity, which
speak peace to their neighbours, but mischief is in their
hearts. 4 Give them according to their deeds, and according to
the wickedness of their endeavours: give them after the work of
their hands; render to them their desert. 5 Because they regard
not the works of the LORD, nor the operation of his hands,
he shall destroy them, and not build them up. 6 Blessed be the
LORD, because he hath heard the voice of my
supplications. 7 The LORD is my strength and my shield;
my heart trusted in him, and I am helped: therefore my
heart greatly rejoiceth; and with my song will I praise
him. 8 The LORD is their strength, and he is the saving strength
of his anointed. 9 Save thy people, and bless thine inheritance:
feed them also, and lift them up for ever.

VERSE OF THE DAY: Psalm 28:7

'The LORD is my strength and my shield; my heart trusted in him, and I am helped: therefore my heart greatly rejoiceth; and with my song will I praise him.'

Do you rejoice in your LORD? David realized that the LORD was his strength, his shield and his help. He trusted in the LORD. He was quick to sing a song of praise to His LORD. Does that describe you?

'*Rejoice in the Lord always, and again I say, Rejoice.*' **(Philippians 4:4)**

# # # # #

DAY #32

READ Psalm 29 (*11 verses*)

1 Give unto the LORD, O ye mighty, give unto the LORD glory
and strength. 2 Give unto the LORD the glory due unto his name;
worship the LORD in the beauty of holiness. 3 The voice of the
LORD is upon the waters: the God of glory thundereth:
the LORD is upon many waters. 4 The voice of the LORD
is powerful; the voice of the LORD is full of majesty. 5 The voice
of the LORD breaketh the cedars; yea, the LORD breaketh the
cedars of Lebanon. 6 He maketh them also to skip like a calf;
Lebanon and Sirion like a young unicorn. 7 The voice of the
LORD divideth the flames of fire. 8 The voice of the LORD
shaketh the wilderness; the LORD shaketh the wilderness of
Kadesh. 9 The voice of the LORD maketh the hinds to calve, and
discovereth the forests: and in his temple doth every one speak
of his glory. 10 The LORD sitteth upon the flood; yea, the LORD
sitteth King for ever. 11 The LORD will give strength unto his
people; the LORD will bless his people with peace.

VERSE OF THE DAY: Psalm 29:11
'The LORD will give strength unto his people; the LORD will bless his people with peace.'

The LORD blesses His people with many things. One of those things is PEACE. Peace is defined as '*the freedom of the mind from annoyance, distraction, anxiety, etc.; tranquility; serenity.*' We live in a world of conflict where wars have been waged almost continually for thousands of years. We live in a world where people are at odds with each other every day. Billions of dollars are spent each year on mental health with California being the state with the most spent (*nearly $6.7 Billion in 2010*). People are seeking one thing: inner peace.The LORD freely gives peace to His people. What a blessing!

'*Thou wilt keep him in perfect peace, whose mind is stayed on thee: because he trusteth in thee.*' **(Isaiah 26:3)**

# # # # #

DAY #33

READ Psalm 30 (*12 verses*)

1 *I will extol thee, O LORD; for thou hast lifted me up, and hast*
not made my foes to rejoice over me. **2** *O LORD my God,*
I cried unto thee, and thou hast healed me. **3** *O LORD, thou hast*
brought up my soul from the grave: thou hast kept me alive, that
I should not go down to the pit. **4** *Sing unto the LORD, O ye saints*
of his, and give thanks at the remembrance of his
holiness. **5** *For his anger endureth but a moment; in his*
favour is life: weeping may endure for a night, but joy cometh in
the morning. **6** *And in my prosperity I said, I shall never be*
moved. **7** *LORD, by thy favour thou hast made my mountain*
to stand strong: thou didst hide thy face, and I was
troubled. **8** *I cried to thee, O LORD; and unto the LORD I made*
supplication. **9** *What profit is there in my blood, when I go down*
to the pit? Shall the dust praise thee? shall it declare thy truth?
10 *Hear, O LORD, and have mercy upon me: LORD, be thou my*
helper. **11** *Thou hast turned for me my mourning into dancing:*
thou hast put off my sackcloth, and girded me with
gladness; **12** *To the end that my glory may sing praise to thee,*
and not be silent. O LORD my God, I will give thanks unto thee
for ever.

VERSE OF THE DAY: Psalm 30:4
'Sing unto the LORD, O ye saints of his, and give thanks at the remembrance of his holiness.'

Easton's Bible Dictionary defines HOLINESS as follows: '*in the highest sense belongs to God* (**Isaiah 6:3; Revelation 15:4**), *and to Christians as consecrated to God's service, and in so far as they are conformed in all things to the will of God* (**Romans 6:19; Romans 6:22; Ephesians 1:4; Titus 1:8; 1 Peter 1:15**).' Holiness, being set apart for God, must be our goal.

'*Because it is written, Be ye holy; for I am holy*' (**I Peter 1:16**).

# # # # #

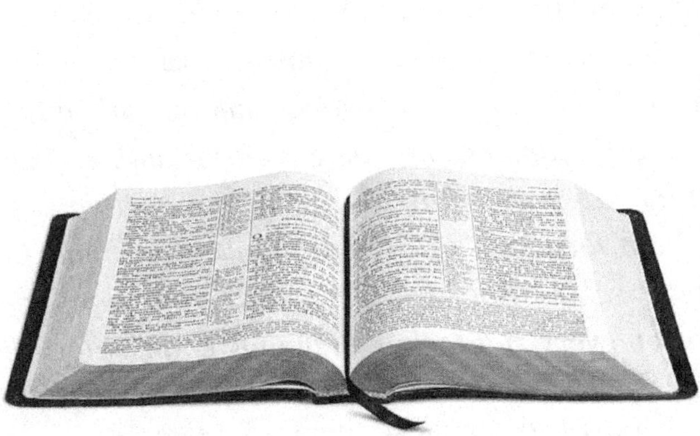

DAY #34

READ Psalm 31:1-15 (*15 verses*)

*1 In thee, O LORD, do I put my trust; let me never be ashamed:
deliver me in thy righteousness. 2 Bow down thine ear to me;
deliver me speedily: be thou my strong rock, for an house of
defence to save me. 3 For thou art my rock and my fortress;
therefore for thy name's sake lead me, and guide me. 4 Pull me
out of the net that they have laid privily for me: for thou art my
strength. 5 Into thine hand I commit my spirit: thou hast
redeemed me, O LORD God of truth. 6 I have hated them that
regard lying vanities: but I trust in the LORD. 7 I will be glad
and rejoice in thy mercy: for thou hast considered my trouble;
thou hast known my soul in adversities; 8 And hast not shut me
up into the hand of the enemy: thou hast set my feet in a large
room. 9 Have mercy upon me, O LORD, for I am in trouble: mine
eye is consumed with grief, yea, my soul and my belly. 10 For my
life is spent with grief, and my years with sighing: my strength
faileth because of mine iniquity, and my bones are
consumed. 11 I was a reproach among all mine enemies,
but especially among my neighbours, and a fear to mine
acquaintance: they that did see me without fled from
me. 12 I am forgotten as a dead man out of mind: I am like a
broken vessel. 13 For I have heard the slander of many:
fear was on every side: while they took counsel together against
me, they devised to take away my life. 14 But I trusted in thee,
O LORD: I said, Thou art my God. 15 My times are in thy hand:*

deliver me from the hand of mine enemies, and from them that persecute me.

VERSES OF THE DAY: Psalm 31:13-14
'For I have heard the slander of many: fear was on every side: while they took counsel together against me, they devised to take away my life. But I trusted in thee, O LORD: I said, Thou art my God.'

The one statement from my seminary schooling that stands out the most is the following shared by my professor in my Evangelism course: '*Of those who claim to be born again Christians, 75% will die never once sharing their faith.*' The #1 reason: **FEAR**. The worst that may happen to me in America by sharing my faith is that I may be mocked. In some nations today the real possible consequence of sharing Jesus is to be imprisoned and killed. People TODAY will kill someone simply because they are a Christian. Someone TODAY will be imprisoned simply for owning a Bible. While people in America are afraid that they will be '*persecuted*' we do not really understand what that entails. Scripture actually tells us that the believer is promised persecution (**II Timothy 3:12**). We should wear it as a badge of honor for our Great God! Put your trust fully in Him. He will be with you and give you the courage and strength to stand up for Him in every situation.

# # # # #

DAY #35

READ Psalm 31:16-24 (*9 verses*)

16 *Make thy face to shine upon thy servant: save me for thy*
mercies' sake. ***17*** *Let me not be ashamed, O LORD; for I have*
called upon thee: let the wicked be ashamed, and let them be
silent in the grave. ***18*** *Let the lying lips be put to silence; which*
speak grievous things proudly and contemptuously against the
righteous. ***19*** *Oh how great is thy goodness, which thou hast laid*
up for them that fear thee; which thou hast wrought for them that
trust in thee before the sons of men! ***20*** *Thou shalt hide them in*
the secret of thy presence from the pride of man: thou shalt keep
them secretly in a pavilion from the strife of
*tongues.****21*** *Blessed be the LORD: for he hath shewed me his*
marvellous kindness in a strong city. ***22*** *For I said in my haste,*
I am cut off from before thine eyes: nevertheless thou heardest
the voice of my supplications when I cried unto thee. ***23*** *O love*
the LORD, all ye his saints: for the LORD preserveth the faithful,
and plentifully rewardeth the proud doer. ***24*** *Be of good courage,*
and he shall strengthen your heart, all ye that hope in the LORD.

VERSE OF THE DAY: Psalm 31:24
'Be of good courage, and he shall strengthen your heart, all ye that hope in the LORD.'

On Day #34 we talked about having courage and strength. This is a great verse to remind us that those whose hope is in the LORD will definitely find courage and strength. We are admonished to rejoice in hope (**Romans 12:12**). In a world that has no hope we have JESUS (**I Timothy 1:1**)!

'*Now the God of hope fill you with all joy and peace in believing, that ye may abound in hope, through the power of the Holy Ghost*' (**Romans 15:13**).

'*Looking for that blessed hope, and the glorious appearing of the great God and our Saviour Jesus Christ*' (**Titus 2:13**).

# # # # #

DAY #36

READ Psalm 32 (*11 verses*)

1 Blessed is he whose transgression is forgiven, whose sin is
covered. 2 Blessed is the man unto whom the LORD imputeth not
iniquity, and in whose spirit there is no guile. 3 When I kept
silence, my bones waxed old through my roaring all the day
long. 4 For day and night thy hand was heavy upon me:
my moisture is turned into the drought of summer.
Selah. 5 I acknowledged my sin unto thee, and mine iniquity have
I not hid. I said, I will confess my transgressions unto the LORD;
and thou forgavest the iniquity of my sin. Selah. 6 For this shall
every one that is godly pray unto thee in a time when thou mayest
be found: surely in the floods of great waters they shall not come
nigh unto him. 7 Thou art my hiding place; thou shalt preserve
me from trouble; thou shalt compass me about with songs of
deliverance. Selah. 8 I will instruct thee and teach thee in the way
which thou shalt go: I will guide thee with mine eye. 9 Be ye not
as the horse, or as the mule, which have no understanding:
whose mouth must be held in with bit and bridle, lest they come
near unto thee. 10 Many sorrows shall be to the wicked:
but he that trusteth in the LORD, mercy shall compass him
about. 11 Be glad in the LORD, and rejoice, ye righteous:
and shout for joy, all ye that are upright in heart.

VERSE OF THE DAY: Psalm 32:1

'Blessed is he whose transgression is forgiven, whose sin is covered.'

What a blessing to know that our sins are forgiven! It still amazes me that a holy God would forgive my sins. They are covered and washed clean by the shed blood of Jesus. I humbly and gratefully shout a resounding AMEN! What a mighty, loving and forgiving God we serve!

'*Blessed are they whose iniquities are forgiven, and whose sins are covered*' (**Romans 4:7**).

# # # # #

DAY #37

READ Psalm 33 (*22 verses*)

*1 Rejoice in the LORD, O ye righteous: for praise is comely for
the upright. 2 Praise the LORD with harp: sing unto him with the
psaltery and an instrument of ten strings. 3 Sing unto him a new
song; play skilfully with a loud noise. 4 For the word of the
LORD is right; and all his works are done in truth. 5 He loveth
righteousness and judgment: the earth is full of the goodness of
the LORD. 6 By the word of the LORD were the heavens
made; and all the host of them by the breath of his
mouth. 7 He gathereth the waters of the sea together as an heap:
he layeth up the depth in storehouses. 8 Let all the earth fear the
LORD: let all the inhabitants of the world stand in awe of
him. 9 For he spake, and it was done; he commanded, and it
stood fast. 10 The LORD bringeth the counsel of the heathen
to nought: he maketh the devices of the people of none
effect. 11 The counsel of the LORD standeth for ever,
the thoughts of his heart to all generations. 12 Blessed is the
nation whose God is the LORD; and the people whom he hath
chosen for his own inheritance. 13 The LORD looketh from
heaven; he beholdeth all the sons of men. 14 From the place of
his habitation he looketh upon all the inhabitants of the
earth. 15 He fashioneth their hearts alike; he considereth all
their works. 16 There is no king saved by the multitude of an host:
a mighty man is not delivered by much strength. 17 An horse is a
vain thing for safety: neither shall he deliver any by his great
strength. 18 Behold, the eye of the LORD is upon them that fear*

him, upon them that hope in his mercy; **19** *To deliver their soul
from death, and to keep them alive in famine.* **20** *Our soul waiteth
for the LORD: he is our help and our shield.* **21** *For our heart
shall rejoice in him, because we have trusted in his holy
name.* **22** *Let thy mercy, O LORD, be upon us, according as we
hope in thee.*

VERSE OF THE DAY: Psalm 33:6
'By the word of the LORD were the heavens made; and all the host of them by the breath of his mouth.'

We see the phrase '*And God said*' many times in the Creation account in **Genesis 1 (verses 3, 6, 9, 11, 14, 20, 24, 26, 29)**. God created all things by His spoken word. Today's verse in the **NLT** says '*He breathed the word, and all the starts were born.*' We are told that He calls the stars by name **(Psalm 147:4)**.

Abraham was promised that his descendants would be '*as the stars of the heavens and as the sand which is on the seashore*' **(Genesis 22:17)**. A group of researchers from the University of Hawaii estimated the number of stars in the universe to be 70 thousand million, million, million (70,000,000,000,000,000,000,000). The estimated grains on sand on earth: seven quintillion, five hundred quadrillion (7,500,000,000,000,000,000). This means that there are more than 9,000 stars for every grain of sand! And to think that He spoke all the stars into existence and knows them individually! What a mighty Creator we serve!

# # # # #

DAY #38

READ Psalm 34 (*22 verses*)

1 *I will bless the LORD at all times: his praise shall continually be in my mouth.* **2** *My soul shall make her boast in the LORD: the humble shall hear thereof, and be glad.* **3** *O magnify the LORD with me, and let us exalt his name together.* **4** *I sought the LORD, and he heard me, and delivered me from all my fears.* **5** *They looked unto him, and were lightened: and their faces were not ashamed.* **6** *This poor man cried, and the LORD heard him, and saved him out of all his troubles.* **7** *The angel of the LORD encampeth round about them that fear him, and delivereth them.* **8** *O taste and see that the LORD is good: blessed is the man that trusteth in him.* **9** *O fear the LORD, ye his saints: for there is no want to them that fear him.* **10** *The young lions do lack, and suffer hunger: but they that seek the LORD shall not want any good thing.* **11** *Come, ye children, hearken unto me: I will teach you the fear of the LORD.* **12** *What man is he that desireth life, and loveth many days, that he may see good?* **13** *Keep thy tongue from evil, and thy lips from speaking guile.* **14** *Depart from evil, and do good; seek peace, and pursue it.* **15** *The eyes of the LORD are upon the righteous, and his ears are open unto their cry.* **16** *The face of the LORD is against them that do evil, to cut off the remembrance of them from the earth.* **17** *The righteous cry, and the LORD heareth, and delivereth them out of all their troubles.* **18** *The LORD is nigh unto them that are of a broken heart; and saveth such as be of a*

contrite spirit. **19** *Many are the afflictions of the righteous: but*
the LORD delivereth him out of them all. **20** *He keepeth all his*
bones: not one of them is broken. **21** *Evil shall slay the wicked:*
and they that hate the righteous shall be desolate. **22** *The LORD*
redeemeth the soul of his servants: and none of them that trust in
him shall be desolate.

VERSE OF THE DAY: Psalm 34:3
'O magnify the LORD with me, and let us exalt his name together.'

I have never understood how believers can come to church and refuse to sing during congregation worship. One man was overheard saying he never sang during a worship service because he wasn't a singer. God is not looking for singers, He is seeking worshippers! I may not have the best voice but I love to sing to my Lord! What a joy it is to come together every week with fellow believers in Christ and magnify the LORD and exalt His name together! Does the music in your church raise high the name of JESUS? I am thankful for the music in our church. I am encouraged each week as we worship the LORD together. Lift high the name of the King of Kings, and Lord of Lords – JESUS!

# # # # #

DAY #39

READ Psalm 35:1-15 (*15 verses*)

*1 Plead my cause, O LORD, with them that strive with me:
fight against them that fight against me. 2 Take hold of shield and
buckler, and stand up for mine help. 3 Draw out also the spear,
and stop the way against them that persecute me: say unto my
soul, I am thy salvation. 4 Let them be confounded and put to
shame that seek after my soul: let them be turned back
and brought to confusion that devise my hurt. 5 Let them be as
chaff before the wind: and let the angel of the LORD
chase them. 6 Let their way be dark and slippery: and let the
angel of the LORD persecute them. 7 For without cause have
they hid for me their net in a pit, which without cause they have
digged for my soul. 8 Let destruction come upon him at
unawares; and let his net that he hath hid catch himself: into that
very destruction let him fall. 9 And my soul shall be joyful in the
LORD: it shall rejoice in his salvation. 10 All my bones shall say,
LORD, who is like unto thee, which deliverest the poor from him
that is too strong for him, yea, the poor and the needy from him
that spoileth him? 11 False witnesses did rise up; they laid to my
charge things that I knew not. 12 They rewarded me evil for
good to the spoiling of my soul. 13 But as for me, when they were
sick, my clothing was sackcloth: I humbled my soul with fasting;
and my prayer returned into mine own bosom. 14 I behaved
myself as though he had been my friend or brother: I bowed
down heavily, as one that mourneth for his mother. 15 But in mine
adversity they rejoiced, and gathered themselves together: yea,*

the abjects gathered themselves together against me, and I knew it not; they did tear me, and ceased not:

VERSE OF THE DAY: Psalm 35:12

'They rewarded me evil for good to the spoiling of my soul.'

Have you ever been treated unfairly? I can't help but be reminded of the case of Joseph being sold into slavery by his own brothers (**Genesis 37:27-28**). What a terrible injustice, but Joseph realized that what his brothers meant for evil God meant for good (**Genesis 50:20**). God allowed this injustice so that many would be saved. What a great reflection of the gospel: Jesus was unjustly crucified so that we could have eternal life through His sacrificial death and resurrection.

When people reward you evil for good, take heart. God is in control. They may try to spoil your soul but God has a plan for your life. Trust that His plan will prevail in spite of our circumstances.

'*And we know that all things work together for good to them that love God, to them who are the called according to His purpose*' (**Romans 8:28**).

# # # # #

DAY #40

READ Psalm 35:16-28 (*13 verses*)

16 *With hypocritical mockers in feasts, they gnashed upon me*
with their teeth. ***17*** *Lord, how long wilt thou look on? rescue my*
soul from their destructions, my darling from the lions. ***18*** *I will*
give thee thanks in the great congregation: I will praise thee
among much people. ***19*** *Let not them that are mine enemies*
wrongfully rejoice over me: neither let them wink with the eye
that hate me without a cause. ***20*** *For they speak not peace:*
but they devise deceitful matters against them that are quiet in
the land. ***21*** *Yea, they opened their mouth wide against*
me, and said, Aha, aha, our eye hath seen it. ***22*** *This thou hast*
seen, O LORD: keep not silence: O Lord, be not far from
me. ***23*** *Stir up thyself, and awake to my judgment, even unto my*
cause, my God and my Lord. ***24*** *Judge me, O LORD my God,*
according to thy righteousness; and let them not rejoice over
me. ***25*** *Let them not say in their hearts, Ah, so would we have it:*
let them not say, We have swallowed him up. ***26*** *Let them be*
ashamed and brought to confusion together that rejoice at mine
hurt: let them be clothed with shame and dishonour that
magnify themselves against me. ***27*** *Let them shout for joy, and be*
glad, that favour my righteous cause: yea, let them say
continually, Let the LORD be magnified, which hath pleasure in
the prosperity of his servant. ***28*** *And my tongue shall speak of thy*
righteousness and of thy praise all the day long.

VERSE OF THE DAY: Psalm 35:28
'And my tongue shall speak of thy righteousness and of thy praise all the day long.'

The book of **James** gives us warnings about the tongue: it is little but boasts great things (**James 3:5**); it is a fire and a world of iniquity (**James 3:6**); it can defile the whole body (**James 3:6**); it cannot be tamed as is full of deadly poison (**James 3:8**). What our tongues says is a true reflection of what is in our heart, either good or bad (**Luke 6:45**). If our heart is right with God it will be reflected in our speech. Use your tongue to give God praise every day, throughout your day. May your tongue be busy praising God today!

# # # # #

DAY #41

READ Psalm 36 (*12 verses*)

*1 The transgression of the wicked saith within my heart, that
there is no fear of God before his eyes. 2 For he flattereth himself
in his own eyes, until his iniquity be found to be
hateful. 3 The words of his mouth are iniquity and deceit: he hath
left off to be wise, and to do good. 4 He deviseth mischief upon
his bed; he setteth himself in a way that is not good; he abhorreth
not evil. 5 Thy mercy, O LORD, is in the heavens; and thy
faithfulness reacheth unto the clouds. 6 Thy righteousness is like
the great mountains; thy judgments are a great deep: O LORD,
thou preservest man and beast. 7 How excellent is thy
lovingkindness, O God! therefore the children of men put their
trust under the shadow of thy wings. 8 They shall be abundantly
satisfied with the fatness of thy house; and thou shalt make them
drink of the river of thy pleasures. 9 For with thee is the fountain
of life: in thy light shall we see light. 10 O continue thy
lovingkindness unto them that know thee; and thy righteousness
to the upright in heart. 11 Let not the foot of pride come against
me, and let not the hand of the wicked remove me. 12 There are
the workers of iniquity fallen: they are cast down, and shall not
be able to rise.*

VERSE OF THE DAY: Psalm 36:7
'How excellent is thy lovingkindness, O God! therefore the children of men put their trust under the shadow of thy wings.'

Psalm 136 has 26 verses. Each verse in the **KJV** ends with the phrase, '*for his mercy endureth forever.*' Each of the 36 verses in **Psalm 136** in the **NASB** ends with the phrase. '*for his lovingkindness is everlasting.*' We serve a God whose lovingkindness, His mercy, is excellent. Have you put your complete trust in Him?

Four times in the **Psalms** we see the phrase, '*shadow of thy wings.*' In addition to here in **Psalm 36:7**, we see it also in the following verses:

- '*Keep me as the apple of the eye, hide me under the shadow of thy wings*' **(Psalm 17:8)**

- '*Be merciful unto me, O God, be merciful unto me: for my soul trusteth in thee: yea, in the shadow of thy wings will I make my refuge, until these calamities be overpast*' **(Psalm 57:7)**

- '*Because thou has been my help, therefore in the shadow of thy wings will I rejoice*' **(Psalm 63:7)**

We find refuge and help in the shadow of His wings. He watches over His own. Find your rest in Him. Now that is excellent lovingkindness toward us - what a wonderful and merciful God we serve!

# # # # #

DAY #42

READ Psalm 37:1-20 (*20 verses*)

*1 Fret not thyself because of evildoers, neither be thou envious
against the workers of iniquity. 2 For they shall soon be cut down
like the grass, and wither as the green herb. 3 Trust in the LORD,
and do good; so shalt thou dwell in the land, and verily thou shalt
be fed. 4 Delight thyself also in the LORD; and he shall give thee
the desires of thine heart. 5 Commit thy way unto the LORD;
trust also in him; and he shall bring it to pass. 6 And he shall
bring forth thy righteousness as the light, and thy judgment as the
noonday. 7 Rest in the LORD, and wait patiently for him:
fret not thyself because of him who prospereth in his way, because
of the man who bringeth wicked devices to pass. 8 Cease from
anger, and forsake wrath: fret not thyself in any wise to do evil.
9 For evildoers shall be cut off: but those that wait upon the
LORD, they shall inherit the earth. 10 For yet a little while, and
the wicked shall not be: yea, thou shalt diligently consider his
place, and it shall not be. 11 But the meek shall inherit the earth;
and shall delight themselves in the abundance of
peace. 12 The wicked plotteth against the just, and gnasheth
upon him with his teeth. 13 The Lord shall laugh at him:
for he seeth that his day is coming. 14 The wicked have drawn
out the sword, and have bent their bow, to cast down the poor
and needy, and to slay such as be of upright conversation.
15 Their sword shall enter into their own heart, and their bows
shall be broken. 16 A little that a righteous man hath is better
than the riches of many wicked. 17 For the arms of the wicked*

shall be broken: but the LORD upholdeth the righteous.
18 *The LORD knoweth the days of the upright: and their*
inheritance shall be for ever. **19** *They shall not be ashamed in the*
evil time: and in the days of famine they shall be
satisfied. **20** *But the wicked shall perish, and the enemies of the*
LORD shall be as the fat of lambs: they shall consume;
into smoke shall they consume away.

VERSE OF THE DAY: Psalm 37:18

'The LORD knoweth the days of the upright: and their inheritance shall be for ever.'

Some people worry about death. How comforting to know the LORD knows the number of our days. When it is our appointed time God will not be surprised. His people are in His hands. Are you making the most of the days He has given to you? We need to share the gospel while we have time. This life is short; it is as a vapor that is here for a little time then fades away (**James 4:14**). On the other hand eternity is long, and our inheritance shall be forever. Live your life with an eternal perspective!

# # # # #

DAY #43

READ Psalm 37:21-40 (*20 verses*)

21 *The wicked borroweth, and payeth not again: but the*
righteous sheweth mercy, and giveth. **22** *For such as be blessed*
of him shall inherit the earth; and they that be cursed of him shall
be cut off. **23** *The steps of a good man are ordered by the LORD:*
and he delighteth in his way. **24** *Though he fall, he shall not be*
utterly cast down: for the LORD upholdeth him with his
hand. **25** *I have been young, and now am old; yet have I not seen*
the righteous forsaken, nor his seed begging bread. **26** *He is ever*
merciful, and lendeth; and his seed is blessed. **27** *Depart from*
evil, and do good; and dwell for evermore. **28** *For the LORD*
loveth judgment, and forsaketh not his saints; they are
preserved for ever: but the seed of the wicked shall be cut
off. **29** *The righteous shall inherit the land, and dwell therein for*
ever. **30** *The mouth of the righteous speaketh wisdom, and his*
tongue talketh of judgment. **31** *The law of his God is in his heart;*
none of his steps shall slide. **32** *The wicked watcheth the*
righteous, and seeketh to slay him. **33** *The LORD will not leave*
him in his hand, nor condemn him when he is judged. **34** *Wait on*
the LORD, and keep his way, and he shall exalt thee to inherit the
land: when the wicked are cut off, thou shalt see it. **35** *I have seen*
the wicked in great power, and spreading himself like a green bay
tree. **36** *Yet he passed away, and, lo, he was not: yea, I sought*
him, but he could not be found. **37** *Mark the perfect man, and*
behold the upright: for the end of that man is peace. **38** *But the*
transgressors shall be destroyed together: the end of the wicked

shall be cut off. **39** *But the salvation of the righteous is of the LORD: he is their strength in the time of trouble.* **40** *And the LORD shall help them, and deliver them: he shall deliver them from the wicked, and save them, because they trust in him.*

VERSE OF THE DAY: Psalm 37:25
'I have been young, and now am old; yet have I not seen the righteous forsaken, nor his seed begging bread.'

Considering the length of one's life, God is faithful throughout. I was saved as a young boy. Some of you may have been saved later in life. Either way we can look back at His steady hand in our lives. He is as faithful today as the day we were saved. He has never forsaken us – HE CAN'T – He has promised He would not forsake us (**Hebrews 13:5**). What a faithful provider! Praise Him today!

# # # # #

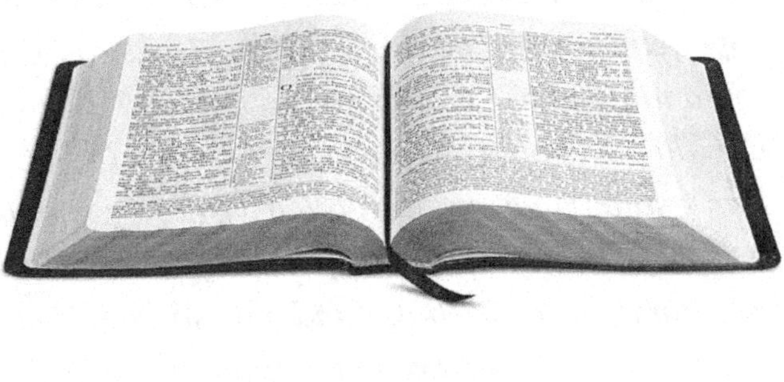

DAY #44

READ Psalm 38 (*22 verses*)

1 *O LORD, rebuke me not in thy wrath: neither chasten me in thy*
hot displeasure. **2** *For thine arrows stick fast in me, and thy hand*
presseth me sore. **3** *There is no soundness in my flesh because of*
thine anger; neither is there any rest in my bones because of my
sin. **4** *For mine iniquities are gone over mine head: as an heavy*
burden they are too heavy for me. **5** *My wounds stink and are*
corrupt because of my foolishness. **6** *I am troubled; I am bowed*
down greatly; I go mourning all the day long. **7** *For my loins are*
filled with a loathsome disease: and there is no soundness in my
flesh. **8** *I am feeble and sore broken: I have roared by reason of*
the disquietness of my heart. **9** *Lord, all my desire is before thee;*
and my groaning is not hid from thee. **10** *My heart panteth,*
my strength faileth me: as for the light of mine eyes, it also is gone
from me. **11** *My lovers and my friends stand aloof from my sore;*
and my kinsmen stand afar off. **12** *They also that seek after my*
life lay snares for me: and they that seek my hurt
speak mischievous things, and imagine deceits all the day
long. **13** *But I, as a deaf man, heard not; and I was as a dumb*
man that openeth not his mouth. **14** *Thus I was as a man that*
heareth not, and in whose mouth are no reproofs. **15** *For in thee,*
O LORD, do I hope: thou wilt hear, O Lord my
God. **16** *For I said, Hear me, lest otherwise they should rejoice*
over me: when my foot slippeth, they magnify themselves against
me. **17** *For I am ready to halt, and my sorrow is continually*
before me. **18** *For I will declare mine iniquity; I will be sorry for*

my sin. **19** *But mine enemies are lively, and they are strong:*
and they that hate me wrongfully are multiplied. **20** *They also*
that render evil for good are mine adversaries; because I
follow the thing that good is. **21** *Forsake me not, O LORD:*
O my God, be not far from me. **22** *Make haste to help me,*
O Lord my salvation.

VERSE OF THE DAY: Psalm 38:15
'For in thee, O LORD, do I hope: thou wilt hear, O Lord my God.'

In the **KJV** the title above this Psalm is '*David appeals to God for mercy in his pitiful case.*' David, called by the LORD as a man after my own heart (**Acts 13:22**), yearned to please the LORD even though he knew his own sinful heart. After sharing his faults in the beginning of the Psalm, David states where he finds his hope – only in the LORD. The Lord HIS God. Our God is personal. He knows each of us better than we know ourselves. He loves us still! Praise You Lord Jesus for loving us, often in spite of us. Praise Your holy name!

# # # # #

DAY #45

READ Psalm 39 (*13 verses*)

1 I said, I will take heed to my ways, that I sin not with my tongue:
I will keep my mouth with a bridle, while the wicked is before
me. 2 I was dumb with silence, I held my peace, even from good;
and my sorrow was stirred. 3 My heart was hot within me,
while I was musing the fire burned: then spake I with my
tongue, 4 LORD, make me to know mine end, and the
measure of my days, what it is; that I may know how frail I am.
5 Behold, thou hast made my days as an handbreadth; and mine
age is as nothing before thee: verily every man at his best
state is altogether vanity. Selah. 6 Surely every man walketh in a
vain shew: surely they are disquieted in vain: he heapeth
up riches, and knoweth not who shall gather them. 7 And now,
Lord, what wait I for? my hope is in thee. 8 Deliver me from
all my transgressions: make me not the reproach of the
foolish. 9 I was dumb, I opened not my mouth; because thou
didst it. 10 Remove thy stroke away from me: I am consumed by
the blow of thine hand. 11 When thou with rebukes dost correct
man for iniquity, thou makest his beauty to consume away like a
moth: surely every man is vanity. Selah. 12 Hear my prayer,
O LORD, and give ear unto my cry; hold not thy peace at my
tears: for I am a stranger with thee, and a sojourner, as all my
fathers were. 13 O spare me, that I may recover strength,
before I go hence, and be no more.

VERSE OF THE DAY: Psalm 39:1
'I said, I will take heed to my ways, that I sin not with my tongue: I will keep my mouth with a bridle, while the wicked is before me.'

We looked at the tongue on Day 40. We must be careful with the words we use. In this **Psalm** David is considering his thoughts and keeping a guard about his tongue. I've heard it said before: '*use your inside words.*' We must be careful not to say everything we think. The wicked world is watching us as Christians. How easy it can be to ruin a testimony in a moment by vulgar or condescending words. We are told in **Proverbs 22:1** that our reputation is priceless.

We are told in **James 1:19**: '*Wherefore, my beloved brethren, let every man be swift to hear, slow to speak, slow to wrath.*' This is addressed to the church – brethren. Wow! That one hits me right between the eyes. Lord, may I be careful with my speech not to harm the cause of Christ!

# # # # #

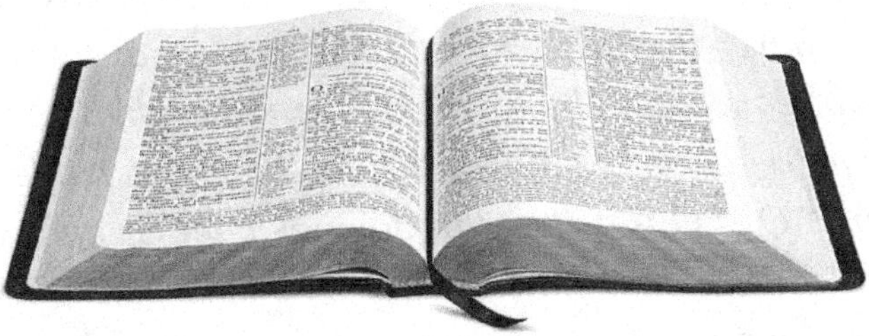

DAY #46

READ Psalm 40 (*17 verses*)

1 *I waited patiently for the LORD; and he inclined unto me, and*
heard my cry. **2** *He brought me up also out of an horrible pit, out*
of the miry clay, and set my feet upon a rock, and established my
goings. **3** *And he hath put a new song in my mouth, even praise*
unto our God: many shall see it, and fear, and shall trust in the
LORD. **4** *Blessed is that man that maketh the LORD his trust,*
and respecteth not the proud, nor such as turn aside to
lies. **5** *Many, O LORD my God, are thy wonderful works which*
thou hast done, and thy thoughts which are to us-ward:
they cannot be reckoned up in order unto thee: if I would declare
and speak of them, they are more than can be numbered.
6 *Sacrifice and offering thou didst not desire; mine ears hast thou*
opened: burnt offering and sin offering hast thou not
required. **7** *Then said I, Lo, I come: in the volume of the book it*
is written of me, **8** *I delight to do thy will, O my God: yea, thy*
law is within my heart. **9** *I have preached righteousness in the*
great congregation: lo, I have not refrained my lips, O LORD,
thou knowest. **10** *I have not hid thy righteousness within my*
heart; I have declared thy faithfulness and thy salvation:
I have not concealed thy lovingkindness and thy truth from the
great congregation. **11** *Withhold not thou thy tender mercies*
from me, O LORD: let thy lovingkindness and thy truth
continually preserve me. **12** *For innumerable evils have*
compassed me about: mine iniquities have taken hold upon me,
so that I am not able to look up; they are more than the hairs of

mine head: therefore my heart faileth me. **13** *Be pleased,*
O LORD, to deliver me: O LORD, make haste to help
me. **14** *Let them be ashamed and confounded together that seek*
after my soul to destroy it; let them be driven backward and put
to shame that wish me evil. **15** *Let them be desolate for a reward*
of their shame that say unto me, Aha, aha. **16** *Let all those that*
seek thee rejoice and be glad in thee: let such as love thy salvation
say continually, The LORD be magnified. **17** *But I am poor and*
needy; yet the Lord thinketh upon me: thou art my help and my
deliverer; make no tarrying, O my God.

VERSE OF THE DAY: Psalm 40:3
'And he hath put a new song in my mouth, even praise unto our God: many shall see it, and fear, and shall trust in the LORD.'

God alone can change the heart of a man. He can change his words from cursing to praising. I am reminded of the story of the demon possessed man in **Luke 8**. Jesus changed a violent, evil man into a pacifist that sat at His feet. Jesus sent him back to the city to '*show how great things God has done unto thee.*' He was radically changed and people could not help but witness it.

Has God made a change in your life? Were you once a hateful person who God has cleansed your heart? God is still in the miracle business – He changes hearts of stone to hearts of flesh every day. Would people trust in the LORD by looking at how Jesus has changed your life? May we live every day in a way that shows that we are new creatures in Christ!

# # # # #

DAY #47

READ Psalm 41 (*13 verses*)

*1 Blessed is he that considereth the poor: the LORD will deliver
him in time of trouble. 2 The LORD will preserve him, and keep
him alive; and he shall be blessed upon the earth: and thou wilt
not deliver him unto the will of his enemies. 3 The LORD will
strengthen him upon the bed of languishing: thou wilt make all
his bed in his sickness. 4 I said, LORD, be merciful unto me:
heal my soul; for I have sinned against thee. 5 Mine enemies
speak evil of me, When shall he die, and his name
perish? 6 And if he come to see me, he speaketh vanity:
his heart gathereth iniquity to itself; when he goeth abroad,
he telleth it. 7 All that hate me whisper together against me:
against me do they devise my hurt. 8 An evil disease, say they,
cleaveth fast unto him: and now that he lieth he shall rise up no
more. 9 Yea, mine own familiar friend, in whom I trusted,
which did eat of my bread, hath lifted up his heel against
me. 10 But thou, O LORD, be merciful unto me, and raise me up,
that I may requite them. 11 By this I know that thou favourest me,
because mine enemy doth not triumph over me. 12 And as for me,
thou upholdest me in mine integrity, and settest me before thy face
for ever. 13 Blessed be the LORD God of Israel from everlasting,
and to everlasting. Amen, and Amen.*

VERSE OF THE DAY: Psalm 41:1

'Blessed is he that considereth the poor: the LORD will deliver him in time of trouble.'

When is the last time you gave something to a poor person? Contemplate how good God has been to you. We have been so blessed! Who can you reach out to? Who can you encourage today? Remember that when Jesus told the story of the sheep and the goats, He said that when we help the least of these you do it unto me (**Matthew 25:40**). Look for an opportunity to be a blessing to someone today who is less fortunate than you.

# # # # #

DAY #48

READ Psalm 42 (*11 verses*)

*1 As the hart panteth after the water brooks, so panteth my soul
after thee, O God. 2 My soul thirsteth for God, for the living God:
when shall I come and appear before God? 3 My tears have been
my meat day and night, while they continually say unto me,
Where is thy God? 4 When I remember these things, I pour out
my soul in me: for I had gone with the multitude, I went with them
to the house of God, with the voice of joy and praise, with a
multitude that kept holyday. 5 Why art thou cast down,
O my soul? and why art thou disquieted in me? hope thou in God:
for I shall yet praise him for the help of his countenance.
6 O my God, my soul is cast down within me: therefore will I
remember thee from the land of Jordan, and of the Hermonites,
from the hill Mizar. 7 Deep calleth unto deep at the noise of thy
waterspouts: all thy waves and thy billows are gone over
me. 8 Yet the LORD will command his lovingkindness in the
daytime, and in the night his song shall be with me, and my
prayer unto the God of my life. 9 I will say unto God my rock,
Why hast thou forgotten me? why go I mourning because of the
oppression of the enemy? 10 As with a sword in my bones,
mine enemies reproach me; while they say daily unto me,
Where is thy God? 11 Why art thou cast down, O my soul?
and why art thou disquieted within me? hope thou in God:
for I shall yet praise him, who is the health of my countenance,
and my God.*

VERSE OF THE DAY: Psalm 42:1
'As the hart panteth after the water brooks, so panteth my soul after thee, O God.'

The word '*hart*' in the **KJV** is a male deer. The Hebrew word **arag** is the word for '*panteth*' and is found in Scripture only twice – both times in this verse. It means '*to long after.*' We see the picture of a male deer longing for a cool drink from the brook. He takes a little at a time and continues until he is satisfied. We also should come to the waters of the Word and long for it, taking in a little at a time until we are satisfied. God's Word should be read in small portions so that have time to meditate on the Word. You should not read your Bible using Evelyn Woods speed reading techniques. Read a small passage. Meditate on it. Ask the Holy Spirit to teach you. Come back for more! Does your soul long for the Word? May it be so in our lives.

# # # # #

DAY #49

READ Psalm 43 (*5 verses*)

1 Judge me, O God, and plead my cause against an
ungodly nation: O deliver me from the deceitful and unjust
man. 2 For thou art the God of my strength: why dost thou cast
me off? why go I mourning because of the oppression of the
enemy? 3 O send out thy light and thy truth: let them lead me;
let them bring me unto thy holy hill, and to thy
tabernacles. 4 Then will I go unto the altar of God, unto God my
exceeding joy: yea, upon the harp will I praise thee, O God my
God. 5 Why art thou cast down, O my soul? and why art thou
disquieted within me? hope in God: for I shall yet praise
him, who is the health of my countenance, and my God.

VERSES OF THE DAY: Psalm 43:3-4

'O send out thy light and thy truth: let them lead me; let them bring me unto thy holy hill, and to thy tabernacles. Then will I go unto the altar of God, unto God my exceeding joy: yea, upon the harp will I praise thee, O God my God O send out thy light and thy truth: let them lead me; let them bring me unto thy holy hill, and to thy tabernacles.'

Psalm 119:105 tells us '*Thy Word is a lamp unto my feet and a light unto my path.*' His Word is our light. It is His truth. When we live our life according to God's Word the result is to find God's exceeding joy. As I look back at my life I know the times that I struggled and had a negative attitude were always the times when I was not spending quality time in the Word. Take time every day to allow God's Word to guide and direct you. But be careful: you might find yourself exceedingly joyful! Proceed with anticipation . . .

I know it is not the Christmas season but it is always the season to worship the LORD! Call me crazy but I enjoy Christmas music all year 'round. Since we are talking about JOY today enjoy this song about unspeakable joy – may we experience it every day in our lives!

# # # # #

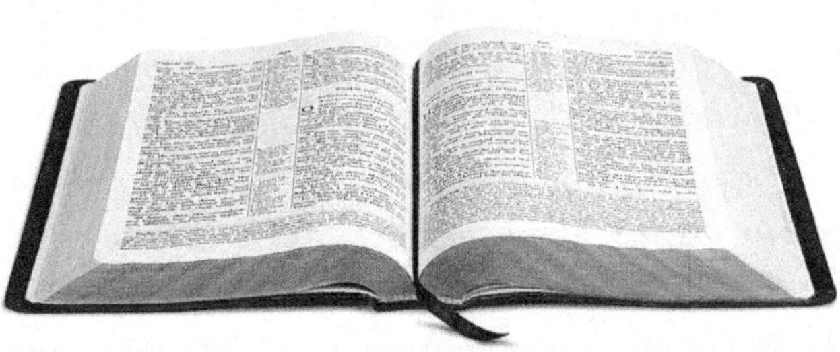

DAY #50

READ Psalm 44:1-16 (*16 verses*)

1 We have heard with our ears, O God, our fathers have told
us, what work thou didst in their days, in the times of
old. 2 How thou didst drive out the heathen with thy hand,
and plantedst them; how thou didst afflict the people, and cast
them out. 3 For they got not the land in possession by their own
sword, neither did their own arm save them: but thy right hand,
and thine arm, and the light of thy countenance, because thou
hadst a favour unto them. 4 Thou art my King, O God: command
deliverances for Jacob. 5 Through thee will we push down our
enemies: through thy name will we tread them under that rise up
against us. 6 For I will not trust in my bow, neither shall my
sword save me. 7 But thou hast saved us from our enemies,
and hast put them to shame that hated us. 8 In God we boast all
the day long, and praise thy name for ever. Selah. 9 But thou hast
cast off, and put us to shame; and goest not forth with our
armies. 10 Thou makest us to turn back from the enemy:
and they which hate us spoil for themselves. 11 Thou hast given
us like sheep appointed for meat; and hast scattered us among
the heathen. 12 Thou sellest thy people for nought, and dost not
increase thy wealth by their price. 13 Thou makest us a reproach
to our neighbours, a scorn and a derision to them that are
round about us. 14 Thou makest us a byword among the
heathen, a shaking of the head among the
people. 15 My confusion is continually before me, and the shame
of my face hath covered me, 16 For the voice of him that

reproacheth and blasphemeth; by reason of the enemy and avenger.

VERSE OF THE DAY: Psalm 44:8
'In God we boast all the day long, and praise thy name for ever. Selah.'

We live in the ME generation. I am always amazed how athletes boast about themselves, even when their team is way behind. It is prevalent in our society, yet it should not be in the church. Paul wrote '*but far be it from me to boast except in the cross of our Lord Jesus Christ . . .*' (**Galatians 6:14**). May we brag about our JESUS before the world!

# # # # #

DAY #51

READ Psalm 44:17-26 (*10 verses*)

*17 All this is come upon us; yet have we not forgotten thee,
neither have we dealt falsely in thy covenant.* **18** *Our heart is not
turned back, neither have our steps declined from thy
way;* **19** *Though thou hast sore broken us in the place of dragons,
and covered us with the shadow of death.* **20** *If we have forgotten
the name of our God, or stretched out our hands to a strange
god;* **21** *Shall not God search this out? for he knoweth the secrets
of the heart.* **22** *Yea, for thy sake are we killed all the day long;
we are counted as sheep for the slaughter.* **23** *Awake, why
sleepest thou, O Lord? arise, cast us not off for ever.*
24 *Wherefore hidest thou thy face, and forgettest our affliction
and our oppression?* **25** *For our soul is bowed down to the dust:
our belly cleaveth unto the earth.* **26** *Arise for our help,
and redeem us for thy mercies' sake.*

VERSES OF THE DAY: Psalm 44:20-21

'If we have forgotten the name of our God, or stretched out our hands to a strange god; Shall not God search this out? for he knoweth the secrets of the heart.'

A '*god*' is anything that we place above the One true God. We live in a culture that has many gods: people place their kids, their job, their possessions, their hobbies, their sports, etc. as priorities in their lives. Think of the time that is spent watching TV. We once challenged our teens for a week to spend as much time reading their Bible as they did watching TV. Not one said they could do it. What has become more important in your life than your walk with Christ? There is nothing wrong with loving your kids, working hard at your job or rooting for your favorite team. But ask yourself: does that come before spending time with the LORD through prayer and Bible reading? God knows the secrets of your heart. May we make JESUS the overriding priority in our lives – PRAISE HIM TODAY!

# # # # #

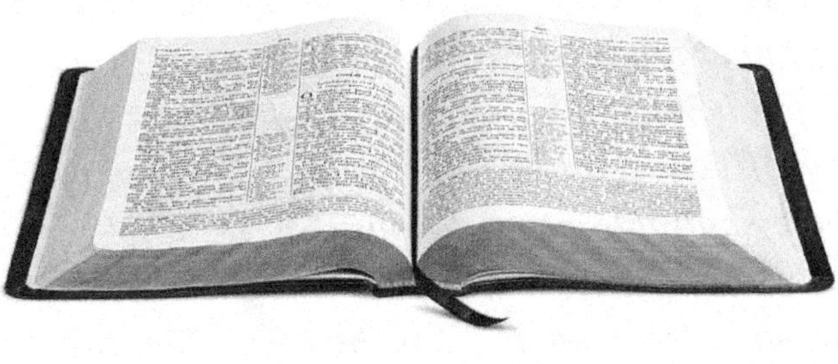

DAY #52

READ Psalm 45 (*17 verses*)

*1 My heart is inditing a good matter: I speak of the things which
I have made touching the king: my tongue is the pen of a
ready writer.* **2** *Thou art fairer than the children of men:
grace is poured into thy lips: therefore God hath blessed thee for
ever.* **3** *Gird thy sword upon thy thigh, O most mighty, with thy
glory and thy majesty.* **4** *And in thy majesty ride prosperously
because of truth and meekness and righteousness; and thy right
hand shall teach thee terrible things.* **5** *Thine arrows are sharp in
the heart of the king's enemies; whereby the people fall under
thee.* **6** *Thy throne, O God, is for ever and ever: the sceptre of thy
kingdom is a right sceptre.* **7** *Thou lovest righteousness,
and hatest wickedness: therefore God, thy God, hath anointed
thee with the oil of gladness above thy fellows.* **8** *All thy
garments smell of myrrh, and aloes, and cassia, out of the ivory
palaces, whereby they have made thee glad.* **9** *Kings' daughters
were among thy honourable women: upon thy right hand did
stand the queen in gold of Ophir.* **10** *Hearken, O daughter,
and consider, and incline thine ear; forget also thine own people,
and thy father's house;* **11** *So shall the king greatly desire thy
beauty: for he is thy Lord; and worship thou him.* **12** *And the
daughter of Tyre shall be there with a gift; even the rich among
the people shall intreat thy favour.* **13** *The king's daughter is all
glorious within: her clothing is of wrought gold.* **14** *She shall be
brought unto the king in raiment of needlework: the virgins
her companions that follow her shall be brought unto*

thee. **15** *With gladness and rejoicing shall they be brought:*
they shall enter into the king's palace. **16** *Instead of thy fathers*
shall be thy children, whom thou mayest make princes in all the
earth. **17** *I will make thy name to be remembered in all*
generations: therefore shall the people praise thee for ever and
ever.

VERSE OF THE DAY: Psalm 45:6

'Thy throne, O God, is for ever and ever: the sceptre of thy kingdom is a right sceptre.'

We serve the King of Kings and Lord of Lords (**Revelation 19:16**). His throne is forever; and forever we shall worship Him! We see the word '*sceptre*' twice in this verse – the only two times this word is used in the entire Old Testament. '*Sceptre*' in the Hebrew is the word **shebet**, meaning '*a stick to punish, fight and rule.*' He shall rule and reign forevermore!

# # # # #

DAY #53

READ Psalm 46 (*11 verses*)

1 God is our refuge and strength, a very present help in trouble
2 Therefore will not we fear, though the earth be removed, and
though the mountains be carried into the midst of the sea;
3 Though the waters thereof roar and be troubled, though the
mountains shake with the swelling thereof. Selah. 4 There is a
river, the streams whereof shall make glad the city of God,
the holy place of the tabernacles of the most High. 5 God is in the
midst of her; she shall not be moved: God shall help her, and
that right early. 6 The heathen raged, the kingdoms were
moved: he uttered his voice, the earth melted. 7 The LORD of
hosts is with us; the God of Jacob is our refuge.
Selah. 8 Come, behold the works of the LORD, what desolations
he hath made in the earth. 9 He maketh wars to cease unto the
end of the earth; he breaketh the bow, and cutteth the spear in
sunder; he burneth the chariot in the fire. 10 Be still, and know
that I am God: I will be exalted among the heathen, I will be
exalted in the earth. 11 The LORD of hosts is with us; the God of
Jacob is our refuge. Selah.

VERSE OF THE DAY: Psalm 46:10
'Be still, and know that I am God: I will be exalted among the heathen, I will be exalted in the earth.'

What a wonderful verse that I have taken to heart often. The word '*still*' is the Hebrew word **raphah**, found here for the only time in the Old Testament. It mean '*to cease, to be faint, to be slothful*'. STOP what you are doing. BE STILL here means to actively stop everything you are doing and be in a conscious state of putting away anything that would distract you from getting the next point; prepare yourself to receive what is about to be shared.

The Hebrew word for '*know*' is **yada** – '*to recognize, to acknowledge, be aware, be certain.*' This word is used 429 times in the Old Testament. The phrase '*shall know that I am the LORD*' is used 60 times in **Ezekiel** alone! He WILL be exalted among the heathen! He WILL be exalted in the earth! HE WILL!

What a great reminder: stop what you're doing and be certain that He is God!

# # # # #

DAY #54

READ Psalm 47 (*9 verses*)

*1 O clap your hands, all ye people; shout unto God with the
voice of triumph. 2 For the LORD most high is terrible; he is a
great King over all the earth. 3 He shall subdue the people under
us, and the nations under our feet. 4 He shall choose our
inheritance for us, the excellency of Jacob whom he loved.
Selah. 5 God is gone up with a shout, the LORD with the sound
of a trumpet. 6 Sing praises to God, sing praises: sing praises
unto our King, sing praises. 7 For God is the King of all the
earth: sing ye praises with understanding. 8 God reigneth
over the heathen: God sitteth upon the throne of his
holiness. 9 The princes of the people are gathered
together, even the people of the God of Abraham: for the shields
of the earth belong unto God: he is greatly exalted.*

VERSE OF THE DAY: Psalm 47:6
'Sing praises to God, sing praises: sing praises unto our King, sing praises.'

When Scripture repeats itself we are to take heed to the message being conveyed. Repeating words bring emphasis. Jesus used the phrase, '*Verily, verily I say unto you*' 25 times in the gospel of **John**. The Greek word for '*verily*' is the same word translated '*amen.*' This word means '*so be it.*' Every time this phrase '*verily, verily*' was followed by an important teaching.

In this verse we see FOUR TIMES the command to SING PRAISES. Obviously it is important that we sing praises to our God. Jesus alone deserves our praise, all of our praise. Give HIM praise today!

# # # # #

DAY #55

READ Psalm 48 (*14 verses*)

1 Great is the LORD, and greatly to be praised in the city of our
God, in the mountain of his holiness. 2 Beautiful for situation,
the joy of the whole earth, is mount Zion, on the sides of the
north, the city of the great King. 3 God is known in her palaces
for a refuge. 4 For, lo, the kings were assembled, they passed by
together. 5 They saw it, and so they marvelled; they were
troubled, and hasted away. 6 Fear took hold upon them
there, and pain, as of a woman in travail. 7 Thou breakest the
ships of Tarshish with an east wind. 8 As we have heard, so have
we seen in the city of the LORD of hosts, in the city of our God:
God will establish it for ever. Selah. 9 We have thought of thy
lovingkindness, O God, in the midst of thy temple. 10 According
to thy name, O God, so is thy praise unto the ends of the earth:
thy right hand is full of righteousness. 11 Let mount Zion rejoice,
let the daughters of Judah be glad, because of thy judgments.
12 Walk about Zion, and go round about her: tell the towers
thereof. 13 Mark ye well her bulwarks, consider her palaces;
that ye may tell it to the generation following. 14 For this
God is our God for ever and ever: he will be our guide even unto
death.

VERSE OF THE DAY: Psalm 48:14

'For this God is our God for ever and ever: he will be our guide even unto death.'

He is our God forever and ever. That means today, tomorrow and for eternity. He will guide us in this life to our last day. He will guide you in the good and in the bad. Even upon our death bed He will be our guide. What a comfort to know that when we see His saints at the end of their days that Jesus is still with them. We do not have to fear death for God is with us!

# # # # #

DAY #56

READ Psalm 49 (*20 verses*)

1 *Hear this, all ye people; give ear, all ye inhabitants of the*
world: ***2*** *Both low and high, rich and poor, together.* ***3*** *My mouth*
shall speak of wisdom; and the meditation of my heart shall be of
understanding. ***4*** *I will incline mine ear to a parable: I will open*
my dark saying upon the harp. ***5*** *Wherefore should I fear in the*
days of evil, when the iniquity of my heels shall compass me
about? ***6*** *They that trust in their wealth, and boast themselves in*
the multitude of their riches; ***7*** *None of them can by any means*
redeem his brother, nor give to God a ransom for him: ***8*** *(For the*
redemption of their soul is precious, and it ceaseth for
ever:) ***9*** *That he should still live for ever, and not see*
corruption. ***10*** *For he seeth that wise men die, likewise the fool*
and the brutish person perish, and leave their wealth to
others. ***11*** *Their inward thought is, that their houses shall*
continue for ever, and their dwelling places to all generations;
they call their lands after their own names. ***12*** *Nevertheless*
man being in honour abideth not: he is like the
beasts that perish. ***13*** *This their way is their folly: yet their*
posterity approve their sayings. Selah. ***14*** *Like sheep they are*
laid in the grave; death shall feed on them; and the upright shall
have dominion over them in the morning; and their beauty shall
consume in the grave from their dwelling. ***15*** *But God will*
redeem my soul from the power of the grave: for he shall receive
me. Selah. ***16*** *Be not thou afraid when one is made rich, when the*
glory of his house is increased; ***17*** *For when he dieth he shall*

carry nothing away: his glory shall not descend after him. **18** *Though while he lived he blessed his soul: and men will praise thee, when thou doest well to thyself.* **19** *He shall go to the generation of his fathers; they shall never see light.* **20** *Man that is in honour, and understandeth not, is like the beasts that perish.*

VERSES OF THE DAY: Psalm 49:6-7

'They that trust in their wealth, and boast themselves in the multitude of their riches; None of them can by any means redeem his brother, nor give to God a ransom for him.'

According to recent reports the number of billionaires living in the United States is 585. I'm going to let you in on a little secret: I am not one of them. Leading the list is Jeff Bezos of amazon.com with an estimated worth exceeding $112,000,000,000. With all that wealth he cannot pay to redeem himself or anyone else. God forbid one of his children were kidnapped. If so I am sure he would be able to pay the ransom that might be demanded. Not so with God. There is not enough money in the world to buy your way to God. Yet He has already paid His way to you! He has paid the ransom through His Son the Lord Jesus Christ!

'*Even as the Son of man came not to be ministered unto, but to minister, and to give His life a ransom for many.*'

(**Matthew 20:28**).

# # # # #

DAY #57

READ Psalm 50 (*23 verses*)

1 *The mighty God, even the LORD, hath spoken, and called the*
earth from the rising of the sun unto the going down
thereof. **2** *Out of Zion, the perfection of beauty, God hath*
shined. **3** *Our God shall come, and shall not keep silence:*
a fire shall devour before him, and it shall be very tempestuous
round about him. **4** *He shall call to the heavens from above,*
and to the earth, that he may judge his people. **5** *Gather my saints*
together unto me; those that have made a covenant with me by
sacrifice. **6** *And the heavens shall declare his righteousness:*
for God is judge himself. Selah. **7** *Hear, O my people, and I will*
speak; O Israel, and I will testify against thee: I am God, even thy
God. **8** *I will not reprove thee for thy sacrifices or thy burnt*
offerings, to have been continually before me. **9** *I will take no*
bullock out of thy house, nor he goats out of thy
folds. **10** *For every beast of the forest is mine, and the cattle upon*
a thousand hills. **11** *I know all the fowls of the mountains:*
and the wild beasts of the field are mine. **12** *If I were hungry,*
I would not tell thee: for the world is mine, and the fulness
thereof. **13** *Will I eat the flesh of bulls, or drink the blood of*
goats? **14** *Offer unto God thanksgiving; and pay thy vows unto*
the most High: **15** *And call upon me in the day of trouble:*
I will deliver thee, and thou shalt glorify me. **16** *But unto the*
wicked God saith, What hast thou to do to declare my
statutes, or that thou shouldest take my covenant in thy
mouth? **17** *Seeing thou hatest instruction, and castest my words*

behind thee. **18** *When thou sawest a thief, then thou consentedst with him, and hast been partaker with adulterers.* **19** *Thou givest thy mouth to evil, and thy tongue frameth deceit.* **20** *Thou sittest and speakest against thy brother; thou slanderest thine own mother's son.* **21** *These things hast thou done, and I kept silence; thou thoughtest that I was altogether such an one as thyself: but I will reprove thee, and set them in order before thine eyes.* **22** *Now consider this, ye that forget God, lest I tear you in pieces, and there be none to deliver.* **23** *Whoso offereth praise glorifieth me: and to him that ordereth his conversation aright will I shew the salvation of God.*

VERSE OF THE DAY: Psalm 50:10

'For every beast of the forest is mine, and the cattle upon a thousand hills.'

The LORD is owner of all, including the cattle upon a thousand hills. There are an estimated number of cattle and calves in the USA is 90,000,000. I once heard a southern preacher say, '*He owns the cattle upon a thousand hills, and the taters under the cattle, and the diamonds under the taters, and the oil under the diamonds. He owns it all!*' He is the Creator of all. He is above all. He is also LORD of all! What a wonderful thing to have a personal relationship with the One who created, and owns, that much cattle!

# # # # #

DAY #58

READ Psalm 51 (*19 verses*)

1 Have mercy upon me, O God, according to thy lovingkindness:
according unto the multitude of thy tender mercies blot out my
transgressions. 2 Wash me throughly from mine iniquity, and
cleanse me from my sin. 3 For I acknowledge my transgressions:
and my sin is ever before me. 4 Against thee, thee only, have I
sinned, and done this evil in thy sight: that thou mightest be
justified when thou speakest, and be clear when thou
judgest. 5 Behold, I was shapen in iniquity; and in sin did my
mother conceive me. 6 Behold, thou desirest truth in the inward
parts: and in the hidden part thou shalt make me to know
wisdom. 7 Purge me with hyssop, and I shall be clean: wash me,
and I shall be whiter than snow. 8 Make me to hear joy and
gladness; that the bones which thou hast broken may
rejoice. 9 Hide thy face from my sins, and blot out all mine
iniquities. 10 Create in me a clean heart, O God; and renew a
right spirit within me. 11 Cast me not away from thy presence;
and take not thy holy spirit from me. 12 Restore unto me the joy
of thy salvation; and uphold me with thy free spirit. 13 Then will
I teach transgressors thy ways; and sinners shall be converted
unto thee. 14 Deliver me from bloodguiltiness, O God, thou God
of my salvation: and my tongue shall sing aloud of thy
righteousness. 15 O Lord, open thou my lips; and my mouth
shall shew forth thy praise. 16 For thou desirest not
sacrifice; else would I give it: thou delightest not in burnt
offering. 17 The sacrifices of God are a broken spirit: a broken

and a contrite heart, O God, thou wilt not despise. **18** *Do good in*
thy good pleasure unto Zion: build thou the walls of
Jerusalem. **19** *Then shalt thou be pleased with the sacrifices of*
righteousness, with burnt offering and whole burnt offering:
then shall they offer bullocks upon thine altar.

VERSE OF THE DAY: Psalm 51:10

'Create in me a clean heart, O God; and renew a right spirit within me.'

David comes broken before His Lord. He has committed adultery with Bathsheba. He pours out his heart before the Lord. Have you ever been there? Have you ever come to the Lord broken in your sin? Our Lord longs for us to confess our sins to Him. He is ready and willing to cleanse us from all unrighteousness when we come to him with a humble, repentant heart (**I John 1:9**). He is the only one who can give us a clean heart. Though our sins be as scarlet they will be as white as snow (**Isaiah 1:18**).

# # # # #

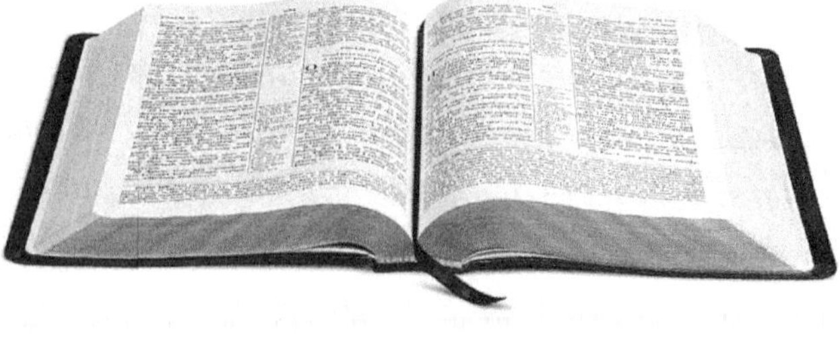

DAY #59

READ Psalm 52 (*9 verses*)

1 Why boastest thou thyself in mischief, O mighty man? the goodness of God endureth continually. 2 Thy tongue deviseth mischiefs; like a sharp razor, working deceitfully. 3 Thou lovest evil more than good; and lying rather than to speak righteousness. Selah. 4 Thou lovest all devouring words, O thou deceitful tongue. 5 God shall likewise destroy thee for ever, he shall take thee away, and pluck thee out of thy dwelling place, and root thee out of the land of the living. Selah. 6 The righteous also shall see, and fear, and shall laugh at him: 7 Lo, this is the man that made not God his strength; but trusted in the abundance of his riches, and strengthened himself in his wickedness. 8 But I am like a green olive tree in the house of God: I trust in the mercy of God for ever and ever. 9 I will praise thee for ever, because thou hast done it: and I will wait on thy name; for it is good before thy saints.

VERSE OF THE DAY: Psalm 52:9
'I will praise thee for ever, because thou hast done it: and I will wait on thy name; for it is good before thy saints.'

David states in this verse that the LORD has done '*it*.' What is the '*it*' that God has done for you? For me the '*it*' that He has done includes salvation, health and many blessings. The '*it's*' that He has given me include family, friends and a wonderful church family. Are you thankful for what He '*hast done*' for you? Praise Him today and every day. God is so good!

# # # # #

DAY #60

READ Psalm 53 (*6 verses*)

1 The fool hath said in his heart, There is no God. Corrupt are
they, and have done abominable iniquity: there is none that doeth
good. 2 God looked down from heaven upon the children of men,
to see if there were any that did understand, that did seek
God. 3 Every one of them is gone back: they are
altogether become filthy; there is none that doeth good, no, not
one. 4 Have the workers of iniquity no knowledge? who eat up
my people as they eat bread: they have not called upon
God. 5 There were they in great fear, where no fear was:
for God hath scattered the bones of him that encampeth
against thee: thou hast put them to shame, because God hath
despised them. 6 Oh that the salvation of Israel were come out of
Zion! When God bringeth back the captivity of his people, Jacob
shall rejoice, and Israel shall be glad.

VERSES OF THE DAY: Psalm 53:2-3
'God looked down from heaven upon the children of men, to see if there were any that did understand, that did seek God. Every one of them is gone back: they are altogether become filthy; there is none that doeth good, no, not one.'

There is a part of the American church that has decided to be '*seeker sensitive.*' I find it interesting that this passage tells us that no one seeks God. Instead everyone has run from God. None do good (**Romans 3:10**). None seek (**Romans 3:11**). Aren't you happy that God sought out you? He has chosen to use us to reach the lost. Are you receiving the blessing that is available by sharing the gospel? May WE be diligent to seek out those in our lives that need Jesus!

# # # # #

DAY #61

READ Psalm 54 (*7 verses*)

1 *Save me, O God, by thy name, and judge me by thy*
strength. **2** *Hear my prayer, O God; give ear to the words of my*
mouth. **3** *For strangers are risen up against me, and oppressors*
seek after my soul: they have not set God before them.
Selah. **4** *Behold, God is mine helper: the Lord is with them that*
uphold my soul. **5** *He shall reward evil unto mine enemies:*
cut them off in thy truth. **6** *I will freely sacrifice unto thee:*
I will praise thy name, O LORD; for it is good. **7** *For he hath*
delivered me out of all trouble: and mine eye hath seen his
desire upon mine enemies.

VERSE OF THE DAY: Psalm 54:4
'Behold, God is mine helper: the Lord is with them that uphold my soul.'

Do you ever need a little help? In **Psalm 30:10** we see the plea: '*Lord, be thou my helper.*' In this verse we see that God IS our helper. Helper is the Hebrew word **azar**, which means '*to surround, to protect, to aid.*' The God of all creation is the One who surrounds you, who protects you, who aids you. Take comfort in that today!

# # # # #

DAY #62

READ Psalm 55 (*23 verses*)

1 Give ear to my prayer, O God; and hide not thyself from my supplication. 2 Attend unto me, and hear me: I mourn in my complaint, and make a noise; 3 Because of the voice of the enemy, because of the oppression of the wicked: for they cast iniquity upon me, and in wrath they hate me. 4 My heart is sore pained within me: and the terrors of death are fallen upon me. 5 Fearfulness and trembling are come upon me, and horror hath overwhelmed me. 6 And I said, Oh that I had wings like a dove! for then would I fly away, and be at rest. 7 Lo, then would I wander far off, and remain in the wilderness. Selah. 8 I would hasten my escape from the windy storm and tempest. 9 Destroy, O Lord, and divide their tongues: for I have seen violence and strife in the city. 10 Day and night they go about it upon the walls thereof: mischief also and sorrow are in the midst of it. 11 Wickedness is in the midst thereof: deceit and guile depart not from her streets. 12 For it was not an enemy that reproached me; then I could have borne it: neither was it he that hated me that did magnify himself against me; then I would have hid myself from him: 13 But it was thou, a man mine equal, my guide, and mine acquaintance. 14 We took sweet counsel together, and walked unto the house of God in company. 15 Let death seize upon them, and let them go down quick into hell: for wickedness is in their dwellings, and among them. 16 As for me, I will call upon God; and the LORD shall save me. 17 Evening, and morning, and at noon, will I pray, and

cry aloud: and he shall hear my voice. **18** *He hath delivered my*
soul in peace from the battle that was against me: for there were
many with me. **19** *God shall hear, and afflict them, even he that*
abideth of old. Selah. Because they have no changes,
therefore they fear not God. **20** *He hath put forth his hands*
against such as be at peace with him: he hath broken his
covenant. **21** *The words of his mouth were smoother than butter,*
but war was in his heart: his words were softer than oil,
yet were they drawn swords. **22** *Cast thy burden upon the LORD,*
and he shall sustain thee: he shall never suffer the righteous to
be moved. **23** *But thou, O God, shalt bring them down into the pit*
of destruction: bloody and deceitful men shall not live out half
their days; but I will trust in thee.

VERSE OF THE DAY: Psalm 55:16
'As for me, I will call upon God; and the LORD shall save me.'

David makes a personal stand: as for ME, I will call upon God. He has confidence that the LORD SHALL save him. He states SHALL not MAYBE. After all, God is his helper (*see Day #61*). Have confidence that our LORD shall be with you. He promised us that in **Hebrews 13:5**: '*I will never leave thee, nor forsake thee.*' Since it is impossible for God to lie that must be true! (**Hebrews 6:18**). Call upon the LORD – He WILL save you!

# # # # #

DAY #63

READ Psalm 56 (*13 verses*)

1 Be merciful unto me, O God: for man would swallow me up;
he fighting daily oppresseth me. 2 Mine enemies would daily
swallow me up: for they be many that fight against me, O thou
most High. 3 What time I am afraid, I will trust in thee. 4 In God
I will praise his word, in God I have put my trust; I will not fear
what flesh can do unto me. 5 Every day they wrest my words:
all their thoughts are against me for evil. 6 They gather
themselves together, they hide themselves, they mark my steps,
when they wait for my soul. 7 Shall they escape by iniquity?
in thine anger cast down the people, O God. 8 Thou tellest my
wanderings: put thou my tears into thy bottle: are they not in thy
book? 9 When I cry unto thee, then shall mine enemies
turn back: this I know; for God is for me. 10 In God will I
praise his word: in the LORD will I praise his word. 11 In God
have I put my trust: I will not be afraid what man can do unto
me. 12 Thy vows are upon me, O God: I will render praises unto
thee. 13 For thou hast delivered my soul from
death: wilt not thou deliver my feet from falling, that I may walk
before God in the light of the living?

VERSE OF THE DAY: Psalm 56:11
'In God have I put my trust: I will not be afraid what man can do unto me.'

The first appeal to have IN GOD WE TRUST placed on our currency came in a letter dated November 13, 1861. The GOD referenced is unquestionably the God of Scripture. The appeal was written to Secretary of the Treasury Salmon P. Chase by

Rev. M. R. Watkinson, Minister of the Gospel from Ridleyville, Pennsylvania, and read (*in part*):

> '*Dear Sir: You are about to submit your annual report to the Congress respecting the affairs of the national finances. One fact touching our currency has hitherto been seriously overlooked. I mean the recognition of the Almighty God in some form on our coins.*'

As a result, Secretary Chase instructed James Pollock, Director of the Mint at Philadelphia, to prepare a motto, in a letter dated November 20, 1861:

> '*Dear Sir: No nation can be strong except in the strength of God, or safe except in His defense. The trust of our people in God should be declared on our national coins. You will cause a device to be prepared without unnecessary delay with a motto expressing in the fewest and tersest words possible this national recognition.*'

IN GOD WE TRUST first appeared on the 1864 two-cent coin. The motto has been in continuous use on the one-cent coin since 1909, and on the ten-cent coin since 1916. It also has appeared on all gold coins and silver dollar coins, half-dollar coins, and quarter-dollar coins struck since July 1, 1908.

Our $20 bill will be changed to display Harriet Tubman instead of Alexander Hamilton beginning in 2020. What other changes to our currency will take place? Will they eventually remove the motto IN GOD WE TRUST? It would not surprise me. As our country changes and sadly moves away from God, can it be said that we as a country still trust in God? We do not have to be afraid of where our country is headed. God is still on the throne. We can still proclaim IN GOD WE TRUST!

# # # # #

DAY #64

READ Psalm 57 (*11 verses*)

*1 Be merciful unto me, O God, be merciful unto me: for my soul
trusteth in thee: yea, in the shadow of thy wings will I make my
refuge, until these calamities be overpast.* **2** *I will cry unto God
most high; unto God that performeth all things for me.* **3** *He shall
send from heaven, and save me from the reproach of him that
would swallow me up. Selah. God shall send forth his mercy and
his truth.* **4** *My soul is among lions: and I lie even among them
that are set on fire, even the sons of men, whose teeth are spears
and arrows, and their tongue a sharp sword.* **5** *Be thou exalted,
O God, above the heavens; let thy glory be above all the
earth.* **6** *They have prepared a net for my steps; my soul is bowed
down: they have digged a pit before me, into the midst whereof
they are fallen themselves. Selah.* **7** *My heart is fixed, O God, my
heart is fixed: I will sing and give praise.* **8** *Awake up, my glory;
awake, psaltery and harp: I myself will awake early.* **9** *I will
praise thee, O Lord, among the people: I will sing unto thee
among the nations.* **10** *For thy mercy is great unto the heavens,
and thy truth unto the clouds.* **11** *Be thou exalted, O God, above
the heavens: let thy glory be above all the earth.*

VERSE OF THE DAY: Psalm 57:7

'My heart is fixed, O God, my heart is fixed: I will sing and give praise.'

The work '*fixed*' is the Hebrew word **kuwn** meaning '*sure, certain, established.*' It is seen twice in this verse and only two other times in the Old Testament (**Psalm 108:1, Psalm 112:7**). In all four occasions the Psalmist's heart is the focus. His faith and trust in God is sure, it is certain, it is established. The result: praise in song. What is the result of your standing with God? Are you certain in your faith? May our faith be sure, and may the result be a song of praise!

# # # # #

DAY #65

READ Psalm 58 (*11 verses*)

*1 Do ye indeed speak righteousness, O congregation? do ye
judge uprightly, O ye sons of men? 2 Yea, in heart ye work
wickedness; ye weigh the violence of your hands in the
earth. 3 The wicked are estranged from the womb: they go astray
as soon as they be born, speaking lies. 4 Their poison is like the
poison of a serpent: they are like the deaf adder that stoppeth her
ear; 5 Which will not hearken to the voice of charmers, charming
never so wisely. 6 Break their teeth, O God, in their mouth:
break out the great teeth of the young lions, O LORD. 7 Let them
melt away as waters which run continually: when he
bendeth his bow to shoot his arrows, let them be as cut in pieces.
8 As a snail which melteth, let every one of them pass
away: like the untimely birth of a woman, that they may not see
the sun. 9 Before your pots can feel the thorns, he shall take
them away as with a whirlwind, both living, and in his
wrath. 10 The righteous shall rejoice when he seeth the
vengeance: he shall wash his feet in the blood of the wicked.
11 So that a man shall say, Verily there is a reward for the
righteous: verily he is a God that judgeth in the earth.*

VERSE OF THE DAY: Psalm 58:6

'Break their teeth, O God, in their mouth: break out the great teeth of the young lions, O LORD.'

Have you ever had problems with your teeth? I had a tooth crack which had to be surgically removed. It was painful for a few days before I could get the surgery scheduled. Last August I had one of my teeth next to my front tooth break – the bottom cracked off. It has taken me months to get a root canal and I am still waiting for my cap to be ready to complete the job. Here we see a plea for God to break the teeth of those who oppose God's people. Not one tooth but many. OUCH! God will take care of His own – and it will be eternally painful for those who stand in God's way!

# # # # #

DAY #66

READ Psalm 59 (*17 verses*)

1 *Deliver me from mine enemies, O my God: defend me from
them that rise up against me.* ***2*** *Deliver me from the workers of
iniquity, and save me from bloody men.* ***3*** *For, lo, they lie in wait
for my soul: the mighty are gathered against me; not for my
transgression, nor for my sin, O LORD.* ***4*** *They run and prepare
themselves without my fault: awake to help me, and
behold.* ***5*** *Thou therefore, O LORD God of hosts, the God of
Israel, awake to visit all the heathen: be not merciful to any
wicked transgressors. Selah.* ***6*** *They return at evening: they make
a noise like a dog, and go round about the city.* ***7*** *Behold, they
belch out with their mouth: swords are in their lips: for who, say
they, doth hear?* ***8*** *But thou, O LORD, shalt laugh at them; thou
shalt have all the heathen in derision.* ***9*** *Because of his strength
will I wait upon thee: for God is my defence.* ***10*** *The God of my
mercy shall prevent me: God shall let me see my desire upon mine
enemies.* ***11*** *Slay them not, lest my people forget: scatter them by
thy power; and bring them down, O Lord our shield.* ***12*** *For the
sin of their mouth and the words of their lips let them even be
taken in their pride: and for cursing and lying which they
speak.* ***13*** *Consume them in wrath, consume them, that
they may not be: and let them know that God ruleth in Jacob unto
the ends of the earth. Selah.* ***14*** *And at evening let them
return; and let them make a noise like a dog, and go round about
the city.* ***15*** *Let them wander up and down for meat, and grudge
if they be not satisfied.* ***16*** *But I will sing of thy power; yea, I will
sing aloud of thy mercy in the morning: for thou hast been my
defence and refuge in the day of my trouble.* ***17*** *Unto thee, O my
strength, will I sing: for God is my defence, and the God of my
mercy.:*

VERSE OF THE DAY: Psalm 59:12
'For the sin of their mouth and the words of their lips let them even be taken in their pride: and for cursing and lying which they speak.'

A great picture of the consequences of pride is given to us in **Daniel 4**. Nebuchadnezzar had a dream that prophesied that his kingdom would be taken from him. In **verse 30** the King looks over his kingdom and declares in his pride: '*Is not this great Babylon, that I have built for the house of the kingdom by the might of my power, and for the honour of my majesty?*' He is caught in his pride in **verse 31**: '*While the word was in the king's mouth, there fell a voice from heaven, saying, O king Nebuchadnezzar, to thee it is spoken; The kingdom is departed from thee.*' He was made to live like an animal as he '*did eat grass as oxen, and his body was wet with the dew of heaven, till his hairs were grown like eagles' feathers, and his nails like birds' claws*' (**verse 33**). He would eventually change his ways and be restored to his kingdom, giving the King of heaven praise and declaring that '*all his acts are just and true, and he is able to humble the proud*' (**verse 37**).

Pride will destroy you. Cursing and lying are characteristics of prideful people. Be careful not to be prideful: we do not want to be humbled by God. Humility is to be found in us as Christians.

'*Pride goeth before destruction, and an haughty spirit before a fall.*' (**Proverbs 16:18**)

'*A man's pride shall bring him low: but honour shall uphold the humble in spirit.*' (**Proverbs 29:23**)

# # # # #

DAY #67

READ Psalm 60 (*12 verses*)

1 *O God, thou hast cast us off, thou hast scattered us, thou hast*
been displeased; O turn thyself to us again. **2** *Thou hast made the*
earth to tremble; thou hast broken it: heal the breaches thereof;
for it shaketh. **3** *Thou hast shewed thy people hard things: thou*
hast made us to drink the wine of astonishment. **4** *Thou hast given*
a banner to them that fear thee, that it may be displayed because
of the truth. Selah. **5** *That thy beloved may be delivered;*
save with thy right hand, and hear me. **6** *God hath spoken in his*
holiness; I will rejoice, I will divide Shechem, and mete out the
valley of Succoth. **7** *Gilead is mine, and Manasseh is mine;*
Ephraim also is the strength of mine head; Judah is my
lawgiver; **8** *Moab is my washpot; over Edom will I cast out my*
shoe: Philistia, triumph thou because of me. **9** *Who will bring*
me into the strong city? who will lead me into Edom? **10** *Wilt not*
thou, O God, which hadst cast us off? and thou,
O God, which didst not go out with our armies? **11** *Give us help*
from trouble: for vain is the help of man. **12** *Through God we*
shall do valiantly: for he it is that shall tread down our enemies.

VERSE OF THE DAY: Psalm 60:12

'Through God we shall do valiantly: for he it is that shall tread down our enemies.'

I find it interesting to read in **I Samuel 14:52**: '*when Saul saw any strong man, or any valiant man, he took him unto him.*' Every valiant man would become a part of Saul's army. We see this verse shortly before Goliath's mockery of God in **I Samuel 17**. One young lad was not considered valiant enough. He would go to see his three older brothers in the army **(I Samuel 17:17-18)**. His brothers, as well as the entire army, did not act valiantly. David, this young shepherd boy, who had been anointed to be the next King **(I Samuel 16:13)**, took care of Goliath, the enemy of God and the army of Israel.

'*Valiant*' by definition means '*boldly courageous; brave; stout-hearted.*' Years later that young shepherd boy would write **Psalm 60**. He knew where his boldness and his bravery came from: through God. He knew that the LORD had taken down Goliath. We can be bold and brave as well. God will go before us as well. God will take care of His own! Boldly stand for Christ! Be valiant!

# # # # #

DAY #68

READ Psalm 61 (*8 verses*)

1 Hear my cry, O God; attend unto my prayer. 2 From the end of
the earth will I cry unto thee, when my heart is overwhelmed:
lead me to the rock that is higher than I. 3 For thou hast been a
shelter for me, and a strong tower from the enemy. 4 I will abide
in thy tabernacle for ever: I will trust in the covert of thy wings.
Selah. 5 For thou, O God, hast heard my vows: thou hast
given me the heritage of those that fear thy name. 6 Thou wilt
prolong the king's life: and his years as many
generations. 7 He shall abide before God for ever: O prepare
mercy and truth, which may preserve him. 8 So will I sing praise
unto thy name for ever, that I may daily perform my vows.

VERSE OF THE DAY: Psalm 61:3
'For thou hast been a shelter for me, and a strong tower from the enemy.'

Sadly there are many in our world that are homeless. Years ago when I worked in the New Center area of Detroit I used to drive by a makeshift cardboard shelter that was constructed under the highway overpass. Spiritually speaking, God has provided us shelter, and not just a cardboard box, but rather a strong tower. Are you thankful for His protection? There are many in our lives that have no spiritual protection. But they can find it in Christ! Who do you know that is spiritually homeless? Who can you share Jesus with today?

# # # # #

DAY #69

READ Psalm 62 (*12 verses*)

1 *Truly my soul waiteth upon God: from him cometh my*
salvation. **2** *He only is my rock and my salvation; he is my*
defence; I shall not be greatly moved. **3** *How long will ye imagine*
mischief against a man? ye shall be slain all of you: as a bowing
wall shall ye be, and as a tottering fence. **4** *They only consult to*
cast him down from his excellency: they delight in lies: they bless
with their mouth, but they curse inwardly. Selah. **5** *My soul,*
wait thou only upon God; for my expectation is from
him. **6** *He only is my rock and my salvation: he is my defence;*
I shall not be moved. **7** *In God is my salvation and my glory:*
the rock of my strength, and my refuge, is in God. **8** *Trust in him*
at all times; ye people, pour out your heart before him: God is a
refuge for us. Selah. **9** *Surely men of low degree*
are vanity, and men of high degree are a lie: to be laid in the
balance, they are altogether lighter than vanity. **10** *Trust not in*
oppression, and become not vain in robbery: if riches increase,
set not your heart upon them. **11** *God hath spoken once;*
twice have I heard this; that power belongeth unto
God. **12** *Also unto thee, O Lord, belongeth mercy: for thou*
renderest to every man according to his work.

VERSE OF THE DAY: Psalm 62:8

'Trust in him at all times; ye people, pour out your heart before him: God is a refuge for us. Selah.'

It is easy to trust God in the good times. We must trust Him at all times, even when life is difficult. We must pour out our heart completely before Him. One commentator put it this way: '*Pour it out as water. Not as milk, whose color remains. Not as wine, whose savor remains. Not as honey, whose taste remains. But as water, of which, when it is poured out, nothing remains.*' Run to Him with all you have – He will be your refuge!

# # # # #

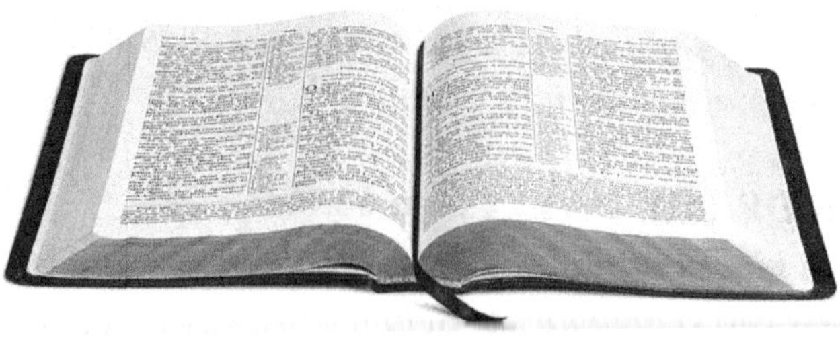

DAY #70

READ Psalm 63 (*11 verses*)

1 O God, thou art my God; early will I seek thee: my soul
thirsteth for thee, my flesh longeth for thee in a dry and thirsty
land, where no water is; 2 To see thy power and thy glory,
so as I have seen thee in the sanctuary. 3 Because thy
lovingkindness is better than life, my lips shall praise
thee. 4 Thus will I bless thee while I live: I will lift up my
hands in thy name. 5 My soul shall be satisfied as with marrow
and fatness; and my mouth shall praise thee with joyful
lips: 6 When I remember thee upon my bed, and meditate on thee
in the night watches. 7 Because thou hast been my help, therefore
in the shadow of thy wings will I rejoice. 8 My soul followeth hard
after thee: thy right hand upholdeth me. 9 But those that seek my
soul, to destroy it, shall go into the lower parts of the
earth. 10 They shall fall by the sword: they shall be a portion for
foxes. 11 But the king shall rejoice in God; every one that
sweareth by him shall glory: but the mouth of them that speak lies
shall be stopped.

VERSE OF THE DAY: Psalm 63:6

'When I remember thee upon my bed, and meditate on thee in the night watches.'

Have you ever laid in bed and reflected on what the LORD has done for you? The word '*meditate*' means to chew on it, as a cow chews its cud. Take your time and remember. At the end of the day think on what the LORD has done for you that day. If we do that every day as we lay down for the night we will realize how good He is to us! Give Him praise today!

DAY #71

READ Psalm 64 (*10 verses*)

1 Hear my voice, O God, in my prayer: preserve my life from fear
of the enemy. 2 Hide me from the secret counsel of the wicked;
from the insurrection of the workers of iniquity: 3 Who whet their
tongue like a sword, and bend their bows to shoot their
arrows, even bitter words: 4 That they may shoot in secret
at the perfect: suddenly do they shoot at him, and fear
not. 5 They encourage themselves in an evil matter:
they commune of laying snares privily; they say, Who shall see
them? 6 They search out iniquities; they accomplish a diligent
search: both the inward thought of every one of them, and the
heart, is deep. 7 But God shall shoot at them with an arrow;
suddenly shall they be wounded. 8 So they shall make their own
tongue to fall upon themselves: all that see them shall flee
away. 9 And all men shall fear, and shall declare the work of
God; for they shall wisely consider of his doing. 10 The righteous
shall be glad in the LORD, and shall trust in him; and all the
upright in heart shall glory.

VERSE OF THE DAY: Psalm 64:10
'The righteous shall be glad in the LORD, and shall trust in him; and all the upright in heart shall glory.'

The word '*glad*' in this verse is the Greek word **sameach**, meaning '*gleeful, joyful, making merry, rejoicing*.' Does that describe how the world sees you? Does the joy of the LORD flow from you? May the world see that we are '*glad in the LORD!*'

# # # # #

DAY #72

READ Psalm 65 (*13 verses*)

*1 Praise waiteth for thee, O God, in Sion: and unto thee shall the
vow be performed. 2 O thou that hearest prayer, unto thee shall
all flesh come. 3 Iniquities prevail against me: as for our
transgressions, thou shalt purge them away. 4 Blessed is the man
whom thou choosest, and causest to approach unto thee, that he
may dwell in thy courts: we shall be satisfied with the goodness
of thy house, even of thy holy temple. 5 By terrible things in
righteousness wilt thou answer us, O God of our
salvation; who art the confidence of all the ends of the
earth, and of them that are afar off upon the sea: 6 Which by his
strength setteth fast the mountains; being girded with power.
7 Which stilleth the noise of the seas, the noise of their waves,
and the tumult of the people. 8 They also that dwell in the
uttermost parts are afraid at thy tokens: thou makest the
outgoings of the morning and evening to rejoice. 9 Thou visitest
the earth, and waterest it: thou greatly enrichest it with the river
of God, which is full of water: thou preparest them corn,
when thou hast so provided for it. 10 Thou waterest the ridges
thereof abundantly: thou settlest the furrows thereof:
thou makest it soft with showers: thou blessest the springing
thereof. 11 Thou crownest the year with thy goodness;
and thy paths drop fatness. 12 They drop upon the
pastures of the wilderness: and the little hills rejoice on every
side. 13 The pastures are clothed with flocks; the valleys also are
covered over with corn; they shout for joy, they also sing.*

VERSE OF THE DAY: Psalm 65:7

'Which stilleth the noise of the seas, the noise of their waves, and the tumult of the people.'

When I read this verse I am reminded of Jesus calming the sea in **Mark 4**. We are told in **verse 37**: '*there arose a great storm of wind, and the waves beat into the ship.*' Jesus told the sea '*Peace, be still*' **(verse 39)**. The result: immediate calm. Can you imagine how loud the winds and crashing waves were, then to be completely calm at Jesus' command? We serve the sovereign God who is in control of all.

What storms are you facing? Jesus can calm them all. Trust in Him, He will deliver you from the crashing waves in your life.

# # # # #

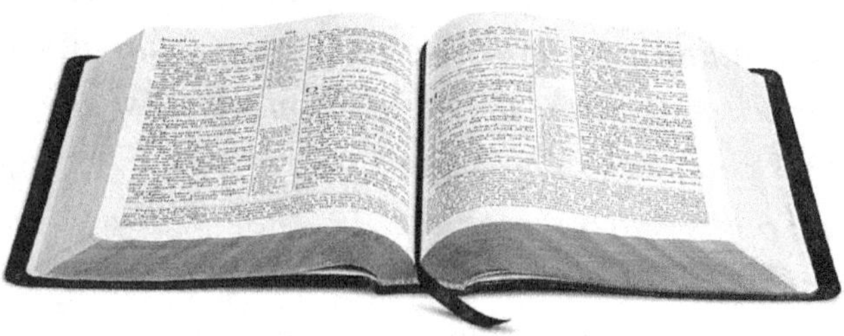

DAY #73

READ Psalm 66 (*20 verses*)

*1 Make a joyful noise unto God, all ye lands: 2 Sing forth the
honour of his name: make his praise glorious. 3 Say unto God,
How terrible art thou in thy works! through the greatness
of thy power shall thine enemies submit themselves unto
thee. 4 All the earth shall worship thee, and shall sing unto thee;
they shall sing to thy name. Selah. 5 Come and see the works
of God: he is terrible in his doing toward the children of
men. 6 He turned the sea into dry land: they went through the
flood on foot: there did we rejoice in him. 7 He ruleth by his
power for ever; his eyes behold the nations: let not the rebellious
exalt themselves. Selah. 8 O bless our God, ye people, and make
the voice of his praise to be heard: 9 Which holdeth our soul in
life, and suffereth not our feet to be moved. 10 For thou, O God,
hast proved us: thou hast tried us, as silver is tried.
11 Thou broughtest us into the net; thou laidst affliction upon our
loins. 12 Thou hast caused men to ride over our heads; we went
through fire and through water: but thou broughtest us out into a
wealthy place. 13 I will go into thy house with burnt offerings:
I will pay thee my vows, 14 Which my lips have uttered, and my
mouth hath spoken, when I was in trouble. 15 I will offer unto
thee burnt sacrifices of fatlings, with the incense of rams;
I will offer bullocks with goats. Selah. 16 Come and hear, all ye
that fear God, and I will declare what he hath done for my
soul. 17 I cried unto him with my mouth, and he was extolled with
my tongue. 18 If I regard iniquity in my heart, the Lord will not*

hear me: **19** *But verily God hath heard me; he hath attended to*
the voice of my prayer. **20** *Blessed be God, which hath not turned*
away my prayer, nor his mercy from me.

VERSE OF THE DAY: Psalm 66:18
'If I regard iniquity in my heart, the Lord will not hear me.'

I am amazed to see those who claim to be Christians but live daily in their sin unrepentantly. I was once told by a man who was caught having an affair with his secretary that, of all those who he knew who had committed adultery, he was the most honorable. My first thought was '*how many people do you associate with who have committed adultery?*' Secondly, I thought, '*don't you understand that your sin makes you dishonorable before God?*'

We cannot continue to live deliberately in sin and expect God to simply look the other way. He WILL discipline His own children (**Hebrews 12:6**). We also see in **Romans 6:1-2**: '*What shall we say then? Shall we continue in sin, that grace may abound? God forbid. How shall we, that are dead to sin, live any longer therein?*'

Repentance on our part will allow us to have our prayers heard by the Most High God! Be sure that you keep short sin accounts with God.

# # # # #

DAY #74

READ Psalm 67 (*7 verses*)

1 God be merciful unto us, and bless us; and cause his face to
shine upon us; Selah. 2 That thy way may be known upon earth,
thy saving health among all nations. 3 Let the people praise thee,
O God; let all the people praise thee. 4 O let the nations be glad
and sing for joy: for thou shalt judge the people righteously, and
govern the nations upon earth. Selah. 5 Let the people praise
thee, O God; let all the people praise thee. 6 Then shall the earth
yield her increase; and God, even our own God, shall bless
us. 7 God shall bless us; and all the ends of the earth shall fear
him.

VERSE OF THE DAY: Psalm 67:1
'God be merciful unto us, and bless us; and cause his face to shine upon us; Selah.'

This verse was displayed on a large sign at my parent's wedding reception behind the bridal table. The sign was hung in the basement of my home for me to see literally thousands of times. What a wonderful prayer that God would be merciful and bless a new home, and that home for years to come. And God continues to display His mercy and His blessing in my parent's marriage and in their family. To have the happy face of God shining upon man is one of the greatest gifts one could have. To know that, as God looks upon you, He is well pleased - not because of who you are, or what you have done, but because you are in Jesus Christ - there is no greater source of peace and power in life. May the LORD's face shine upon you today!

# # # # #

DAY #75

READ Psalm 68:1-18 (*18 verses*)

*1 Let God arise, let his enemies be scattered: let them also that
hate him flee before him. 2 As smoke is driven
away, so drive them away: as wax melteth before the fire, so let
the wicked perish at the presence of God. 3 But let the righteous
be glad; let them rejoice before God: yea, let them exceedingly
rejoice. 4 Sing unto God, sing praises to his name: extol him that
rideth upon the heavens by his name JAH, and rejoice before
him. 5 A father of the fatherless, and a judge of the
widows, is God in his holy habitation. 6 God setteth the solitary
in families: he bringeth out those which are bound with chains:
but the rebellious dwell in a dry land. 7 O God, when thou
wentest forth before thy people, when thou didst march through
the wilderness; Selah: 8 The earth shook, the heavens also
dropped at the presence of God: even Sinai itself was moved at
the presence of God, the God of Israel. 9 Thou, O God, didst send
a plentiful rain, whereby thou didst confirm thine inheritance,
when it was weary. 10 Thy congregation hath dwelt therein: thou,
O God, hast prepared of thy goodness for the poor. 11 The Lord
gave the word: great was the company of those that published it.
12 Kings of armies did flee apace: and she that tarried at home
divided the spoil. 13 Though ye have lien among the pots, yet
shall ye be as the wings of a dove covered with silver, and her
feathers with yellow gold. 14 When the Almighty scattered kings
in it, it was white as snow in Salmon. 15 The hill of God is as the
hill of Bashan; an high hill as the hill of Bashan. 16 Why leap ye,*

*ye high hills? this is the hill which God desireth to dwell in; yea,
the LORD will dwell in it for ever.* **17** *The chariots of God are
twenty thousand, even thousands of angels: the Lord is among
them, as in Sinai, in the holy place.* **18** *Thou hast ascended on
high, thou hast led captivity captive: thou hast received gifts for
men; yea, for the rebellious also, that the LORD God might
dwell among them.*

VERSE OF THE DAY: Psalm 68:3

'But let the righteous be glad; let them rejoice before God: yea, let them exceedingly rejoice.'

We looked at the word '*glad*' this past Sunday. In the life of the believer, gladness and rejoicing go hand in hand. We see **gladness** and **rejoicing** listed together 17 times in the **Psalms (Psalm 9:2, Psalm 14:7, Psalm 31:7, Psalm 32:11, Psalm 40:16, Psalm 45:15, Psalm 48:11, Psalm 51:8, Psalm 53:6, Psalm 68:3, Psalm 70:4, Psalm 90:14, Psalm 96:11, Psalm 97:1, Psalm 97:8, Psalm 106:5, Psalm 118:24)**. Gladness leads to rejoicing. Rejoicing produces more rejoicing. Be gleeful and joyful in the LORD! Rejoice, rejoice, rejoice!

# # # # #

DAY #76

READ Psalm 68:19-35 (*17 verses*)

19 Blessed be the Lord, who daily loadeth us with benefits,
even the God of our salvation. Selah. 20 He that is our God is the
God of salvation; and unto GOD the Lord belong the issues from
death. 21 But God shall wound the head of his enemies, and the
hairy scalp of such an one as goeth on still in his
trespasses. 22 The Lord said, I will bring again from
Bashan, I will bring my people again from the depths of
the sea: 23 That thy foot may be dipped in the
blood of thine enemies, and the tongue of thy dogs in the
same. 24 They have seen thy goings, O God; even the goings of
my God, my King, in the sanctuary. 25 The singers went before,
the players on instruments followed after; among them were the
damsels playing with timbrels. 26 Bless ye God in the
congregations, even the Lord, from the fountain of Israel.
27 There is little Benjamin with their ruler, the princes of
Judah and their council, the princes of Zebulun, and the princes
of Naphtali. 28 Thy God hath commanded thy strength:
strengthen, O God, that which thou hast wrought for
us. 29 Because of thy temple at Jerusalem shall kings bring
presents unto thee. 30 Rebuke the company of spearmen,
the multitude of the bulls, with the calves of the people, till every
one submit himself with pieces of silver: scatter thou the
people that delight in war. 31 Princes shall come out of Egypt;
Ethiopia shall soon stretch out her hands unto God. 32 Sing unto
God, ye kingdoms of the earth; O sing praises unto the Lord;

Selah: 33 To him that rideth upon the heavens of heavens, which were of old; lo, he doth send out his voice, and that a mighty /voice. 34 Ascribe ye strength unto God: his excellency is over Israel, and his strength is in the clouds. 35 O God, thou art terrible out of thy holy places: the God of Israel is he that giveth strength and power unto his people. Blessed be God.

VERSE OF THE DAY: Psalm 68:19
'Blessed be the Lord, who daily loadeth us with benefits, even the God of our salvation. Selah.'

I love that the **KJV** uses the word '*loadeth*' to describe the many benefits that the Lord gives us every day. It is a picture of being filled to capacity. We are daily given love, mercy, grace, comfort, strength and many other benefits. And in addition to our daily bounty, He has provided us salvation, a way to be freed from our sin and enjoy a personal relationship with the God of Scripture. Blessed be the Lord indeed!

# # # # #

DAY #77

READ Psalm 69:1-18 (*18 verses*)

*1 Save me, O God; for the waters are come in
unto my soul. 2 I sink in deep mire, where there is no
standing: I am come into deep waters, where the floods overflow
me. 3 I am weary of my crying: my throat is dried: mine eyes fail
while I wait for my God. 4 They that hate me without a cause are
more than the hairs of mine head: they that would destroy me,
being mine enemies wrongfully, are mighty: then I restored that
which I took not away. 5 O God, thou knowest my foolishness;
and my sins are not hid from thee. 6 Let not them that wait on
thee, O Lord GOD of hosts, be ashamed for my sake: let not those
that seek thee be confounded for my sake, O God of Israel.
7 Because for thy sake I have borne reproach; shame hath
covered my face. 8 I am become a stranger unto my brethren, and
an alien unto my mother's children. 9 For the zeal of thine house
hath eaten me up; and the reproaches of them that reproached
thee are fallen upon me. 10 When I wept, and chastened my soul
with fasting, that was to my reproach. 11 I made sackcloth also
my garment; and I became a proverb to them. 12 They that sit in
the gate speak against me; and I was the song of the drunkards.
13 But as for me, my prayer is unto thee, O LORD, in an
acceptable time: O God, in the multitude of thy mercy hear me,
in the truth of thy salvation. 14 Deliver me out of the mire,
and let me not sink: let me be delivered from them that hate me,
and out of the deep waters. 15 Let not the waterflood overflow
me, neither let the deep swallow me up, and let not the pit shut*

her mouth upon me. **16** *Hear me, O LORD; for thy*
lovingkindness is good: turn unto me according to the multitude
of thy tender mercies. **17** *And hide not thy face from thy servant;*
for I am in trouble: hear me speedily. **18** *Draw nigh unto my*
soul, and redeem it: deliver me because of mine enemies.

VERSE OF THE DAY: Psalm 69:13

'But as for me, my prayer is unto thee, O LORD, in an acceptable time: O God, in the multitude of thy mercy hear me, in the truth of thy salvation.'

David recognized a number of things in this verse. First, his personal prayers were offered to the LORD. God desire to hear our praises and our petitions. Secondly, it was an acceptable time to pray. It is always an acceptable time to go to the LORD with our prayers. Thirdly, God's mercy is great. His mercy (*compassion toward an offender*) is non-ending. Lastly, His salvation is true. David looked to God for His salvation. We must do that as well. Salvation is of the LORD! (**Jonah 2:9**). What a great verse to remind us of the greatness of our personal God.

# # # # #

DAY #78

READ Psalm 69:19-36 (*18 verses*)

*19 Thou hast known my reproach, and my shame, and my
dishonour: mine adversaries are all before thee. 20 Reproach
hath broken my heart; and I am full of heaviness: and I looked for
some to take pity, but there was none; and for comforters, but I
found none. 21 They gave me also gall for my meat; and in my
thirst they gave me vinegar to drink. 22 Let their table become a
snare before them: and that which should have
been for their welfare, let it become a trap. 23 Let their eyes be
darkened, that they see not; and make their loins continually to
shake. 24 Pour out thine indignation upon them, and let thy
wrathful anger take hold of them. 25 Let their habitation be
desolate; and let none dwell in their tents. 26 For they
persecute him whom thou hast smitten; and they talk to the
grief of those whom thou hast wounded. 27 Add iniquity unto
their iniquity: and let them not come into thy
righteousness. 28 Let them be blotted out of the book of the living,
and not be written with the righteous. 29 But I am poor and
sorrowful: let thy salvation, O God, set me up on high. 30 I will
praise the name of God with a song, and will magnify him with
thanksgiving. 31 This also shall please the LORD better than an
ox or bullock that hath horns and hoofs. 32 The humble shall
see this, and be glad: and your heart shall live that seek
God. 33 For the LORD heareth the poor, and despiseth not his
prisoners. 34 Let the heaven and earth praise him, the seas,
and every thing that moveth therein. 35 For God will save Zion,*

and will build the cities of Judah: that they may dwell there,
and have it in possession. **36** *The seed also of his servants shall*
inherit it: and they that love his name shall dwell therein.

VERSE OF THE DAY: Psalm 69:30

'I will praise the name of God with a song, and will magnify him with thanksgiving.'

Are you thankful for God's blessings in your life? The Hebrew word **gadal** meaning to '*lift up*' is translated here '*magnify*.' Do you lift up the LORD and give Him thanks? May it be so with us!

# # # # #

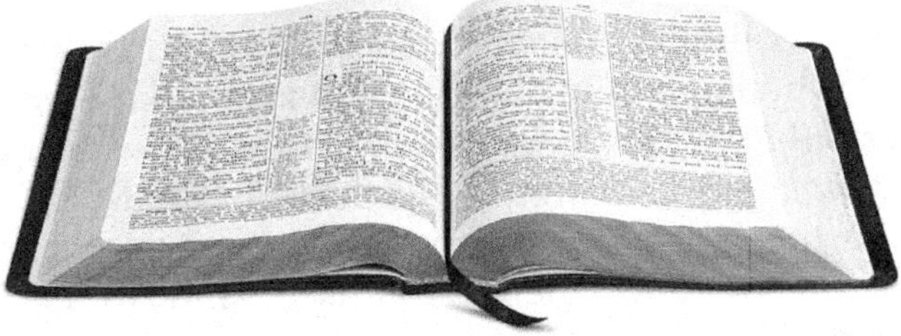

DAY #79

READ Psalm 70 (*5 verses*)

1 Make haste, O God, to deliver me; make haste to help me,
O LORD. 2 Let them be ashamed and confounded that seek after
my soul: let them be turned backward, and put to confusion,
that desire my hurt. 3 Let them be turned back for a reward of
their shame that say, Aha, aha. 4 Let all those that seek thee
rejoice and be glad in thee: and let such as love thy salvation say
continually, Let God be magnified. 5 But I am poor and needy:
make haste unto me, O God: thou art my help and my deliverer;
O LORD, make no tarrying.

VERSE OF THE DAY: Psalm 70:5
'But I am poor and needy: make haste unto me, O God: thou art my help and my deliverer; O LORD, make no tarrying.'

We are born sinners, speaking lies from the womb (**Psalm 58:3 NIV**). Spiritually we are poor and needy sinners who need a deliverer. In addition to today's verse, the Psalms tell us that God is our deliverer (**Psalm 18:2, Psalm 40:17, Psalm 144:2**) and our helper (**Psalm 27:9, Psalm 33:20, Psalm 40:17, Psalm 46:1, Psalm 63:7, Psalm 94:17, Psalm 115:9-11**).

Psalm 40:17 is the only other verse in the **Psalms** that says that our LORD is both our **help** and our **deliverer**: '*But I am poor and needy; yet the Lord thinketh upon me: thou art my help and my deliverer; make no tarrying, O my God.*' In the **NLT** it says that '*the Lord is thinking about me right now.*' Yet another reminder that our help and deliverer is ALWAYS THERE! (**Hebrews 13:5**).

# # # # #

DAY #80

READAD Psalm 71:1-14 (*14 verses*)

1 In thee, O LORD, do I put my trust: let me never be put to
confusion. 2 Deliver me in thy righteousness, and cause me to
escape: incline thine ear unto me, and save me. 3 Be thou my
strong habitation, whereunto I may continually resort:
thou hast given commandment to save me; for thou art my rock
and my fortress. 4 Deliver me, O my God, out of the hand
of the wicked, out of the hand of the unrighteous and cruel man.
5 For thou art my hope, O Lord GOD: thou art my trust from my
youth. 6 By thee have I been holden up from the womb: thou art
he that took me out of my mother's bowels: my praise shall
be continually of thee. 7 I am as a wonder unto many;
but thou art my strong refuge. 8 Let my mouth be filled with thy
praise and with thy honour all the day. 9 Cast me not off
in the time of old age; forsake me not when my strength
faileth. 10 For mine enemies speak against me; and they that lay
wait for my soul take counsel together, 11 Saying, God hath
forsaken him: persecute and take him; for there is none to
deliver him. 12 O God, be not far from me: O my God,
make haste for my help. 13 Let them be
confounded and consumed that are adversaries to my soul;
let them be covered with reproach and dishonour that seek my
hurt. 14 But I will hope continually, and will yet praise thee more
and more.

VERSES OF THE DAY: Psalm 71:10-11

'For mine enemies speak against me; and they that lay wait for my soul take counsel together, Saying, God hath forsaken him: persecute and take him; for there is none to deliver him.'

When you take a stand for Christ people will watch you. They will wait for you to have difficulty and see how you react. They would love nothing more than to see you stumble and act out in a way that is displeasing to God. When trouble arises they will say '*where is your God?*' Take heart believer: the Lord IS your deliverer. We looked at that last week. God has not forsaken you. He will deliver you. YOU CAN COUNT ON IT: HE WILL!

# # # # #

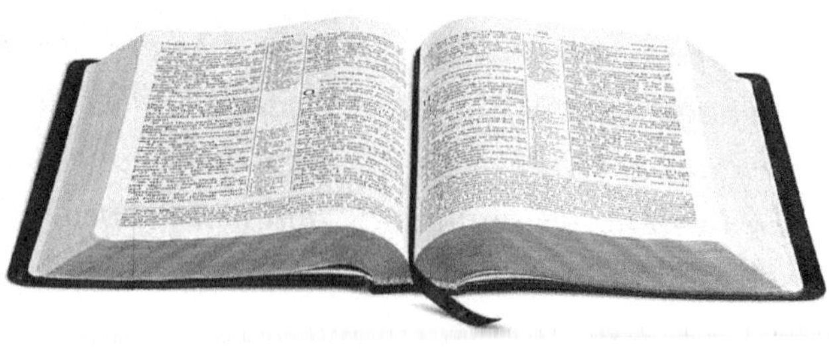

DAY #81

READ Psalm 71:15-24 (*10 verses*)

15 *My mouth shall shew forth thy righteousness and thy salvation*
all the day; for I know not the numbers thereof. **16** *I will go in the*
strength of the Lord GOD: I will make mention of thy
righteousness, even of thine only. **17** *O God, thou hast taught me*
from my youth: and hitherto have I declared thy wondrous
works. **18** *Now also when I am old and grayheaded,*
O God, forsake me not; until I have shewed thy strength
unto this generation, and thy power to every one that is to
come. **19** *Thy righteousness also, O God, is very high, who hast*
done great things: O God, who is like unto thee! **20** *Thou, which*
hast shewed me great and sore troubles, shalt quicken
me again, and shalt bring me up again from the depths of the
earth. **21** *Thou shalt increase my greatness, and comfort me on*
every side. **22** *I will also praise thee with the psaltery, even thy*
truth, O my God: unto thee will I sing with the harp, O thou Holy
One of Israel. **23** *My lips shall greatly rejoice when I sing unto*
thee; and my soul, which thou hast redeemed. **24** *My tongue also*
shall talk of thy righteousness all the day long: for they are
confounded, for they are brought unto shame, that seek my hurt.

VERSE OF THE DAY: Psalm 71:22

'I will also praise thee with the psaltery, even thy truth, O my God: unto thee will I sing with the harp, O thou Holy One of Israel.'

The psaltery and the harp were stringed instruments used in biblical times to offer praise to God. Do you play a musical instrument? Can your musical abilities be used in your local church? If God has given you a gift be sure to use it before you lose it! Praise God with the psaltery, with the harp, with the guitar or piano, or whatever instrument you play!

# # # # #

DAY #82

READ Psalm 72 (*20 verses*)

1 *Give the king thy judgments, O God, and thy righteousness unto*
the king's son. **2** *He shall judge thy people with righteousness,*
and thy poor with judgment. **3** *The mountains shall bring peace*
to the people, and the little hills, by righteousness. **4** *He shall*
judge the poor of the people, he shall save the children of the
needy, and shall break in pieces the oppressor. **5** *They shall fear*
thee as long as the sun and moon endure, throughout all
generations. **6** *He shall come down like rain upon the mown*
grass: as showers that water the earth. **7** *In his days shall the*
righteous flourish; and abundance of peace so long as the moon
endureth. **8** *He shall have dominion also from sea to sea,*
and from the river unto the ends of the earth. **9** *They that dwell in*
the wilderness shall bow before him; and his enemies shall
lick the dust. **10** *The kings of Tarshish and of the isles*
shall bring presents: the kings of Sheba and Seba shall offer
gifts. **11** *Yea, all kings shall fall down before him: all nations*
shall serve him. **12** *For he shall deliver the needy when he crieth;*
the poor also, and him that hath no helper. **13** *He shall spare the*
poor and needy, and shall save the souls of the needy. **14** *He shall*
redeem their soul from deceit and violence: and precious shall
their blood be in his sight. **15** *And he shall live, and to him shall*
be given of the gold of Sheba: prayer also shall be made for him
continually; and daily shall he be praised. **16** *There shall be an*
handful of corn in the earth upon the top of the mountains;
the fruit thereof shall shake like Lebanon: and they of the city

shall flourish like grass of the earth. **17** *His name shall endure*
for ever: his name shall be continued as long as the sun:
and men shall be blessed in him: all nations shall call him
blessed. **18** *Blessed be the LORD God, the God of Israel,*
who only doeth wondrous things. **19** *And blessed be his glorious*
name for ever: and let the whole earth be filled with his glory;
Amen, and Amen. **20** *The prayers of David the son of Jesse are*
ended.

VERSE OF THE DAY: Psalm 72:5
'They shall fear thee as long as the sun and moon endure, throughout all generations.'

To fear God is to have a holy reverence. We must revere God as long as the sun and the moon are still in the sky. That will be all of our days, as well as the days of generations to come, should the Lord tarry. In other words, continually live righteously before the Lord.

# # # # #

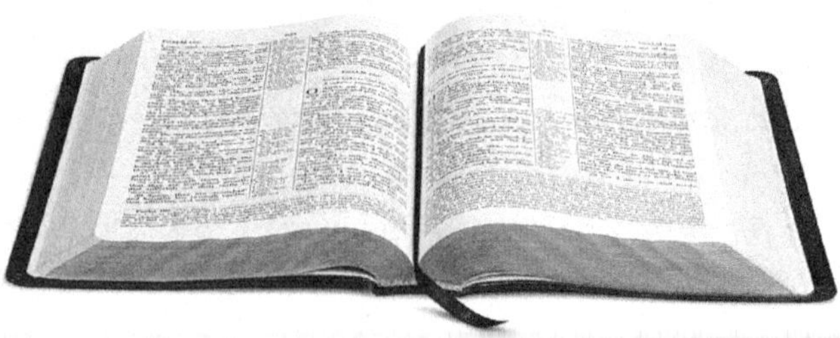

DAY #83

READ Psalm 73:1-17 (*17 verses*)

1 Truly God is good to Israel, even to such as are of a clean
heart. 2 But as for me, my feet were almost gone; my steps had
well nigh slipped. 3 For I was envious at the foolish, when I saw
the prosperity of the wicked. 4 For there are no bands in their
death: but their strength is firm. 5 They are not in trouble as
other men; neither are they plagued like other men. 6 Therefore
pride compasseth them about as a chain; violence covereth
them as a garment. 7 Their eyes stand out with fatness: they have
more than heart could wish. 8 They are corrupt, and speak
wickedly concerning oppression: they speak loftily. 9 They set
their mouth against the heavens, and their tongue walketh
through the earth. 10 Therefore his people return hither:
and waters of a full cup are wrung out to them. 11 And they say,
How doth God know? and is there knowledge in the most
High? 12 Behold, these are the ungodly, who prosper in the
world; they increase in riches. 13 Verily I have cleansed
my heart in vain, and washed my hands in innocency. 14 For all
the day long have I been plagued, and chastened every morning.
15 If I say, I will speak thus; behold, I should offend against the
generation of thy children. 16 When I thought to know this,
it was too painful for me; 17 Until I went into the sanctuary of
God; then understood I their end.

VERSE OF THE DAY: Psalm 73:1
'Truly God is good to Israel, even to such as are of a clean heart.'

We see throughout the Old Testament that the Lord loved Israel and was very patient with them. When they sinned against Him He would punish them but restore them once they repented. We see this cycle repeated over and over. What a great reminder that God loves us yet He will chasten us when needed (**Hebrews 12:6**). How much easier it must be for our Lord to love us and bless us when we live obediently before Him. May we strive every day to live before Him with a clean heart!

# # # # #

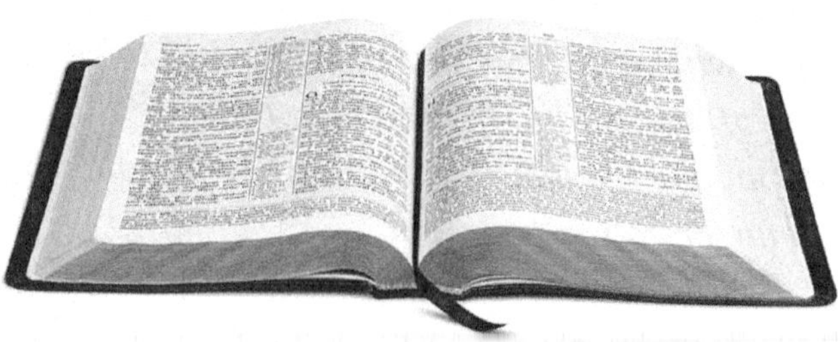

DAY #84

READ Psalm 73:18-28 (*11 verses*)

18 *Surely thou didst set them in slippery places: thou castedst*
them down into destruction. **19** *How are they brought into*
desolation, as in a moment! they are utterly consumed with
terrors. **20** *As a dream when one awaketh; so, O Lord, when thou*
awakest, thou shalt despise their image. **21** *Thus my heart was*
grieved, and I was pricked in my reins. **22** *So foolish was I, and*
ignorant: I was as a beast before thee. **23** *Nevertheless*
I am continually with thee: thou hast holden me by my right
hand. **24** *Thou shalt guide me with thy counsel, and afterward*
receive me to glory. **25** *Whom have I in heaven but thee?*
and there is none upon earth that I desire beside thee. **26** *My*
flesh and my heart faileth: but God is the strength of my heart,
and my portion for ever. **27** *For, lo, they that are far from thee*
shall perish: thou hast destroyed all them that go a whoring from
thee. **28** *But it is good for me to draw near to God: I have put my*
trust in the Lord GOD, that I may declare all thy works.

VERSE OF THE DAY: Psalm 73:28
'But it is good for me to draw near to God: I have put my trust in the Lord GOD, that I may declare all thy works.'

I find it puzzling to see those who claim to be Christians but have little time for God. As a sinner saved by the grace of a loving, living God I cannot be close enough to my Redeemer. It is my prayer that I am closer to my Lord day by day. Do you have a desire to be drawn nearer to God with each passing day? I believe that God would desire that for us. Lord, may it be so in my life to the glory of my Jesus, my Savior, my Redeemer. Amen and amen.

# # # # #

DAY #85

READ Psalm 74 (*23 verses*)

1 *O God, why hast thou cast us off for ever? why doth thine anger*
smoke against the sheep of thy pasture? **2** *Remember thy*
congregation, which thou hast purchased of old; the rod of thine
inheritance, which thou hast redeemed; this mount Zion, wherein
thou hast dwelt. **3** *Lift up thy feet unto the perpetual*
desolations; even all that the enemy hath done wickedly in the
sanctuary. **4** *Thine enemies roar in the midst of thy*
congregations; they set up their ensigns for signs. **5** *A man was*
famous according as he had lifted up axes upon the thick
trees. **6** *But now they break down the carved work thereof at once*
with axes and hammers. **7** *They have cast fire into thy sanctuary,*
they have defiled by casting down the dwelling place of thy name
to the ground. **8** *They said in their hearts, Let us destroy them*
together: they have burned up all the synagogues of God in the
land. **9** *We see not our signs: there is no more any prophet:*
neither is there among us any that knoweth how long. **10** *O God,*
how long shall the adversary reproach? shall the enemy
blaspheme thy name for ever? **11** *Why withdrawest thou thy*
hand, even thy right hand? pluck it out of thy bosom. **12** *For*
God is my King of old, working salvation in the midst of the
earth. **13** *Thou didst divide the sea by thy strength: thou brakest*
the heads of the dragons in the waters. **14** *Thou brakest the heads*
of leviathan in pieces, and gavest him to be meat to the people
inhabiting the wilderness. **15** *Thou didst cleave the fountain and*
the flood: thou driedst up mighty rivers. **16** *The day is thine, the*
night also is thine: thou hast prepared the light and the
sun. **17** *Thou hast set all the borders of the earth: thou hast made*
summer and winter. **18** *Remember this, that the enemy hath*
reproached, O LORD, and that the foolish people have

blasphemed thy name. **19** *O deliver not the soul of thy turtledove unto the multitude of the wicked: forget not the congregation of thy poor for ever.* **20** *Have respect unto the covenant: for the dark places of the earth are full of the habitations of cruelty.* **21** *O let not the oppressed return ashamed: let the poor and needy praise thy name.* **22** *Arise, O God, plead thine own cause: remember how the foolish man reproacheth thee daily.* **23** *Forget not the voice of thine enemies: the tumult of those that rise up against thee increaseth continually.*

VERSE OF THE DAY: Psalm 74:18

'Remember this, that the enemy hath reproached, O LORD, and that the foolish people have blasphemed thy name.'

I have often heard the name of Jesus Christ used in a blasphemous, cursing way. Yet I have never heard Muhammad, Buddha, Confucious or any other religious leader's name used to curse. The fool has said in his heart that there is no God (**Psalm 14:1, Psalm 53:1**) even though Jesus is the only name given among men by which we must be saved (**Acts 4:12**). The fool blasphemes the name of the Holy One continually. Those who love the world are the enemies of God (**James 4:4**). They have reproached, meaning to defy and blaspheme, God.

Never forget that before we were saved we were enemies with God. Praise God by faith through grace we can become His children (**Ephesians 2:8-9**). While we were yet sinners Christ died for us (**Romans 5:8**). For those that we know that are currently enemies with God – there is hope for them in Christ Jesus. Ask the Lord who you might be able to share the gospel with even today. May we see His mocking enemies find salvation through JESUS.

'For if, when we were enemies, we were reconciled to God by the death of his Son, much more, being reconciled, we shall be saved by his life' (**Romans 5:10**)

# # # # #

DAY #86

READ Psalm 75 (*10 verses*)

***1** Unto thee, O God, do we give thanks, unto thee do we give*
thanks: for that thy name is near thy wondrous works
*declare. **2** When I shall receive the congregation I will judge*
*uprightly. **3** The earth and all the inhabitants thereof are*
*dissolved: I bear up the pillars of it. Selah. **4** I said unto the fools,*
*Deal not foolishly: and to the wicked, Lift not up the horn: **5** Lift*
*not up your horn on high: speak not with a stiff neck. **6** For*
promotion cometh neither from the east, nor from the west, nor
*from the south. **7** But God is the judge: he putteth down one, and*
*setteth up another. **8** For in the hand of the LORD there is a cup,*
and the wine is red; it is full of mixture; and he poureth out of the
same: but the dregs thereof, all the wicked of the earth shall
*wring them out, and drink them. **9** But I will declare for ever; I*
*will sing praises to the God of Jacob. **10** All the horns of the*
wicked also will I cut off; but the horns of the righteous shall be
exalted.

VERSE OF THE DAY: Psalm 75:1
'Unto thee, O God, do we give thanks, unto thee do we give thanks: for that thy name is near thy wondrous works declare.'

As we have seen several times in **Psalms** to repeat a phrase is to emphasize the content of the statement. We must be thankful to God. We must be thankful to God. His wonderful works in our lives is evident that He is worthy of our thanksgiving. Far too often we go to God only when in need. May we often go to Him simply to say, '*Thank You Father!*'

# # # # #

DAY #87

READ Psalm 76 (*12 verses*)

1 In Judah is God known: his name is great in Israel. 2 In Salem
also is his tabernacle, and his dwelling place in Zion. 3 There
brake he the arrows of the bow, the shield, and the sword, and
the battle. Selah. 4 Thou art more glorious and excellent than the
mountains of prey. 5 The stouthearted are spoiled, they have
slept their sleep: and none of the men of might have found their
hands. 6 At thy rebuke, O God of Jacob, both the chariot and
horse are cast into a dead sleep. 7 Thou, even thou, art to be
feared: and who may stand in thy sight when once thou art
angry? 8 Thou didst cause judgment to be heard from heaven;
the earth feared, and was still, 9 When God arose to judgment, to
save all the meek of the earth. Selah. 10 Surely the wrath of man
shall praise thee: the remainder of wrath shalt thou
restrain. 11 Vow, and pay unto the LORD your God: let all that
be round about him bring presents unto him that ought to be
feared. 12 He shall cut off the spirit of princes: he is terrible to
the kings of the earth.

VERSE OF THE DAY: Psalm 76:7
Thou, even thou, art to be feared: and who may stand in thy sight when once thou art angry?

The Lord God deserves our holy reverence: to be feared. **Reverence** is defined as '*a feeling or attitude of deep respect tinged with awe.*' Does that describe your feelings toward the Lord? It should. Woe to those who do not stand before God with a holy fear. May we live each day aware of the greatness of our God!

# # # # #

DAY #88

READ Psalm 77 (*20 verses*)

1 *I cried unto God with my voice, even unto God with my voice;*
and he gave ear unto me. **2** *In the day of my trouble I sought the*
Lord: my sore ran in the night, and ceased not: my soul
refused to be comforted. **3** *I remembered God, and was*
troubled: I complained, and my spirit was overwhelmed.
Selah. **4** *Thou holdest mine eyes waking: I am so troubled that I*
cannot speak. **5** *I have considered the days of old, the years of*
ancient times. **6** *I call to remembrance my song in the night:*
I commune with mine own heart: and my spirit made diligent
search. **7** *Will the Lord cast off for ever? and will he be*
favourable no more? **8** *Is his mercy clean gone for ever?*
doth his promise fail for evermore? **9** *Hath God forgotten to be*
gracious? hath he in anger shut up his tender mercies?
Selah. **10** *And I said, This is my infirmity: but I will remember the*
years of the right hand of the most High. **11** *I will remember the*
works of the LORD: surely I will remember thy wonders of
old. **12** *I will meditate also of all thy work, and talk of thy*
doings. **13** *Thy way, O God, is in the sanctuary: who is so great*
a God as our God? **14** *Thou art the God that doest wonders:*
thou hast declared thy strength among the people. **15** *Thou hast*
with thine arm redeemed thy people, the sons of Jacob and
Joseph. Selah. **16** *The waters saw thee, O God, the waters*
saw thee; they were afraid: the depths also were
troubled. **17** *The clouds poured out water: the skies sent out a*
sound: thine arrows also went abroad. **18** *The voice of thy*
thunder was in the heaven: the lightnings lightened the world:
the earth trembled and shook. **19** *Thy way is in the sea, and thy*
path in the great waters, and thy footsteps are not

known. 20 *Thou leddest thy people like a flock by the hand of Moses and Aaron.*

VERSE OF THE DAY: Psalm 77:11
'I will remember the works of the LORD: surely I will remember thy wonders of old.'

In **Joshua 24**, Joshua gathered the Israelites and gave them a history lesson of what God had done for them. They had been told to REMEMBER. They were told to remember the day they were taken out of Egypt (**Exodus 13:3; Deuteronomy 5:15, Deuteronomy 15:15, Deuteronomy 16:13**). They were told to remember the Sabbath day and to keep it holy (**Exodus 20:8**). They were told to remember the commandments of the LORD (**Numbers 15:39-40**). They were told to remember how He had led them through the wilderness in spite of their rebelliousness (**Deuteronomy 8:2, Deuteronomy 9:7**). They were told to remember how God had been faithful to them (**Deuteronomy 32:7**). They were told to remember what God had given to them (**Joshua 1:13**). They seemingly had forgotten everything.

Today when the local church meets for communion, we partake in remembrance of the sacrifice that our LORD has made for us through the shed blood and broken body of the Lord Jesus (**I Corinthians 11:24-25**). We must never cease to remember not only the great works that are recorded in Scripture but the wonders we have seen in our own lives. May we never forget what great things the LORD has done for us – we have a lot to be thankful for!

'*Yes, the LORD has done amazing things for us! What joy!*'
Psalm 126:3 (NLT)

# # # # #

DAY #89

READ Psalm 78:1-17 (*17 verses*)

*1 Give ear, O my people, to my law: incline your ears to the
words of my mouth. 2 I will open my mouth in a parable: I will
utter dark sayings of old: 3 Which we have heard and known, and
our fathers have told us. 4 We will not hide them from their
children, shewing to the generation to come the praises of the
LORD, and his strength, and his wonderful works that he hath
done. 5 For he established a testimony in Jacob, and appointed a
law in Israel, which he commanded our fathers, that they should
make them known to their children: 6 That the generation to
come might know them, even the children which should be
born; who should arise and declare them to their
children: 7 That they might set their hope in God, and not forget
the works of God, but keep his commandments: 8 And might not
be as their fathers, a stubborn and rebellious generation; a
generation that set not their heart aright, and whose spirit was
not stedfast with God. 9 The children of
Ephraim, being armed, and carrying bows, turned back in the
day of battle. 10 They kept not the covenant of God, and refused
to walk in his law; 11 And forgat his works, and his wonders that
he had shewed them. 12 Marvellous things did he in the
sight of their fathers, in the land of Egypt, in the field of
Zoan. 13 He divided the sea, and caused them to pass through;
and he made the waters to stand as an heap. 14 In the daytime
also he led them with a cloud, and all the night with a light of
fire. 15 He clave the rocks in the wilderness, and gave them drink*

as out of the great depths. **16** *He brought streams also out of the rock, and caused waters to run down like rivers.* **17** *And they sinned yet more against him by provoking the most High in the wilderness.*

VERSE OF THE DAY: Psalm 78:4

'We will not hide them from their children, shewing to the generation to come the praises of the LORD, and his strength, and his wonderful works that he hath done.'

We looked last week at the need to remember what God has done. Not only remembering, but we must share it with others. What a privilege to share Christ with a child, whether it is your children or working with other children at church. May the younger generations see us praise the LORD and follow our lead!

# # # # #

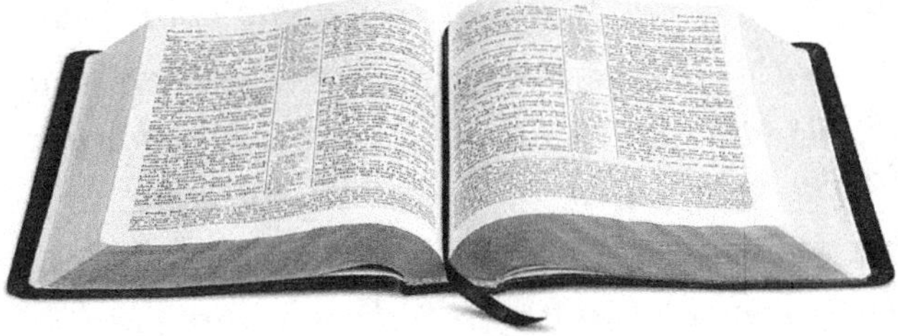

DAY #90

READ Psalm 78:18-38 (*21 verses*)

18 *And they tempted God in their heart by asking meat for their*
lust. **19** *Yea, they spake against God; they said, Can God furnish*
a table in the wilderness? **20** *Behold, he smote the rock, that the*
waters gushed out, and the streams overflowed; can he give
bread also? can he provide flesh for his people? **21** *Therefore the*
LORD heard this, and was wroth: so a fire was kindled against
Jacob, and anger also came up against Israel; **22** *Because they*
believed not in God, and trusted not in his salvation: **23** *Though*
he had commanded the clouds from above, and opened the doors
of heaven, **24** *And had rained down manna upon them to eat, and*
had given them of the corn of heaven. **25** *Man did eat angels'*
food: he sent them meat to the full. **26** *He caused an east wind to*
blow in the heaven: and by his power he brought in the south
wind. **27** *He rained flesh also upon them as dust, and feathered*
fowls like as the sand of the sea: **28** *And he let it fall in the midst*
of their camp, round about their habitations. **29** *So they did eat,*
and were well filled: for he gave them their own desire; **30** *They*
were not estranged from their lust. But while their meat was yet
in their mouths, **31** *The wrath of God came upon them, and slew*
the fattest of them, and smote down the chosen men of Israel.
32 *For all this they sinned still, and believed not for his wondrous*
works. **33** *Therefore their days did he consume in vanity, and*
their years in trouble. **34** *When he slew them, then they sought*
him: and they returned and enquired early after God. **35** *And they*
remembered that God was their rock, and the high God their

redeemer. 36 Nevertheless they did flatter him with their mouth,
and they lied unto him with their tongues. 37 For their heart was
not right with him, neither were they stedfast in his
covenant. 38 But he, being full of compassion,
forgave their iniquity, and destroyed them not: yea, many a time
turned he his anger away, and did not stir up all his wrath.

VERSE OF THE DAY: Psalm 78:35
'And they remembered that God was their rock, and the high God their redeemer.'

Continuing for the 3rd week the need to remember, we see today the Psalmist's remembrance of God's provision for His people. He had provided water from a rock (**Psalm 78:20, Exodus 17:6**) and rained manna from heaven (**Psalm 78:24, Exodus 16**). He met their physical needs. Consider the ways that God has provided for you so that you can afford groceries. Personally I have never gone hungry in my life. Many today are not so fortunate.

The Psalmist also remembered that God had met their spiritual needs. He is their redeemer. Jesus has provided salvation for us. Be thankful that you have food to eat. Remember those who are without; pray for them and reach out to them. Be thankful for your redemption. Remember those who still need Jesus; pray for them and reach out to them. You have the bread of life that will satisfy a starving soul!

# # # # #

DAY #91

READ Psalm 78:39-58 (*20 verse*)

39 *For he remembered that they were but flesh; a wind that*
passeth away, and cometh not again. **40** *How oft did they provoke*
him in the wilderness, and grieve him in the desert! **41** *Yea, they*
turned back and tempted God, and limited the Holy One of
Israel. **42** *They remembered not his hand, nor the day when he*
delivered them from the enemy. **43** *How he had wrought his signs*
in Egypt, and his wonders in the field of Zoan: **44** *And had turned*
their rivers into blood; and their floods, that they could not
drink. **45** *He sent divers sorts of flies among them, which*
devoured them; and frogs, which destroyed them. **46** *He gave*
also their increase unto the caterpiller, and their labour unto the
locust. **47** *He destroyed their vines with hail, and their sycomore*
trees with frost. **48** *He gave up their cattle also to the hail, and*
their flocks to hot thunderbolts. **49** *He cast upon them the*
fierceness of his anger, wrath, and indignation, and trouble, by
sending evil angels among them. **50** *He made a way to his anger;*
he spared not their soul from death, but gave their life over to the
pestilence; **51** *And smote all the firstborn in Egypt; the chief*
of their strength in the tabernacles of Ham: **52** *But made his own*
people to go forth like sheep, and guided them in the wilderness
like a flock. **53** *And he led them on safely, so that they feared not:*
but the sea overwhelmed their enemies. **54** *And he brought them*
to the border of his sanctuary, even to this mountain, which his
right hand had purchased. **55** *He cast out the heathen also before*
them, and divided them an inheritance by line, and made the

tribes of Israel to dwell in their tents. **56** *Yet they tempted*
and provoked the most high God, and kept not his
testimonies: **57** *But turned back, and dealt unfaithfully like their*
fathers: they were turned aside like a deceitful bow. **58** *For they*
provoked him to anger with their high places, and moved him to
jealousy with their graven images.

VERSE OF THE DAY: Psalm 78:56

'Yet they tempted and provoked the most high God, and kept not his testimonies.'

Our Psalm of remembrance continues. Today's verse remembers how the Israelites had done the wrong thing. **Verse 41** tells us '*they turned back and tempted God*' and **verse 42** says '*they remembered not his hand, nor the day when he delivered them from the enemy.*' **Verses 43-55** remind us of all the Lord had done for the Israelites. How sad to see that they did not remember God's goodness to them. How important it is every day to recognized God's goodness to us. May we live day to day thankful for all that He has done for us!

# # # # #

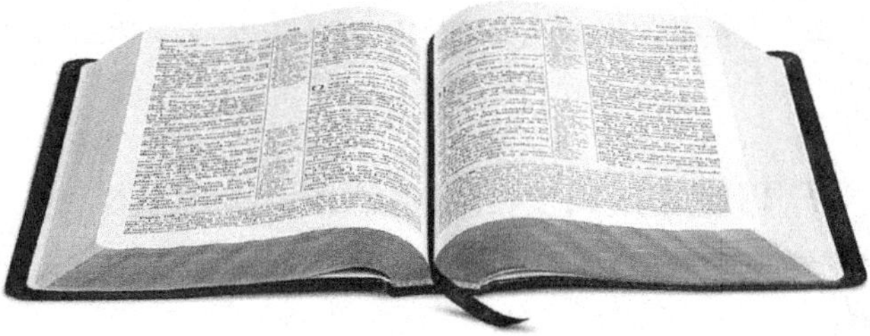

DAY #92

READAD Psalm 78:59-72 (*14 verses*)

59 When God heard this, he was wroth, and greatly abhorred
Israel: 60 So that he forsook the tabernacle of Shiloh, the
tent which he placed among men; 61 And delivered his strength
into captivity, and his glory into the enemy's hand. 62 He gave
his people over also unto the sword; and was wroth with his
inheritance. 63 The fire consumed their young men; and their
maidens were not given to marriage. 64 Their priests fell by the
sword; and their widows made no lamentation. 65 Then the Lord
awaked as one out of sleep, and like a mighty man that shouteth
by reason of wine. 66 And he smote his enemies in the hinder
parts: he put them to a perpetual reproach. 67 Moreover he
refused the tabernacle of Joseph, and chose not the tribe of
Ephraim: 68 But chose the tribe of Judah, the mount Zion which
he loved. 69 And he built his sanctuary like high palaces, like the
earth which he hath established for ever. 70 He chose David also
his servant, and took him from the sheepfolds: 71 From following
the ewes great with young he brought him to feed Jacob his
people, and Israel his inheritance. 72 So he fed them according
to the integrity of his heart; and guided them by the skilfulness of
his hands.

VERSE OF THE DAY: Psalm 78:70
'He chose David also his servant, and took him from the sheepfolds.'

I Samuel 17 records the story of God sending Samuel to the house of Jesse to select a new King. Son after son were paraded before Samuel until there were none left, except one. He was out in the fields with the sheep. The one who was the least likely to be chosen from the perspective of man was the one that God would choose to rule over His people.

David was out with the sheep. He was there out of obedience to his father Jesse. Where are you? Are you where you are in life out of obedience to your Heavenly Father? If you are where He wants you, He can use you. If the Lord has chosen you and has saved your soul, He desires to use you. He has great plans for you. Be willing to serve Him – right where you are!

# # # # #

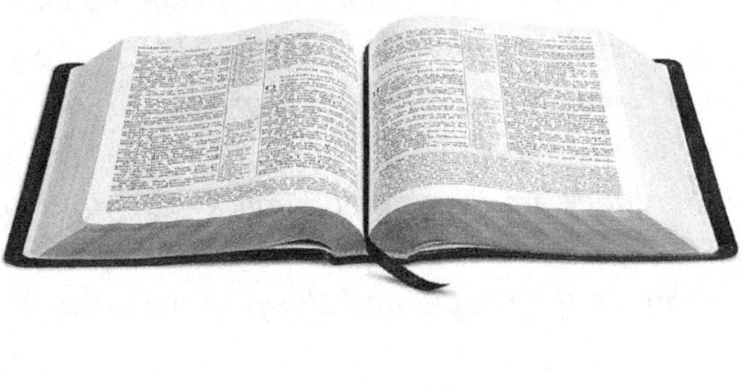

DAY #93

READ Psalm 79 (*13 verses*)

1 *O God, the heathen are come into thine inheritance; thy holy*
temple have they defiled; they have laid Jerusalem on
heaps. **2** *The dead bodies of thy servants have they given to*
be meat unto the fowls of the heaven, the flesh of thy saints unto
the beasts of the earth. **3** *Their blood have they shed like*
water round about Jerusalem; and there was none to
bury them. **4** *We are become a reproach to our neighbours, a*
scorn and derision to them that are round about us. **5** *How long,*
LORD? wilt thou be angry for ever? shall thy jealousy burn like
fire? **6** *Pour out thy wrath upon the heathen that have not known*
thee, and upon the kingdoms that have not called upon thy
name. **7** *For they have devoured Jacob, and laid waste his*
dwelling place. **8** *O remember not against us former iniquities:*
let thy tender mercies speedily prevent us: for we are brought
very low. **9** *Help us, O God of our salvation, for the glory of thy*
name: and deliver us, and purge away our sins, for thy name's
sake. **10** *Wherefore should the heathen say, Where is their God?*
let him be known among the heathen in our sight by the revenging
of the blood of thy servants which is shed. **11** *Let the sighing of*
the prisoner come before thee; according to the greatness
of thy power preserve thou those that are appointed to
die; **12** *And render unto our neighbours sevenfold into their*
bosom their reproach, wherewith they have reproached thee,
O Lord. **13** *So we thy people and sheep of thy pasture will give*

thee thanks for ever: we will shew forth thy praise to all generations.

VERSE OF THE DAY: Psalm 79:9
'Help us, O God of our salvation, for the glory of thy name: and deliver us, and purge away our sins, for thy name's sake.'

We have seen through our study of Psalms that the Lord is both our helper and our deliverer. Today reflect on how God has been that for you. Remember the day that you came to the saving knowledge of Jesus' finished work on the cross. Realize that your sins have been purged away. The Hebrew word here for '*purge*' is **kaphar**, meaning '*atoned for, forgiven, pardoned.*' Atonement has been made. You are forgiven. You have been pardoned. Praise Him today! Amen and amen!

# # # # #

DAY #94

READ Psalm 80 (*19 verses*)

*1 Give ear, O Shepherd of Israel, thou that leadest Joseph like a
flock; thou that dwellest between the cherubims, shine
forth. 2 Before Ephraim and Benjamin and Manasseh stir up thy
strength, and come and save us. 3 Turn us again, O God, and
cause thy face to shine; and we shall be saved. 4 O LORD God
of hosts, how long wilt thou be angry against the prayer of thy
people? 5 Thou feedest them with the bread of tears; and givest
them tears to drink in great measure. 6 Thou makest us a strife
unto our neighbours: and our enemies laugh among
themselves. 7 Turn us again, O God of hosts, and cause thy face
to shine; and we shall be saved. 8 Thou hast brought a
vine out of Egypt: thou hast cast out the heathen, and planted
it. 9 Thou preparedst room before it, and didst cause it to take
deep root, and it filled the land. 10 The hills were covered with
the shadow of it, and the boughs thereof were like the goodly
cedars. 11 She sent out her boughs unto the sea, and her branches
unto the river. 12 Why hast thou then broken down her hedges,
so that all they which pass by the way do pluck her? 13 The boar
out of the wood doth waste it, and the wild beast of the field doth
devour it. 14 Return, we beseech thee, O God of hosts: look down
from heaven, and behold, and visit this vine; 15 And the vineyard
which thy right hand hath planted, and the branch that thou
madest strong for thyself. 16 It is burned with fire, it is cut down:
they perish at the rebuke of thy countenance. 17 Let thy hand be
upon the man of thy right hand, upon the son of man whom thou*

madest strong for thyself. **18** *So will not we go back from thee: quicken us, and we will call upon thy name.* **19** *Turn us again, O LORD God of hosts, cause thy face to shine; and we shall be saved.*

VERSE OF THE DAY: Psalm 80:19
'Turn us again, O LORD God of hosts, cause thy face to shine; and we shall be saved.'

We are told that the Psalmist Asaph wrote this Psalm complaining about the miseries of God's people. As members of the church we are well aware that we are nothing more than a collection of forgiven sinners who struggle with many different sins day by day. It has been said that the church is a hospital for sinners.

We see Asaph's cry here in **verse 19** that God's people would turn back to Him. Notice that his plea in **verse 19** is the same plea given in **verse 7**. We must continually be seeking God and keep our sin accounts short before a holy God. May we consciously continue to turn toward our Lord!

# # # # #

DAY #95

READ Psalm 81 (*16 verses*)

1 *Sing aloud unto God our strength: make a joyful noise unto the*
God of Jacob. **2** *Take a psalm, and bring hither the timbrel, the*
pleasant harp with the psaltery. **3** *Blow up the trumpet in the new*
moon, in the time appointed, on our solemn feast day. **4** *For this*
was a statute for Israel, and a law of the God of Jacob. **5** *This he*
ordained in Joseph for a testimony, when he went out through the
land of Egypt: where I heard a language that I understood
not. **6** *I removed his shoulder from the burden: his hands were*
delivered from the pots. **7** *Thou calledst in trouble, and I*
delivered thee; I answered thee in the secret place of thunder:
I proved thee at the waters of Meribah. Selah. **8** *Hear, O my*
people, and I will testify unto thee: O Israel, if thou wilt hearken
unto me; **9** *There shall no strange god be in thee; neither shalt*
thou worship any strange god. **10** *I am the LORD thy God, which*
brought thee out of the land of Egypt: open thy mouth wide, and
I will fill it. **11** *But my people would not hearken to my voice; and*
Israel would none of me. **12** *So I gave them up unto their own*
hearts' lust: and they walked in their own counsels. **13** *Oh that*
my people had hearkened unto me, and Israel had walked in my
ways! **14** *I should soon have subdued their enemies, and turned*
my hand against their adversaries. **15** *The haters of the LORD*
should have submitted themselves unto him: but their time should
have endured for ever. **16** *He should have fed them also with the*
finest of the wheat: and with honey out of the rock should I have
satisfied thee.

VERSE OF THE DAY: Psalm 81:1

'Sing aloud unto God our strength: make a joyful noise unto the God of Jacob.'

I remember overhearing a gentleman in the foyer of my church tell a friend, '*I don't sing in church. I'm not much of a singer.*' God is not searching for '*singers*' but rather '*worshippers.*' We see the term '*joyful noise*' 7 times in the **Psalms (Psalm 66:1, Psalm 81:1, Psalm 95:1, Psalm 95:2, Psalm 98:4, Psalm 98:6, Psalm 100:1)**. I don't think the Lord is as focused on the '*noise*' as He is on the '*joyful*' attitude of the noise. Do you sing with all your heart unto the Lord? May we not be shy in our attitude of worship: sing loudly unto the Lord from a joyful and thankful heart!

# # # # #

DAY #96

READ Psalm 82 (*8 verses*)

1 God standeth in the congregation of the mighty; he judgeth
among the gods. 2 How long will ye judge unjustly, and accept
the persons of the wicked? Selah. 3 Defend the poor and
fatherless: do justice to the afflicted and needy. 4 Deliver the
poor and needy: rid them out of the hand of the
wicked. 5 They know not, neither will they understand; they walk
on in darkness: all the foundations of the earth are out of
course. 6 I have said, Ye are gods; and all of you are children of
the most High. 7 But ye shall die like men, and fall like one of the
princes. 8 Arise, O God, judge the earth: for thou shalt inherit all
nations.

VERSE OF THE DAY: Psalm 82:8
'Arise, O God, judge the earth: for thou shalt inherit all nations.'

This verse speaks of the sovereignty of God. He is over all and above all. He WILL judge. One commentator put it this way: '*As rightful sovereign of earth, God is invoked personally to correct the evils of His representatives.*'

We also see that He WILL inherit all nations. He will save people from all nations. What a challenge for us to believe in and support global missions! We must declare the good news to every creature (**Mark 16:15**).

Your world may be right where you are. Is God calling you to expand your world? Be open to His leading in your life. May we be like Isaiah: '*Here am I, send me*' **(Isaiah 6:8)**.

'And they sang a new song with these words: "You are worthy to take the scroll and break its seals and open it. For you were killed, and your blood has ransomed people for God from every tribe and language and people and nation."'

(Revelation 5:9 NLT).

# # # # #

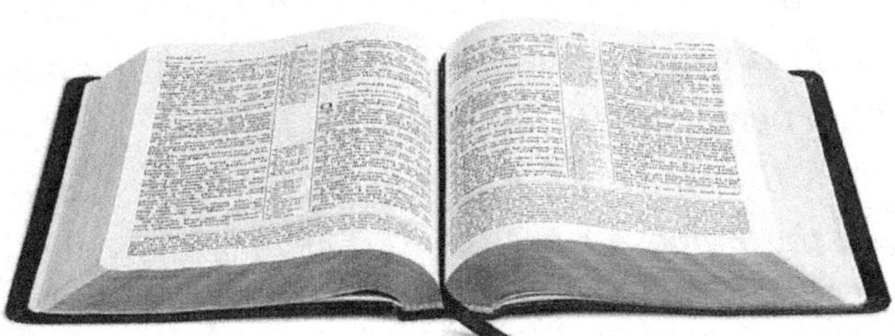

DAY #97

READ Psalm 83 (*18 verses*)

1 *Keep not thou silence, O God: hold not thy peace, and be not*
still, O God. **2** *For, lo, thine enemies make a tumult: and they that*
hate thee have lifted up the head. **3** *They have taken crafty*
counsel against thy people, and consulted against thy hidden
ones. **4** *They have said, Come, and let us cut them off*
from being a nation; that the name of Israel may be no more in
remembrance. **5** *For they have consulted together with one*
consent: they are confederate against thee: **6** *The tabernacles of*
Edom, and the Ishmaelites; of Moab, and the
Hagarenes; **7** *Gebal, and Ammon, and Amalek; the Philistines*
with the inhabitants of Tyre; **8** *Assur also is joined with them:*
they have holpen the children of Lot. Selah. **9** *Do unto them*
as unto the Midianites; as to Sisera, as to Jabin, at the brook of
Kison: **10** *Which perished at Endor: they became as dung for the*
earth. **11** *Make their nobles like Oreb, and like Zeeb: yea, all*
their princes as Zebah, and as Zalmunna: **12** *Who said, Let us*
take to ourselves the houses of God in possession. **13** *O my God,*
make them like a wheel; as the stubble before the wind. **14** *As the*
fire burneth a wood, and as the flame setteth the mountains on
fire; **15** *So persecute them with thy tempest, and make them*
afraid with thy storm. **16** *Fill their faces with shame; that they*
may seek thy name, O LORD. **17** *Let them be confounded and*
troubled for ever; yea, let them be put to shame, and
perish. **18** *That men may know that thou, whose name alone is*
JEHOVAH, art the most high over all the earth.

VERSE OF THE DAY: Psalm 83:18
'That men may know that thou, whose name alone is JEHOVAH, art the most high over all the earth.'

JEHOVAH is the English transliteration of Hebrew text's current reading of the divine name Yahweh. We see many variations of Jehovah in Scripture:

- **Jehovah-Jireh**. *"Yahweh will provide"* **(Genesis 22:14)**
- **Jehovah-Nissi**. *"Yahweh is my banner"* **(Exodus 17:15)**
- **Jehovah-Shalom**. *"Yahweh is peace"* **(Judges 6:24)**
- **Jehovah-Shamma**. *"The Lord is there"* **(Ezekiel 48:35)**
- **Jehovah-Tsidkenu**. *"The Lord is our righteousness"* **(Jeremiah 23:6, Jeremiah 33:16)**

JEHOVAH is the most high! He reigns over all the earth! Offer Him your praise and worship today for His everlasting goodness toward us!

'For the LORD Most High is awesome. He is the great King of all the earth.' **(Psalm 47:2 NLT)**.

# # # # #

DAY #98

READ Psalm 84 (*12 verses*)

*1 How amiable are thy tabernacles, O LORD of hosts! 2 My soul
longeth, yea, even fainteth for the courts of the LORD: my heart
and my flesh crieth out for the living God. 3 Yea, the sparrow
hath found an house, and the swallow a nest for herself, where
she may lay her young, even thine altars, O LORD of hosts, my
King, and my God. 4 Blessed are they that dwell in thy house:
they will be still praising thee. Selah. 5 Blessed is the man whose
strength is in thee; in whose heart are the ways of them.
6 Who passing through the valley of Baca make it a well; the rain
also filleth the pools. 7 They go from strength to strength, every
one of them in Zion appeareth before God. 8 O LORD God of
hosts, hear my prayer: give ear, O God of Jacob. Selah. 9 Behold,
O God our shield, and look upon the face of thine
anointed. 10 For a day in thy courts is better than a thousand.
I had rather be a doorkeeper in the house of my God, than to
dwell in the tents of wickedness. 11 For the LORD God is a sun
and shield: the LORD will give grace and glory:
no good thing will he withhold from them that walk
uprightly. 12 O LORD of hosts, blessed is the man that trusteth
in thee.*

VERSE OF THE DAY: Psalm 84:10

'For a day in thy courts is better than a thousand. I had rather be a doorkeeper in the house of my God, than to dwell in the tents of wickedness.'

A very popular praise chorus of today comes from this verse. Better is one day in your courts, better is one day in your house, better is one day in your courts than thousands elsewhere. The Psalmist states that there is no better place to be than in the service of God. The lowest servant in His kingdom is far greater, and in a far better place, than the greatest of the ungodly.

The Hebrew word used here for '*doorkeeper*' is **caphaph**. This is the only time this word is used in the Old Testament. It pictures a servant waiting at the threshold. He is waiting for his opportunity to be of service. Are you one who is waiting for the Lord to use you? Are you a doorkeeper in the house of God? Where are you serving in your local church? Be ready and useful for the Lord!

# # # # #

DAY #99

READ Psalm 85 (*13 verses*)

*1 LORD, thou hast been favourable unto thy land: thou hast
brought back the captivity of Jacob. 2 Thou hast forgiven the
iniquity of thy people, thou hast covered all their sin.
Selah. 3 Thou hast taken away all thy wrath: thou hast
turned thyself from the fierceness of thine anger. 4 Turn us,
O God of our salvation, and cause thine anger toward us to
cease. 5 Wilt thou be angry with us for ever? wilt thou draw out
thine anger to all generations? 6 Wilt thou not revive us again:
that thy people may rejoice in thee? 7 Shew us thy mercy,
O LORD, and grant us thy salvation. 8 I will hear what God the
LORD will speak: for he will speak peace unto his people, and to
his saints: but let them not turn again to folly. 9 Surely his
salvation is nigh them that fear him; that glory may dwell in our
land. 10 Mercy and truth are met together; righteousness and
peace have kissed each other. 11 Truth shall spring out of the
earth; and righteousness shall look down from
heaven. 12 Yea, the LORD shall give that which is good; and our
land shall yield her increase. 13 Righteousness shall go before
him; and shall set us in the way of his steps.*

VERSE OF THE DAY: Psalm 85:7
'Shew us thy mercy, O LORD, and grant us thy salvation.'

Mercy is defined as '*compassionate or kindly forbearance shown toward an offender, an enemy, or other person in one's power.*'

God's mercy is a prominent theme in the **Psalms**. We see **mercy** mentioned 130 in the **Psalms**. We are told '*for his mercy endureth forever*' in all 26 verses in **Psalm 136**.

Through His mercy He has provided salvation for us through His Son, the Lord Jesus Christ. '*Blessed be the God and Father of our Lord Jesus Christ, which according to his abundant mercy hath begotten us again unto a lively hope by the resurrection of Jesus Christ from the dead*' (**I Peter 1:3**). Thank the LORD for His mercy today!

'*Blessed be God, even the Father of our Lord Jesus Christ, the Father of mercies, and the God of all comfort.*'

(II Corinthians 1:3).

# # # # #

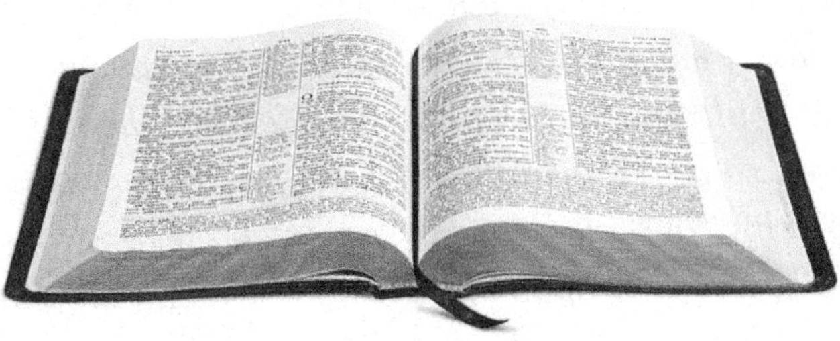

DAY #100

READ Psalm 86 (*17 verses*)

1 Bow down thine ear, O LORD, hear me: for I am poor and
needy. 2 Preserve my soul; for I am holy: O thou my God, save
thy servant that trusteth in thee. 3 Be merciful unto me, O Lord:
for I cry unto thee daily. 4 Rejoice the soul of thy servant: for unto
thee, O Lord, do I lift up my soul. 5 For thou, Lord, art good, and
ready to forgive; and plenteous in mercy unto all them that call
upon thee. 6 Give ear, O LORD, unto my prayer; and attend to
the voice of my supplications. 7 In the day of my trouble I will
call upon thee: for thou wilt answer me. 8 Among the gods there
is none like unto thee, O Lord; neither are there any works like
unto thy works. 9 All nations whom thou hast made shall come
and worship before thee, O Lord; and shall glorify thy name.
10 For thou art great, and doest wondrous things: thou art God
alone. 11 Teach me thy way, O LORD; I will walk in thy truth:
unite my heart to fear thy name. 12 I will praise thee, O Lord my
God, with all my heart: and I will glorify thy name for
evermore. 13 For great is thy mercy toward me: and thou hast
delivered my soul from the lowest hell. 14 O God, the proud are
risen against me, and the assemblies of violent men have sought
after my soul; and have not set thee before them. 15 But thou,
O Lord, art a God full of compassion, and gracious,
longsuffering, and plenteous in mercy and truth. 16 O turn unto
me, and have mercy upon me; give thy strength unto thy servant,
and save the son of thine handmaid. 17 Shew me a token for

good; that they which hate me may see it, and be ashamed: because thou, LORD, hast holpen me, and comforted me.

VERSE OF THE DAY: Psalm 86:15

'But thou, O Lord, art a God full of compassion, and gracious, longsuffering, and plenteous in mercy and truth.'

The word '*plenteous*' is the Hebrew word **rab** which is a word describing large measurement. The word '*plenteous*' used here in the **KJV** is translated in other translations as abundant, abounding, great, full, filled, rich, always, immense and much. Regardless of the word used, this is a great example that our English language cannot adequately describe the greatness of our God. If you could imagine the largest measure of compassion, grace, longsuffering, mercy and truth possible it would still fall far short from the accurate measurement. The amount of our God's compassion, grace, longsuffering, mercy and truth is beyond comprehension. Stand in awe of Him today!

# # # # #

DAY #101

READ Psalm 87 (*7 verses*)

1 His foundation is in the holy mountains. 2 The LORD loveth the
gates of Zion more than all the dwellings of Jacob. 3 Glorious
things are spoken of thee, O city of God. Selah. 4 I will make
mention of Rahab and Babylon to them that know me: behold
Philistia, and Tyre, with Ethiopia; this man was born
there. 5 And of Zion it shall be said, This and that man was born
in her: and the highest himself shall establish her. 6 The LORD
shall count, when he writeth up the people, that this man was
born there. Selah. 7 As well the singers as the players on
instruments shall be there: all my springs are in thee.

VERSE OF THE DAY: Psalm 87:1
'His foundation is in the holy mountains.'

God's foundations are there in the holy mountains. Their holiness is due to God's presence there, not the other way around. God is not there because the mountains are holy, but they are holy because God is there.

Christ Himself is the Foundation of the church. The glorious things spoken of Zion were all typical of Christ. Is Jesus the foundation of your faith?

'For other foundation can no man lay than that is laid, which is Jesus Christ.' **(I Corinthians 3:11)**

'And are built upon the foundation of the apostles and prophets, Jesus Christ himself being the chief corner stone.'

(Ephesians 2:20)

# # # # #

DAY #102

READ Psalm 88 (*18 verses*)

1 O LORD God of my salvation, I have cried day and night before
thee: 2 Let my prayer come before thee: incline thine ear unto my
cry; 3 For my soul is full of troubles: and my life draweth nigh
unto the grave. 4 I am counted with them that go down into the
pit: I am as a man that hath no strength: 5 Free among the dead,
like the slain that lie in the grave, whom thou rememberest no
more: and they are cut off from thy hand. 6 Thou hast laid me in
the lowest pit, in darkness, in the deeps. 7 Thy wrath lieth hard
upon me, and thou hast afflicted me with all thy waves.
Selah. 8 Thou hast put away mine acquaintance far from me;
thou hast made me an abomination unto them: I am shut up, and
I cannot come forth. 9 Mine eye mourneth by reason of affliction:
LORD, I have called daily upon thee, I have stretched out my
hands unto thee. 10 Wilt thou shew wonders to the dead? shall
the dead arise and praise thee? Selah. 11 Shall thy
lovingkindness be declared in the grave? or thy faithfulness in
destruction? 12 Shall thy wonders be known in the dark? and thy
righteousness in the land of forgetfulness? 13 But unto thee have
I cried, O LORD; and in the morning shall my prayer prevent
thee. 14 LORD, why castest thou off my soul? why hidest thou thy
face from me? 15 I am afflicted and ready to die from my youth
up: while I suffer thy terrors I am distracted. 16 Thy fierce wrath
goeth over me; thy terrors have cut me off. 17 They came round
about me daily like water; they compassed me about

together. ***18*** *Lover and friend hast thou put far from me, and mine acquaintance into darkness.*

VERSE OF THE DAY: Psalm 88:1
'O LORD God of my salvation, I have cried day and night before thee.'

We can cry to our God during the day: '*In the day when I cried thou answeredst me, and strengthenedst me with strength in my soul*' (**Psalm 138:3**). We can cry to our God during the night: '*Arise, cry out in the night in the beginning of the watched pour out thine heart like water before the face of the Lord: lift up thy hands toward him for the life of thy young children, that faint for hunger in the top of every street*' (**Lamentations 2:19**). He hears our cries whenever we call out to Him: '*In sudden fear I had cried out, "I have been cut off from the LORD!" But you heard my cry for mercy and answered my call for help.*' (**Psalm 31:22 NLT**).

Talk to your Heavenly Father in the day or in the night. We are told to pray without ceasing, that means at any time (**I Thessalonians 5:17**). The God of our salvation has a listening ear to the cries of His children! He is there for you!

# # # # #

DAY #103

READ Psalm 89:1-16 (*16 verses*)

1 *I will sing of the mercies of the LORD for ever: with my mouth*
will I make known thy faithfulness to all generations. **2** *For I have*
said, Mercy shall be built up for ever: thy faithfulness shalt thou
establish in the very heavens. **3** *I have made a covenant with my*
chosen, I have sworn unto David my servant, **4** *Thy seed will I*
establish for ever, and build up thy throne to all generations.
Selah. **5** *And the heavens shall praise thy wonders, O LORD: thy*
faithfulness also in the congregation of the saints. **6** *For who in*
the heaven can be compared unto the LORD? who among the
sons of the mighty can be likened unto the LORD? **7** *God is*
greatly to be feared in the assembly of the saints, and to be had
in reverence of all them that are about him. **8** *O LORD God of*
hosts, who is a strong LORD like unto thee? or to thy faithfulness
round about thee? **9** *Thou rulest the raging of the sea: when the*
waves thereof arise, thou stillest them. **10** *Thou hast broken*
Rahab in pieces, as one that is slain; thou hast scattered thine
enemies with thy strong arm. **11** *The heavens are thine, the earth*
also is thine: as for the world and the fulness thereof, thou hast
founded them. **12** *The north and the south thou hast created*
them: Tabor and Hermon shall rejoice in thy name. **13** *Thou hast*
a mighty arm: strong is thy hand, and high is thy right
hand. **14** *Justice and judgment are the habitation of thy throne:*
mercy and truth shall go before thy face. **15** *Blessed is the people*
that know the joyful sound: they shall walk, O LORD, in the light

of thy countenance. **16** *In thy name shall they rejoice all the day: and in thy righteousness shall they be exalted.*

VERSE OF THE DAY: Psalm 89:1

'I will sing of the mercies of the LORD for ever: with my mouth will I make known thy faithfulness to all generations.'

The **Psalms** were the hymnbook for Israel. Not every Psalm was sung but their congregational praise were comprised of singing of Psalms. Today a popular song's lyrics are the words from today's verse. This praise chorus from today gives us a glimpse into what it might have been like as the congregation sang from the **Psalms**. Do you long to sing of the mercies of the LORD forever? When you meet together in corporate worship or just driving in your car sing with all your heart. May we make the faithfulness of our great God known to all generations.

# # # # #

DAY #104

READ Psalm 89:17-33 (*17 verses*)

*17 For thou art the glory of their strength: and in thy favour our
horn shall be exalted. 18 For the LORD is our defence; and the
Holy One of Israel is our king. 19 Then thou spakest in vision to
thy holy one, and saidst, I have laid help upon one that is mighty;
I have exalted one chosen out of the people. 20 I have found
David my servant; with my holy oil have I anointed
him: 21 With whom my hand shall be established: mine arm also
shall strengthen him. 22 The enemy shall not exact upon him; nor
the son of wickedness afflict him. 23 And I will beat down his foes
before his face, and plague them that hate him. 24 But my
faithfulness and my mercy shall be with him: and in my name
shall his horn be exalted. 25 I will set his hand also in the sea,
and his right hand in the rivers. 26 He shall cry unto me,
Thou art my father, my God, and the rock of my
salvation. 27 Also I will make him my firstborn, higher than the
kings of the earth. 28 My mercy will I keep for him for evermore,
and my covenant shall stand fast with him. 29 His seed also will
I make to endure for ever, and his throne as the days of
heaven. 30 If his children forsake my law, and walk not in my
judgments; 31 If they break my statutes, and keep not my
commandments; 32 Then will I visit their transgression with the
rod, and their iniquity with stripes. 33 Nevertheless my
lovingkindness will I not utterly take from him, nor suffer my
faithfulness to fail.*

VERSE OF THE DAY: Psalm 89:29
'His seed also will I make to endure for ever, and his throne as the days of heaven.'

This Psalm tells of the Messiah who would come through the line of David. This was prophesied in **Jeremiah 23:5**: '*Behold, the days come, saith the LORD, that I will raise unto David a righteous Branch, and a King shall reign and prosper, and shall execute judgment and justice in the earth.*' The genealogies set forth in **Luke 3** and **Matthew 1** prove this to be true. Jesus is the promised Messiah. He will reign forever! Blessed be the name of the LORD!

# # # # #

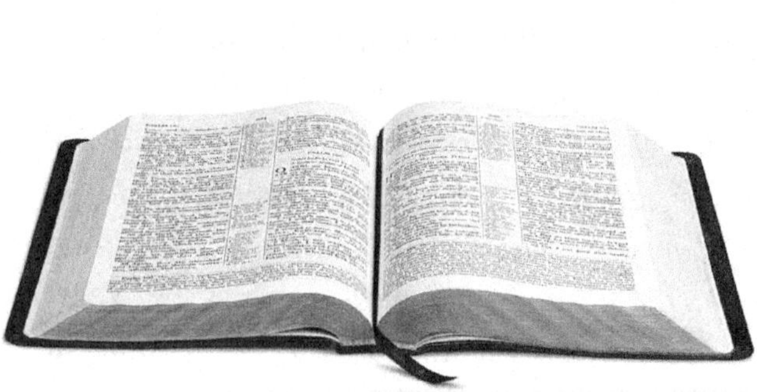

DAY #105

READ Psalm 89:34-52 (*19 verses*)

34 *My covenant will I not break, nor alter the thing that is gone*
out of my lips. **35** *Once have I sworn by my holiness that I will*
not lie unto David. **36** *His seed shall endure for ever, and his*
throne as the sun before me. **37** *It shall be established for ever as*
the moon, and as a faithful witness in heaven. Selah. **38** *But thou*
hast cast off and abhorred, thou hast been wroth with thine
anointed. **39** *Thou hast made void the covenant of thy servant:*
thou hast profaned his crown by casting it to the ground.
40 *Thou hast broken down all his hedges; thou hast brought his*
strong holds to ruin. **41** *All that pass by the way spoil him: he is*
a reproach to his neighbours. **42** *Thou hast set up the right hand*
of his adversaries; thou hast made all his enemies to rejoice.
43 *Thou hast also turned the edge of his sword, and hast not made*
him to stand in the battle. **44** *Thou hast made his glory to cease,*
and cast his throne down to the ground. **45** *The days of his youth*
hast thou shortened: thou hast covered him with shame.
Selah. **46** *How long, LORD? wilt thou hide thyself for ever? shall*
thy wrath burn like fire? **47** *Remember how short my time is:*
wherefore hast thou made all men in vain? **48** *What man is he*
that liveth, and shall not see death? shall he deliver his soul from
the hand of the grave? Selah. **49** *Lord, where are thy former*
lovingkindnesses, which thou swarest unto David in thy
truth? **50** *Remember, Lord, the reproach of thy servants; how I*
do bear in my bosom the reproach of all the mighty
people; **51** *Wherewith thine enemies have reproached, O LORD;*

wherewith they have reproached the footsteps of thine anointed.
52 *Blessed be the LORD for evermore. Amen, and Amen.*

VERSE OF THE DAY: Psalm 89:52
'Blessed be the LORD for evermore. Amen, and Amen.'

Three times in the **Psalms** we see the phrase, '*Amen and amen.*' We see it in **Psalm 41:13, Psalm 72:19** and here in **Psalm 89:52**. In each case it is following the recognition that the Lord is blessed forever. The Hebrew word for '*blessed*' here is **barak** which implies kneeling in an act of abundant adoration. May we kneel before our great God forever with obedient lives. Amen and amen!

# # # # #

DAY #106

READ Psalm 90 (*17 verses*)

1 Lord, thou hast been our dwelling place in all
generations. 2 Before the mountains were brought forth, or ever
thou hadst formed the earth and the world, even from everlasting
to everlasting, thou art God. 3 Thou turnest man to destruction;
and sayest, Return, ye children of men. 4 For a thousand years in
thy sight are but as yesterday when it is past, and as a watch in
the night. 5 Thou carriest them away as with a flood; they
are as a sleep: in the morning they are like grass which groweth
up. 6 In the morning it flourisheth, and groweth up; in the evening
it is cut down, and withereth. 7 For we are consumed by thine
anger, and by thy wrath are we troubled. 8 Thou hast set our
iniquities before thee, our secret sins in the light of thy
countenance. 9 For all our days are passed away in thy wrath:
we spend our years as a tale that is told. 10 The days of our
years are threescore years and ten; and if by reason of
strength they be fourscore years, yet is their strength labour and
sorrow; for it is soon cut off, and we fly away. 11 Who knoweth
the power of thine anger? even according to thy fear, so is thy
wrath. 12 So teach us to number our days, that we may
apply our hearts unto wisdom. 13 Return, O LORD, how long?
and let it repent thee concerning thy servants. 14 O satisfy us
early with thy mercy; that we may rejoice and be glad all our
days. 15 Make us glad according to the days wherein thou hast
afflicted us, and the years wherein we have seen evil. 16 Let thy
work appear unto thy servants, and thy glory unto their

children. 17 *And let the beauty of the LORD our God be upon us: and establish thou the work of our hands upon us; yea, the work of our hands establish thou it.*

VERSE OF THE DAY: Psalm 90:12
'So teach us to number our days, that we may apply our hearts unto wisdom.'

We need to understand that this life is short. We are told in **James 4:14** that our life '*is as a vapour that appeareth for a little time, and then vanisheth away.*' Time here on earth is short, especially when viewed from an eternal perspective. Through the same lens eternity is immeasurably long. We must see the urgency of sharing Christ with those we love who are without our Savior so they can spend eternity with Him. We must realize that our days are numbered and use them wisely for the furtherance of the gospel. May our hearts be filled with wisdom as we seek to serve our great King, the Lord Jesus!

# # # # #

DAY #107

READ Psalm 91 (*16 verses*)

1 *He that dwelleth in the secret place of the most High shall abide*
under the shadow of the Almighty. ***2*** *I will say of the LORD, He*
is my refuge and my fortress: my God; in him will I
trust. ***3*** *Surely he shall deliver thee from the snare of the*
fowler, and from the noisome pestilence. ***4*** *He shall cover thee*
with his feathers, and under his wings shalt thou trust: his
truth shall be thy shield and buckler. ***5*** *Thou shalt not be afraid*
for the terror by night; nor for the arrow that flieth by
day; ***6*** *Nor for the pestilence that walketh in darkness; nor for*
the destruction that wasteth at noonday. ***7*** *A thousand shall fall*
at thy side, and ten thousand at thy right hand; but it shall not
come nigh thee. ***8*** *Only with thine eyes shalt thou behold and see*
the reward of the wicked. ***9*** *Because thou hast made the*
LORD, which is my refuge, even the most High, thy
habitation; ***10*** *There shall no evil befall thee, neither shall any*
plague come nigh thy dwelling. ***11*** *For he shall give his angels*
charge over thee, to keep thee in all thy ways. ***12*** *They shall bear*
thee up in their hands, lest thou dash thy foot against a
stone. ***13*** *Thou shalt tread upon the lion and adder: the young*
lion and the dragon shalt thou trample under feet. ***14*** *Because he*
hath set his love upon me, therefore will I deliver him: I will set
him on high, because he hath known my name. ***15*** *He shall call*
upon me, and I will answer him: I will be with him in trouble;
I will deliver him, and honour him. ***16*** *With long life will I satisfy*
him, and shew him my salvation.

VERSE OF THE DAY: Psalm 91:2
'I will say of the LORD, He is my refuge and my fortress: my God; in him will I trust.'

We see two words here that describe the LORD's protection: refuge and fortress. '*Refuge*' is the Hebrew word **machaceh**, being a place of shelter. The LORD is our refuge (**II Samuel 22:3; Psalm 2:12; Psalm 7:1; Psalm 11:1; Psalm 14:6; Psalm 16:1; Psalm 17:7; Psalm 18:2,30; Psalm 25:20; Psalm 31:1, 19; Psalm 46:1; Psalm 57:1; Psalm 61:3-4; Psalm 62:7-8; Psalm 71:1; Psalm 73:28; Psalm 91:2, 9; Psalm 94:22; Psalm 118:8-9; Psalm 141:8; Psalm 142:5; Proverbs 30:5; Isaiah 57:13; Joel 3:16; Zephaniah 3:12**). '*Fortress*' is the Hebrew word **matsuwd**, signifying a large strong tower, much like a castle. The LORD is our fortress (**II Samuel 22:2, Psalm 18:2, Psalm 31:3, Psalm 71:3, Psalm 91:2, Psalm 144:2, Jeremiah 16:19**). How wonderful to trust in such a strong and safe protector!

# # # # #

DAY #108

READ Psalm 92 (*15 verses*)

1 *It is a good thing to give thanks unto the LORD, and to sing*
praises unto thy name, O most High: **2** *To shew forth thy*
lovingkindness in the morning, and thy faithfulness every
night, **3** *Upon an instrument of ten strings, and upon the psaltery;*
upon the harp with a solemn sound. **4** *For thou, LORD, hast*
made me glad through thy work: I will triumph in the works of
thy hands. **5** *O LORD, how great are thy works! and thy thoughts*
are very deep. **6** *A brutish man knoweth not; neither doth a fool*
understand this. **7** *When the wicked spring as the grass, and when*
all the workers of iniquity do flourish; it is that they shall be
destroyed for ever: **8** *But thou, LORD, art most high for*
evermore. **9** *For, lo, thine enemies, O LORD, for, lo, thine*
enemies shall perish; all the workers of iniquity shall be
scattered. **10** *But my horn shalt thou exalt like the horn of an*
unicorn: I shall be anointed with fresh oil. **11** *Mine eye also shall*
see my desire on mine enemies, and mine ears shall hear my
desire of the wicked that rise up against me. **12** *The righteous*
shall flourish like the palm tree: he shall grow like a cedar in
Lebanon. **13** *Those that be planted in the house of the LORD*
shall flourish in the courts of our God. **14** *They shall still bring*
forth fruit in old age; they shall be fat and
flourishing; **15** *To shew that the LORD is upright: he is my rock,*
and there is no unrighteousness in him.

VERSE OF THE DAY: Psalm 92:13
'Those that be planted in the house of the LORD shall flourish in the courts of our God.'

This verse reminds me of the blessed man in **Psalm 1:3**: '*And he shall be like a tree planted by the rivers of water, that bringeth forth his fruit in his season; his leaf also shall not wither; and whatsoever he doeth shall prosper.*' How important it is to be planted deep in the faith. That is done through daily time in the Word and in prayer. That is one of the reasons we are doing this study through the **Psalms**. May it instill in each of us a need to be in His Word every day so that we can flourish in our Christian faith to the glory of God!

# # # # #

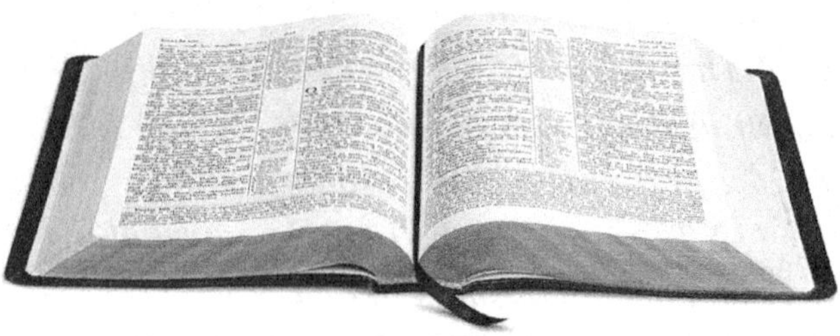

DAY #109

READ Psalm 93 (*5 verses*)

1 The LORD reigneth, he is clothed with majesty; the LORD is
clothed with strength, wherewith he hath girded himself:
the world also is stablished, that it cannot be moved.
2 Thy throne is established of old: thou art from
everlasting. 3 The floods have lifted up, O LORD, the floods have
lifted up their voice; the floods lift up their waves. 4 The LORD
on high is mightier than the noise of many waters, yea, than the
mighty waves of the sea. 5 Thy testimonies are very sure: holiness
becometh thine house, O LORD, for ever.

VERSE OF THE DAY: Psalm 93:4
'The LORD on high is mightier than the noise of many waters, yea, than the mighty waves of the sea.'

The mightiest rush of water I have ever heard was during my visit to Niagara Falls. The roar of the falls is powerful. The falls roar and roar. There is no way to make it stop. I am reminded of the account of Jesus speaking to the raging waves: '*Peace be still*' (**Mark 4:39**). The Lord God is much more powerful that the roar of the mightiest waters. In the midst of the storms of life, we can find peace in Jesus. He is mightier than any trial you may be facing. Put your trust in Him. He will be with you despite the storms in your life! He will make a way, for mighty is He!

# # # # #

DAY #110

READ Psalm 94 (*23 verses*)

*1 O LORD God, to whom vengeance belongeth; O God, to whom
vengeance belongeth, shew thyself. 2 Lift up thyself, thou judge
of the earth: render a reward to the proud. 3 LORD, how long
shall the wicked, how long shall the wicked triumph? 4 How long
shall they utter and speak hard things? and all the workers of
iniquity boast themselves? 5 They break in pieces thy people, O
LORD, and afflict thine heritage. 6 They slay the widow and the
stranger, and murder the fatherless. 7 Yet they say, The LORD
shall not see, neither shall the God of Jacob regard it.
8 Understand, ye brutish among the people: and ye fools, when
will ye be wise? 9 He that planted the ear, shall he not hear? he
that formed the eye, shall he not see? 10 He that chastiseth the
heathen, shall not he correct? he that teacheth man
knowledge, shall not he know? 11 The LORD knoweth the
thoughts of man, that they are vanity. 12 Blessed is the man
whom thou chastenest, O LORD, and teachest him out of thy
law; 13 That thou mayest give him rest from the days of adversity,
until the pit be digged for the wicked. 14 For the LORD will
not cast off his people, neither will he forsake his
inheritance. 15 But judgment shall return unto righteousness:
and all the upright in heart shall follow it. 16 Who will rise up for
me against the evildoers? or who will stand up for me against the
workers of iniquity? 17 Unless the LORD had been my help, my
soul had almost dwelt in silence. 18 When I said, My foot
slippeth; thy mercy, O LORD, held me up. 19 In the multitude of*

my thoughts within me thy comforts delight my soul. **20** *Shall the*
throne of iniquity have fellowship with thee, which frameth
mischief by a law? **21** *They gather themselves together*
against the soul of the righteous, and condemn the innocent
blood. **22** *But the LORD is my defence; and my God is the rock*
of my refuge. **23** *And he shall bring upon them their own iniquity,*
and shall cut them off in their own wickedness; yea, the LORD
our God shall cut them off.

VERSE OF THE DAY: Psalm 94:11
'The LORD knoweth the thoughts of man, that they are vanity.'

Samuel was sent to anoint Saul as King of Israel when they demanded a King in **I Samuel 8**. In **I Samuel 9:19** Saul was told that Samuel the next day would '*tell thee all that is in thine heart.*' If someone was able to see the thought s and intents of your heart, what would you think? Would that change your thoughts? We see in the gospels that Jesus knew the thoughts of people (**Matthew 9:1-8, Matthew 12:22-25, Luke 6:6-10**).

We are told in today's verse that the LORD knows that the thought of man are '*vanity*' the Hebrew word **hebel** which means '*unsatisfactory.*' What does God see when he looks at our heart? May we seek to live with a pure heart!

# # # # #

DAY #111

READ Psalm 95 (*11 verses*)

1 *O come, let us sing unto the LORD: let us make a joyful noise*
to the rock of our salvation. ***2*** *Let us come before his presence*
with thanksgiving, and make a joyful noise unto him with
psalms. ***3*** *For the LORD is a great God, and a great King above*
all gods. ***4*** *In his hand are the deep places of the earth: the*
strength of the hills is his also. ***5*** *The sea is his, and he made it:*
and his hands formed the dry land. ***6*** *O come, let us worship*
and bow down: let us kneel before the LORD our
maker. ***7*** *For he is our God; and we are the people of his pasture,*
and the sheep of his hand. To day if ye will hear his
voice, ***8*** *Harden not your heart, as in the*
provocation, and as in the day of temptation in the
wilderness: ***9*** *When your fathers tempted me, proved me, and saw*
my work. ***10*** *Forty years long was I grieved with this generation,*
and said, It is a people that do err in their heart, and they have
not known my ways: ***11*** *Unto whom I sware in my wrath that they*
should not enter into my rest.

VERSES OF THE DAY: Psalm 95:6-7

'O come, let us worship and bow down: let us kneel before the LORD our maker. For he is our God; and we are the people of his pasture, and the sheep of his hand. Today if ye will hear his voice.'

We see in these verses two titles of our God. The first is that of our maker, or Creator. Our understanding of the doctrine of creation is important because of its effect on our understanding of other biblical doctrines. We find belief in the **Genesis** account of creation throughout both the Old and New Testaments.

The Old Testament refers to the creation account many times outside of the book of **Genesis**. **Job 10:9** states that God has made man from the earth. In **Job 38** we see God asking Job where he was when God created all things. The **Psalms** declare God's marvelous craftsmanship (**Psalm 19:1**), the heavens were made by the breath of His mouth (**Psalm 33:5-6**) and that God created all in His wisdom (**Psalm 104:24**) and by His Spirit (**Psalm 104:30**). **Ecclesiastes 12:1** mandates that we remember that God is the Creator. In **Isaiah 40:26-28** we are instructed to behold the Lord, the Creator of the ends of the earth who fainteth not.

The New Testament is full of passages that talk about the creation account. The foundation of the world is referred to on numerous occasions (**Matthew 13:35, 25:34; Luke 11:50; John 17:24; Ephesians 1:4; Hebrews 4:3, 9:26; I Peter 1:20; Revelation 13:8, 17:8**). References to the beginning of creation abound as well (**Matthew 24:21; Mark 10:6, 13:19; Romans 1:20; Hebrews 1:10; II Peter 3:4; Revelation 3:14**). The following passages confirm the belief in the creation account given in Genesis:

- **Mark 13:19** – *God created in the beginning*
- **John 1:1-3** – *all things were created by Jesus Christ*
- **Acts 17:24** – *God made the world and all things therein*

- **Romans 1:20** - *The invisible things of Him from the creation of the world are clearly seen*
- **Romans 5:12-21** – *sin and death entered the world by the first created man Adam*
- **I Corinthians 11:8-9** – *woman was created from man and for man*
- **I Corinthians 15:21** – *sin entered the world through Adam*
- **I Corinthians 15:45** – *The first man, Adam, was made a living soul*
- **I Corinthians 15:47** – *Adam was made of the earth*
- **Ephesians 3:9** – *all things were created by Jesus Christ*
- **I Timothy 2:13** – *Adam was created before Eve*
- **Hebrews 11:3** – *the worlds were framed by the word of God*
- **Revelation 4:11** – *God created all things for His pleasure*

Secondly we see that the LORD is the Great Shepherd (**Psalm 23:1, Hebrews 13:20**). He is the shepherd and we are His sheep. What a great comparison, seeing that sheep may be the dumbest of all animals who have no way to protect themselves. It shows the need to rely on the Shepherd. Jesus said: '*My sheep hear my voice, and I know them, and they follow Me*' (**John 10:27**).

Aren't you glad that the One who created all things watches over us as a loving Shepherd! May we worship and bow down before the Lord, our God, our Maker this day!

# # # # #

DAY #112

READ Psalm 96 (*13 verses*)

*1 O sing unto the LORD a new song: sing unto the LORD, all the
earth. 2 Sing unto the LORD, bless his name; shew forth his
salvation from day to day. 3 Declare his glory among the
heathen, his wonders among all people. 4 For the
LORD is great, and greatly to be praised: he is to be
feared above all gods. 5 For all the gods of the nations are idols:
but the LORD made the heavens. 6 Honour and
majesty are before him: strength and beauty are in his
sanctuary. 7 Give unto the LORD, O ye kindreds of the people,
give unto the LORD glory and strength. 8 Give unto the LORD
the glory due unto his name: bring an offering, and come into his
courts. 9 O worship the LORD in the beauty of holiness: fear
before him, all the earth. 10 Say among the heathen that the
LORD reigneth: the world also shall be established that it shall
not be moved: he shall judge the people righteously. 11 Let the
heavens rejoice, and let the earth be glad; let the sea roar, and
the fulness thereof. 12 Let the field be joyful, and all
that is therein: then shall all the trees of the wood
rejoice 13 Before the LORD: for he cometh, for he cometh to
judge the earth: he shall judge the world with righteousness, and
the people with his truth.*

VERSE OF THE DAY: Psalm 96:5

'For all the gods of the nations are idols: but the LORD made the heavens.'

The Old Testament is full of the gods of other nations. Sadly the Israelites at times in their history turned their back on Jehovah their Creator and followed other gods: '*And the children of Israel did evil again in the sight of the LORD, and served Baalim, and Ashtaroth, and the gods of Syria, and the gods of Zidon, and the gods of Moab, and the gods of the children of Ammon, and the gods of the Philistines, and forsook the LORD, and served not him.*' (**Judges 10:6**). We can look at them and think 'how could they ever forsake God?' Yet when we place anything above God like our job, our children, our possessions, our favorite team – anything - we made them idols. There is nothing wrong with taking pride in your work, loving your children, having a nice home or rooting for your favorite team. But we need to make sure that we do not place them above the LORD. We serve the Creator of the heavens. May we be diligent to give Him the rightful place in our lives – LORD above all idols – above everything. May Jesus be Lord of all! Amen and amen . . .

# # # # #

DAY #113

READ Psalm 97 (*12 verses*)

*1 The LORD reigneth; let the earth rejoice; let the multitude of
isles be glad thereof. 2 Clouds and darkness are round about
him: righteousness and judgment are the habitation of his
throne. 3 A fire goeth before him, and burneth up his enemies
round about. 4 His lightnings enlightened the world: the earth
saw, and trembled. 5 The hills melted like wax at the
presence of the LORD, at the presence of the Lord of the whole
earth. 6 The heavens declare his righteousness, and all the
people see his glory. 7 Confounded be all they that serve graven
images, that boast themselves of idols: worship him, all ye
gods. 8 Zion heard, and was glad; and the daughters of Judah
rejoiced because of thy judgments, O LORD. 9 For thou,
LORD, art high above all the earth: thou art exalted far above
all gods. 10 Ye that love the LORD, hate evil: he preserveth the
souls of his saints; he delivereth them out of the hand of the
wicked. 11 Light is sown for the righteous, and gladness for the
upright in heart. 12 Rejoice in the LORD, ye righteous; and give
thanks at the remembrance of his holiness.*

VERSE OF THE DAY: Psalm 97:9
'For thou, LORD, art high above all the earth: thou art exalted far above all gods.'

Not only is our LORD above all gods, but He is exalted FAR above all gods. There is no comparison. No god (*small g*) compares to the Almighty Creator God (*large G*). Today's question: do you exalt Him above all? Lenny LeBlanc wrote a song titled '*Above All.*' What a wonderful song! The lyrics are listed below. May we exalt our Lord Jesus above all!

ABOVE ALL

Above all powers, above all kings
Above all nature and all created things
Above all wisdom and all the ways of man
You were here before the world began
Above all kingdoms, above all thrones
Above all wonders the world has ever known
Above all wealth and treasures of the earth
There's no way to measure what You're worth
Crucified, laid behind the stone
You lived to die, rejected and alone
Like a rose trampled on the ground
You took the fall and thought of me
Above all

# # # # #

DAY #114

READ Psalm 98 (*9 verses*)

*1 O sing unto the LORD a new song; for he hath done marvellous
things: his right hand, and his holy arm, hath gotten him the
victory. 2 The LORD hath made known his salvation:
his righteousness hath he openly shewed in the sight of the
heathen. 3 He hath remembered his mercy and his truth toward
the house of Israel: all the ends of the earth have seen the
salvation of our God. 4 Make a joyful noise unto the LORD,
all the earth: make a loud noise, and rejoice, and sing
praise. 5 Sing unto the LORD with the harp; with the harp, and
the voice of a psalm. 6 With trumpets and sound of cornet make
a joyful noise before the LORD, the King. 7 Let the sea roar,
and the fulness thereof; the world, and they that dwell
therein. 8 Let the floods clap their hands: let the hills be joyful
together 9 Before the LORD; for he cometh to judge the earth:
with righteousness shall he judge the world, and the people with
equity.*

VERSE OF THE DAY: Psalm 98:1
'O sing unto the LORD a new song; for he hath done marvellous things: his right hand, and his holy arm, hath gotten him the victory.'

The debate over musical styles makes me wonder: Does God prefer hymns or praise choruses? As we see in this verse, God loves music that is new (**Psalm 33:3, Psalm 96:1, Psalm 98:1,**

Psalm 149:1, Isaiah 42:10, Revelation 5:9, Revelation 14:3). The word '*new*' in the Old Testament verses referenced is the Hebrew word **chadash**, meaning '*fresh.*' The verses referenced from the book of **Revelation** use the Greek work **kainos** for new, meaning '*freshness.*' God is seeking worshippers who sing songs to Him that are fresh, not stale or faded. A lot of this has to do with the attitude of our heart. He longs to hear a song of praise that comes from a heart of worship that is daily renewed through the victory of our Lord Jesus! Whether you sing praise choruses or hymns, sing with all your heart out of joy and thanksgiving – for He hath done marvelous things for us!

# # # # #

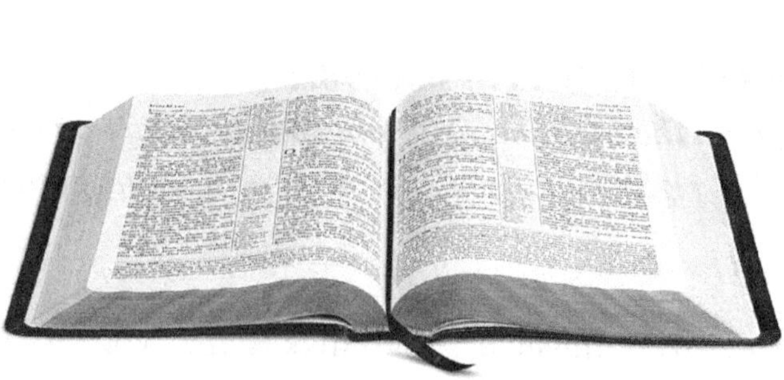

DAY #115

READ Psalm 99 (*9 verses*)

1 The LORD reigneth; let the people tremble:
he sitteth between the cherubims; let the earth be
moved. 2 The LORD is great in Zion; and he is high above all the
people. 3 Let them praise thy great and terrible
name; for it is holy. 4 The king's strength also loveth judgment;
thou dost establish equity, thou executest judgment and
righteousness in Jacob. 5 Exalt ye the LORD our God, and
worship at his footstool; for he is holy. 6 Moses and Aaron among
his priests, and Samuel among them that call upon his name; they
called upon the LORD, and he answered them. 7 He spake unto
them in the cloudy pillar: they kept his testimonies, and the
ordinance that he gave them. 8 Thou answeredst them, O LORD
our God: thou wast a God that forgavest them, though thou
tookest vengeance of their inventions. 9 Exalt the LORD our
God, and worship at his holy hill; for the LORD our God is holy.

VERSE OF THE DAY: Psalm 99:6
'Moses and Aaron among his priests, and Samuel among them that call upon his name; they called upon the LORD, and he answered them.'

When we read through the Old Testament accounts of the lives of great biblical figures like Moses and Samuel we see that God did some mighty things. They called upon the LORD, and He answered them. I think that we sometimes forget that we serve the same God as did Moses and Samuel. We pray to the same God. He speaks to us through His Word. We serve a great God who desires to spread His gospel through us. He can use us, like He used Moses and Samuel, if we are obedient and willing. Trust Him today to use you to reach a lost world for Christ!

# # # # #

DAY #116

READ Psalm 100 (*5 verses*)

*1 Make a joyful noise unto the LORD, all ye lands. 2 Serve the
LORD with gladness: come before his presence with
singing. 3 Know ye that the LORD he is God: it is he that made
us, and not we ourselves; we are his people, and the sheep of his
pasture. 4 Enter into his gates with thanksgiving, and into his
courts with praise: be thankful unto him, and bless his
name. 5 For the LORD is good; his mercy is everlasting; and his
truth endureth to all generations.*

VERSE OF THE DAY: Psalm 100:2
'Serve the LORD with gladness: come before his presence with singing.'

Other than the **23rd Psalm**, today's reading, the **100th Psalm**, may be the most well-known **Psalm**. We are commanded to serve the LORD with gladness. That may be difficult for some of us to do, especially during these volatile days with the coronavirus scare that has attacked our world. But when we consider all that He has done for us we should serve Him with gladness, with a heart of thanksgiving. If we are to come before His presence with singing, should we constantly have a song in our heart? Are we not constantly before Him? Do you ever find yourself humming or whistling a song during your day? I do. As I am driving my car I often have music playing that praises the Lord. I find myself singing along only to see the person in the car next to me staring at me as if something is wrong with me.

When alone I sing from my heart. Then again, I am never alone, for I am always in His presence as He has promised to never leave me (**Hebrews 13:5**). Sing from your heart. Sing gladly. Even during these troubled times. It will put a smile on your face!

'Thou hast put gladness in my heart . . .' (**Psalm 4:7**)

# # # # #

DAY #117

READ Psalm 101 (*8 verses*)

1 *I will sing of mercy and judgment: unto thee, O LORD, will I*
sing. 2 *I will behave myself wisely in a perfect way. O when wilt*
thou come unto me? I will walk within my house with a
perfect heart. 3 *I will set no wicked thing before mine eyes:*
I hate the work of them that turn aside; it shall not cleave to
me. 4 *A froward heart shall depart from me: I will not know a*
wicked person. 5 *Whoso privily slandereth his neighbour, him*
will I cut off: him that hath an high look and a proud heart will
not I suffer. 6 *Mine eyes shall be upon the faithful of the land,*
that they may dwell with me: he that walketh in a perfect way, he
shall serve me. 7 *He that worketh deceit shall not dwell within my*
house: he that telleth lies shall not tarry in my sight. 8 *I will early*
destroy all the wicked of the land; that I may cut off all wicked
doers from the city of the LORD.

VERSE OF THE DAY: Psalm 101:3
'I will set no wicked thing before mine eyes: I hate the work of them that turn aside; it shall not cleave to me.'

I have been saddened to see men in the church who would gawk at a beautiful woman. I heard one man say '*I'm married, not dead.*' Not too long after that he left his wife for another woman. We see that Job stated, 'I made a covenant with my eyes not to look with lust upon a young woman' (**Job 31:1 NLT**). We need to make a covenant before God to keep ourselves pure. We need to '*keep away from every kind of evil*' (**I Thessalonians 5:22**). May you '*cleave unto the LORD your God, as ye have done unto this day*' (**Joshua 23:8**). Lord, give us the strength to flee the world and cleave to You!

'Let love be without dissimulation. Abhor that which is evil; cleave to that which is good.' (**Romans 12:9**).

# # # # #

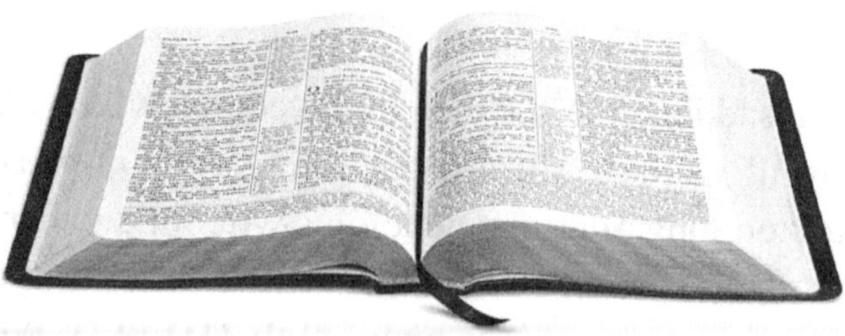

DAY #118

READ Psalm 102:1-14 (*14 verses*)

*1 Hear my prayer, O LORD, and let my cry come unto
thee. 2 Hide not thy face from me in the day when I am in trouble;
incline thine ear unto me: in the day when I call answer me
speedily. 3 For my days are consumed like smoke, and my bones
are burned as an hearth. 4 My heart is smitten, and withered like
grass; so that I forget to eat my bread. 5 By reason of the voice
of my groaning my bones cleave to my skin. 6 I am like a pelican
of the wilderness: I am like an owl of the desert. 7 I watch, and
am as a sparrow alone upon the house top. 8 Mine enemies
reproach me all the day; and they that are mad against me are
sworn against me. 9 For I have eaten ashes like bread, and
mingled my drink with weeping, 10 Because of thine indignation
and thy wrath: for thou hast lifted me up, and cast me
down. 11 My days are like a shadow that declineth; and I am
withered like grass. 12 But thou, O LORD, shalt endure for ever;
and thy remembrance unto all generations. 13 Thou shalt
arise, and have mercy upon Zion: for the time to favour her, yea,
the set time, is come. 14 For thy servants take pleasure in her
stones, and favour the dust thereof.*

VERSE OF THE DAY: Psalm 102:8

'Mine enemies reproach me all the day; and they that are mad against me are sworn against me.'

If you take a stand for Christian beliefs people get mad! It is a reminder to me to stand firm in my Christian beliefs, regardless of what people think. As long as we do it in a loving way, we can agree to disagree, but we must stand firmly on biblical principles. I find that when I go out of my way to be nice to someone who has opposite views than I do it is so much easier to get along. Who knows, maybe they will like me in spite of our differences. We are told to love our enemies (**Matthew 5:44**). Live to please the Lord. That is always the best solution.

'When a man's ways please the LORD, he maketh even his enemies to be at peace with him' (**Proverbs 16:7**).

# # # # #

DAY #119

READ Psalm 102:15-28 (*14 verses*)

*15 So the heathen shall fear the name of the LORD, and all the
kings of the earth thy glory. 16 When the LORD shall build up
Zion, he shall appear in his glory. 17 He will regard the prayer
of the destitute, and not despise their prayer. 18 This shall be
written for the generation to come: and the people which shall be
created shall praise the LORD. 19 For he hath looked down from
the height of his sanctuary; from heaven did the LORD behold
the earth; 20 To hear the groaning of the prisoner; to loose those
that are appointed to death; 21 To declare the name of the LORD
in Zion, and his praise in Jerusalem; 22 When the people
are gathered together, and the kingdoms, to serve the
LORD. 23 He weakened my strength in the way; he shortened my
days. 24 I said, O my God, take me not away in the midst of my
days: thy years are throughout all generations. 25 Of old hast
thou laid the foundation of the earth: and the heavens are the
work of thy hands. 26 They shall perish, but thou shalt endure:
yea, all of them shall wax old like a garment; as a vesture shalt
thou change them, and they shall be changed: 27 But thou art the
same, and thy years shall have no end. 28 The children of thy
servants shall continue, and their seed shall be established before
thee.*

VERSE OF THE DAY: Psalm 102:17
'He will regard the prayer of the destitute, and not despise their prayer.'

The word '*destitute*' in this verse is the Hebrew word **arar**, meaning '*naked and poor.*' I know some people who might be considered poor, but they have clothes to wear. When God looks down on the poorest of the poor, He loves them and hears their prayers. What a great example of the lowest of the low speaking to the highest of the high! The prayer of a naked beggar in an alley can reach the throne of Heaven!

First of all, are you thankful that you are not poor and naked? Secondly, do you take for granted that the God of the universe hears your prayers? Be thankful today and call on Him. Let Him know how much you love Him. Worship Him! What a mighty God we serve!

# # # # #

DAY #120

READ Psalm 103 (*22 verses*)

1 Bless the LORD, O my soul: and all that is within me, bless his
holy name. 2 Bless the LORD, O my soul, and forget not all his
benefits: 3 Who forgiveth all thine iniquities; who healeth all thy
diseases; 4 Who redeemeth thy life from destruction;
who crowneth thee with lovingkindness and tender
mercies; 5 Who satisfieth thy mouth with good things; so
that thy youth is renewed like the eagle's. 6 The LORD
executeth righteousness and judgment for all that are
oppressed. 7 He made known his ways unto Moses, his acts unto
the children of Israel. 8 The LORD is merciful and gracious,
slow to anger, and plenteous in mercy. 9 He will not always
chide: neither will he keep his anger for ever. 10 He hath not
dealt with us after our sins; nor rewarded us according to our
iniquities. 11 For as the heaven is high above the earth, so great
is his mercy toward them that fear him. 12 As far as the east is
from the west, so far hath he removed our transgressions from
us. 13 Like as a father pitieth his children, so the LORD pitieth
them that fear him. 14 For he knoweth our frame; he
remembereth that we are dust. 15 As for man, his days are as
grass: as a flower of the field, so he flourisheth. 16 For the wind
passeth over it, and it is gone; and the place thereof shall know
it no more. 17 But the mercy of the LORD is from everlasting to
everlasting upon them that fear him, and his righteousness unto
children's children; 18 To such as keep his covenant, and to those
that remember his commandments to do them. 19 The LORD hath

prepared his throne in the heavens; and his kingdom ruleth over
all. **20** *Bless the LORD, ye his angels, that excel in strength, that*
do his commandments, hearkening unto the voice of his
word. **21** *Bless ye the LORD, all ye his hosts; ye ministers of his,*
that do his pleasure. **22** *Bless the LORD, all his works in all*
places of his dominion: bless the LORD, O my soul.

VERSE OF THE DAY: Psalm 103:1
'Bless the LORD, O my soul: and all that is within me, bless his holy name.'

What a great verse that talks about our commitment to Christ. Do you bless the LORD with ALL that is within you? We are to dedicate our whole life to Him. He is to be our priority. He is to be our everything! He is to be LORD, master over all! I remember my Pastor in my youth saying many times, '*If He is not LORD OF all He is not LORD AT all.*' May we bless the LORD today with our whole heart, with all that is within us! Bless His holy name!

# # # # #

DAY #121

READ Psalm 104:1-15 (*15 verses*)

1 *Bless the LORD, O my soul. O LORD my God, thou art*
very great; thou art clothed with honour and
majesty. **2** *Who coverest thyself with light as with a garment:*
who stretchest out the heavens like a curtain: **3** *Who layeth the*
beams of his chambers in the waters: who maketh the clouds his
chariot: who walketh upon the wings of the wind: **4** *Who maketh*
his angels spirits; his ministers a flaming fire: **5** *Who laid the*
foundations of the earth, that it should not be removed for
ever. **6** *Thou coveredst it with the deep as with a garment: the*
waters stood above the mountains. **7** *At thy rebuke they fled;*
at the voice of thy thunder they hasted away. **8** *They go up by the*
mountains; they go down by the valleys unto the place which thou
hast founded for them. **9** *Thou hast set a bound that they*
may not pass over; that they turn not again to cover the
earth. **10** *He sendeth the springs into the valleys, which run*
among the hills. **11** *They give drink to every beast of the field: the*
wild asses quench their thirst. **12** *By them shall the fowls of the*
heaven have their habitation, which sing among the
branches. **13** *He watereth the hills from his chambers: the earth*
is satisfied with the fruit of thy works. **14** *He causeth the grass to*
grow for the cattle, and herb for the service of man: that he may
bring forth food out of the earth; **15** *And wine that maketh glad*
the heart of man, and oil to make his face to shine,
and bread which strengtheneth man's heart.

VERSE OF THE DAY: Psalm 104:14

'He causeth the grass to grow for the cattle, and herb for the service of man: that he may bring forth food out of the earth.'

I hear all the time in my house that there is nothing to eat, yet we have never gone without a meal. We have truly never gone without. I am amazed at God's creation as the earth replenishes itself with food for the inhabitants of the earth. I have been blessed. I think of those in the world that are less fortunate. There is not a day that goes by where someone on our earth does not die of starvation. There are those today that are hurting financially due to the virus situation that has hit our nation. May we seek ways to provide for others, even if that means simply praying for their provision. Next week we will continue in **Psalm 104**, continuing to look at our great God, our provider.

# # # # #

DAY #122

READ Psalm 104:16-25 (*10 verses*)

1 The trees of the LORD are full of sap; the cedars of Lebanon,
which he hath planted; 2 Where the birds make their
nests: as for the stork, the fir trees are her
house 3 The high hills are a refuge for the wild goats; and the
rocks for the conies. 4 He appointed the moon for seasons:
the sun knoweth his going down. 5 Thou makest darkness,
and it is night: wherein all the beasts of the forest do
creep forth. 6 The young lions roar after their prey, and seek
their meat from God. 7 The sun ariseth, they gather themselves
together, and lay them down in their dens. 8 Man goeth forth unto
his work and to his labour until the evening. 9 O LORD, how
manifold are thy works! in wisdom hast thou made them all:
the earth is full of thy riches. 10 So is this great and wide sea,
wherein are things creeping innumerable, both small and great
beasts.

VERSE OF THE DAY: Psalm 104:24
'O LORD, how manifold are thy works! in wisdom hast thou made them all: the earth is full of thy riches.'

We see in today's reading the provision of God. Whether it is the fullness of the sap (**v. 16**), nests and trees for birds (**v. 17**), the hills and rocks for various animals (**v. 18**), morning and night (**v. 19-20**), meat for the lions (**v. 21**) or work for mankind (**v. 24**), He is the great provider (**Psalm 65:9**). I have never truly known hunger. I have always had a place to dwell. God is so good. He has provided for me and continues to do so. How manifold are His blessings toward me! Praise You Lord Jesus!

# # # # #

DAY #123

READ Psalm 104:26-35 (*10 verses*)

26 *There go the ships: there is that leviathan, whom thou hast*
made to play therein. ***27*** *These wait all upon thee; that thou*
mayest give them their meat in due season. ***28*** *That thou givest*
them they gather: thou openest thine hand, they are filled with
good. ***29*** *Thou hidest thy face, they are troubled: thou takest*
away their breath, they die, and return to their dust. ***30*** *Thou*
sendest forth thy spirit, they are created: and thou renewest the
face of the earth. ***31*** *The glory of the LORD shall endure for ever:*
the LORD shall rejoice in his works. ***32*** *He looketh on the earth,*
and it trembleth: he toucheth the hills, and they smoke. ***33*** *I will*
sing unto the LORD as long as I live: I will sing praise to my God
while I have my being. ***34*** *My meditation of him shall be sweet:*
I will be glad in the LORD. ***35*** *Let the sinners be consumed out*
of the earth, and let the wicked be no more. Bless thou the LORD,
O my soul. Praise ye the LORD.

VERSE OF THE DAY: Psalm 104:34
'My meditation of him shall be sweet: I will be glad in the LORD.'

I once heard of a Pastor who had a picture of the Chicago Bears Hall of Fame Running Back Walter Payton on the screen as he began to preach. His sermon was about how sweet God was. Since Walter Payton's nickname was '*sweetness*' he thought it was appropriate to display his picture. He quoted a few brief verses about the sweetness of God and the sermon was over.

A man approached the preacher after the service and corrected him: the picture displayed was of Chicago Bears great Gale Sayers, not Payton.

It was a sermon that was thrown together quickly and carelessly. We must not approach our Lord in a quick and callous manner. We must meditate on His goodness. He truly is sweet! May we not miss His sweetness to us in a daily and complete and continual way. O how sweet the LORD is to us! How sweet is His precious Word! May our daily time in His Word remind us – sweet is the Lord! Rejoice and be glad in Him!

'How sweet are thy words unto my taste! Yea, sweeter than honey to my mouth!' **(Psalm 119:103)**

# # # # #

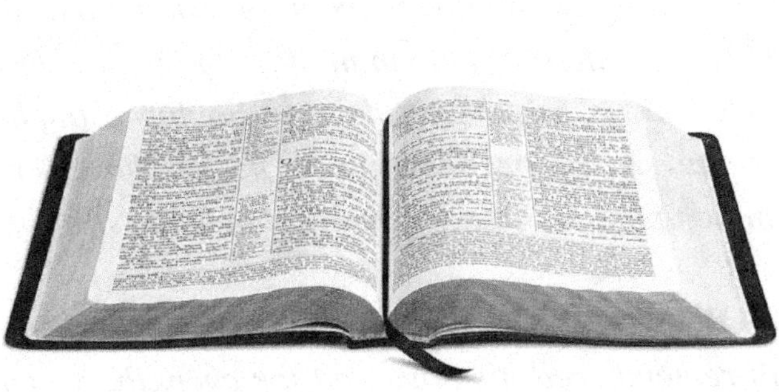

DAY #124

READAD Psalm 105:1-16 (*16 verses*)

*1 O give thanks unto the LORD; call upon his name: make known
his deeds among the people. 2 Sing unto him, sing psalms unto
him: talk ye of all his wondrous works. 3 Glory ye in his
holy name: let the heart of them rejoice that seek the
LORD. 4 Seek the LORD, and his strength: seek his face
evermore. 5 Remember his marvellous works that he hath done;
his wonders, and the judgments of his mouth; 6 O ye seed of
Abraham his servant, ye children of Jacob his chosen. 7 He is the
LORD our God: his judgments are in all the earth. 8 He hath
remembered his covenant for ever, the word which he
commanded to a thousand generations. 9 Which covenant he
made with Abraham, and his oath unto Isaac; 10 And confirmed
the same unto Jacob for a law, and to Israel for an everlasting
covenant: 11 Saying, Unto thee will I give the land of Canaan,
the lot of your inheritance: 12 When they were but a few men in
number; yea, very few, and strangers in it. 13 When they went
from one nation to another, from one kingdom to another
people; 14 He suffered no man to do them wrong: yea,
he reproved kings for their sakes; 15 Saying, Touch not mine
anointed, and do my prophets no harm. 16 Moreover he called
for a famine upon the land: he brake the whole staff of bread.*

VERSE OF THE DAY: Psalm 105:8

'He hath remembered his covenant for ever, the word which he commanded to a thousand generations.'

What a great reminder that our God's promises are everlasting. We know that Scripture tells us that God cannot lie (**Titus 1:2, Hebrews 6:18**). What a blessing to know that when God tells us He will not leave or forsake us that is true (**Hebrews 13:5**). What a comfort to know that when God tells us when we confess our sins He is faithful and just to forgive us our sins and cleanse us from all unrighteousness (**I John 1:9**). What a joy to know that Jesus is preparing a place for us and will return to take us there (**John 14:3**). O the endless promises of our Lord to His people – all true and trustworthy. Thank You Lord Jesus! I praise You this day!

# # # # #

DAY #125

READ Psalm 105:17-35 (*19 verses*)

17 He sent a man before them, even Joseph, who was sold for a
*servant: **18** Whose feet they hurt with fetters: he was laid in*
*iron: **19** Until the time that his word came: the word of the LORD*
*tried him. **20** The king sent and loosed him; even the ruler of the*
*people, and let him go free. **21** He made him lord of his house,*
*and ruler of all his substance: **22** To bind his princes at his*
*pleasure; and teach his senators wisdom. **23** Israel also came*
*into Egypt; and Jacob sojourned in the land of Ham. **24** And he*
increased his people greatly; and made them stronger than their
*enemies. **25** He turned their heart to hate his people, to deal*
*subtilly with his servants. **26** He sent Moses his*
*servant; and Aaron whom he had chosen. **27** They shewed his*
*signs among them, and wonders in the land of Ham. **28** He sent*
darkness, and made it dark; and they rebelled not against his
*word. **29** He turned their waters into blood, and slew their*
*fish. **30** Their land brought forth frogs in abundance, in the*
*chambers of their kings. **31** He spake, and there came divers sorts*
*of flies, and lice in all their coasts. **32** He gave them hail for*
*rain, and flaming fire in their land. **33** He smote their*
vines also and their fig trees; and brake the trees of their
*coasts. **34** He spake, and the locusts came, and caterpillers,*
*and that without number, **35** And did eat up all the herbs in their*
land, and devoured the fruit of their ground.

VERSE OF THE DAY: Psalm 105:26
'He sent Moses his servant; and Aaron whom he had chosen.'

In **verses 27-35** today we begin a reminder of the greatness of the LORD and what He did for His people. We will see more of that tomorrow. I see two key words in today's verse: **SENT** and **CHOSEN**. God decided to choose a poor, scared, awkward speaker to declare His message: '*And Moses said unto the LORD, O my Lord, I am not eloquent, neither heretofore, nor since thou has spoken unto thy servant: but I am slow of speech, and of a slow tongue*' (**Exodus 4:10**). The **NLT** translates this verse this way: '*O Lord, I'm just not a good speaker. I have never been, and I'm not now, even after you have spoken to me. I'm clumsy with words*.' Moses was hand-picked by God. He was chosen.

Secondly, Moses was sent. He was given a mission and told to go. He would not send him alone, his brother Aaron would go with him. But do not forget: Moses was the one to speak not Aaron. God promised to go with him and give him the words to say (**Exodus 4:12**). Moses was told to go to Pharoah and speak God's message in **Exodus 6:11, Exodus 8:1, Exodus 9:1** and **Exodus 10:1**. We see the CHOSEN messenger being SENT repeatedly and we see obedience. God would free His people and Moses was His chosen sent one used to accomplish His will.

Has God chosen you? Where has He sent you to share the gospel? Ask Him today to lead you, to be with you, to give you the words to say. Our Lord does not always seek the eloquent of speech to share His message, rather just willing and obedient servants. May He send us today to someone who needs Jesus and may we do our best to lovingly share the truth of the gospel! Amen and amen . . .

# # # # #

DAY #126

READ Psalm 105:36-45 (*10 verses*)

*36 He smote also all the firstborn in their land, the chief of all
their strength. 37 He brought them forth also with silver and
gold: and there was not one feeble person among their
tribes. 38 Egypt was glad when they departed: for the fear of
them fell upon them. 39 He spread a cloud for a covering;
and fire to give light in the night. 40 The people asked, and he
brought quails, and satisfied them with the bread of
heaven. 41 He opened the rock, and the waters gushed out;
they ran in the dry places like a river. 42 For he remembered his
holy promise, and Abraham his servant. 43 And he brought forth
his people with joy, and his chosen with gladness: 44 And gave
them the lands of the heathen: and they inherited the labour of
the people; 45 That they might observe his statutes, and keep his
laws. Praise ye the LORD.*

VERSE OF THE DAY: Psalm 105:39
'He spread a cloud for a covering; and fire to give light in the night.'

Again today in **Psalm 105** we see God's provision: He provided food (**v. 40**), drink (**v. 41**), and a new land (**v. 44**). In today's verse we see that the LORD gave them direction. He led them with a cloud by day and by fire by night: '*And the LORD went before them by day in a pillar of a cloud, to lead them the way, and by night in a pillar of fire, to give them light, to go by day and night*'

(**Exodus 13:21**). Today He still guides our way with a light, the light of His Word: '*Thy Word is a lamp unto my feet, and a light unto my path*' (**Psalm 119:105**). How important to spend time every day in His Word. Do not proceed in the dark; go forward by the light of His Word! He will guide your way!

'Trust in the LORD with all thine heart; and lean not unto thine own understanding. In all thy ways acknowledge Him, and He shall direct thy paths.' (**Proverbs 3:5-6**).

# # # # #

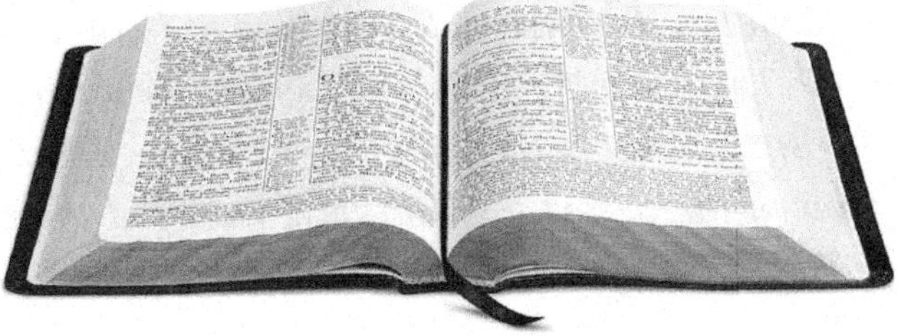

DAY #127

READ Psalm 106:1-15 (*15 verses*)

*1 Praise ye the LORD. O give thanks unto the LORD; for he
is good: for his mercy endureth for ever. 2 Who can utter the
mighty acts of the LORD? who can shew forth all his
praise? 3 Blessed are they that keep judgment, and he that doeth
righteousness at all times. 4 Remember me, O LORD, with the
favour that thou bearest unto thy people: O visit me with thy
salvation; 5 That I may see the good of thy chosen, that I may
rejoice in the gladness of thy nation, that I may glory with thine
inheritance. 6 We have sinned with our fathers, we have
committed iniquity, we have done wickedly. 7 Our fathers
understood not thy wonders in Egypt; they remembered not the
multitude of thy mercies; but provoked him at the sea, even at the
Red sea. 8 Nevertheless he saved them for his name's sake, that
he might make his mighty power to be known. 9 He rebuked the
Red sea also, and it was dried up: so he led them through the
depths, as through the wilderness. 10 And he saved them from the
hand of him that hated them, and redeemed them from the hand
of the enemy. 11 And the waters covered their enemies: there was
not one of them left. 12 Then believed they his words; they sang
his praise. 13 They soon forgat his works; they waited not for his
counsel: 14 But lusted exceedingly in the wilderness, and
tempted God in the desert. 15 And he gave them their request;
but sent leanness into their soul.*

VERSE OF THE DAY: Psalm 106:8

'Nevertheless he saved them for his name's sake, that he might make his mighty power to be known.'

Although God's mighty power is seen throughout Scripture, this verse is the only verse in the Psalms where we see the term, '*mighty power.*' The word '*nevertheless*' means '*in spite of, however.*' The title above this **Psalm** is '*The psalmist exhorts men to praise God.*' Jehovah had done many great works to display His mighty power to His people. They did not always remember God's goodness to them. The LORD saved them in spite of them and their lack of remembrance or thankfulness. How often do we take for granted the goodness of the LORD in our lives? He often loves us in spite of us. He can use us to share His gospel in spite of us and our shortcomings. May we be thankful. May we remember all His mercies toward us. As He made His mighty power known, may be eager to share His gospel each day!

'I pray that you will begin to understand the incredible greatness of his power for us who believe him. This is the same mighty power that raised Christ from the dead and seated him in the place of honor at God's right hand in the heavenly realms.' **(Ephesians 1:19-20 NLT)**

# # # # #

DAY #128

READ Psalm 106:16-35 (*20 verses*)

*16 They envied Moses also in the camp, and Aaron the saint of
the LORD. 17 The earth opened and swallowed up Dathan, and
covered the company of Abiram. 18 And a fire was kindled in
their company; the flame burned up the wicked. 19 They made a
calf in Horeb, and worshipped the molten image. 20 Thus they
changed their glory into the similitude of an ox that eateth
grass. 21 They forgat God their saviour, which had done great
things in Egypt; 22 Wondrous works in the land of
Ham, and terrible things by the Red sea. 23 Therefore he said
that he would destroy them, had not Moses his chosen stood
before him in the breach, to turn away his wrath, lest he should
destroy them. 24 Yea, they despised the pleasant land, they
believed not his word: 25 But murmured in their
tents, and hearkened not unto the voice of the
LORD. 26 Therefore he lifted up his hand against them,
to overthrow them in the wilderness: 27 To overthrow their
seed also among the nations, and to scatter them in the
lands. 28 They joined themselves also unto Baalpeor, and ate the
sacrifices of the dead. 29 Thus they provoked him to
anger with their inventions: and the plague brake in upon
them. 30 Then stood up Phinehas, and executed judgment:
and so the plague was stayed. 31 And that was counted
unto him for righteousness unto all generations for
evermore. 32 They angered him also at the waters of strife,
so that it went ill with Moses for their sakes: 33 Because they*

provoked his spirit, so that he spake unadvisedly with his
lips. 34 *They did not destroy the nations, concerning whom the*
LORD commanded them: 35 *But were mingled among the*
heathen, and learned their works.

VERSE OF THE DAY: Psalm 106:23
'*Therefore he said that he would destroy them, had not Moses his chosen stood before him in the breach, to turn away his wrath, lest he should destroy them.*'

In this verse we see the power of intercessory prayer. The Israelites had forsaken the LORD when Moses was on Mt. Sinai receiving the Ten Commandments (**Exodus 32:7**). The LORD was about to '*consume them*' (**Exodus 32:10**). We see Moses interceding for the Israelites in **Exodus 32:11-13**. God's response to Moses' prayer: '*And the LORD repented of the evil which He thought to do unto His people*' (**Exodus 32:14**).

The word '*intercede*' means to act or interpose on behalf of someone in difficulty or trouble, as by pleading or petition. Were the Israelites in trouble? Absolutely! Moses interceded on their behalf. Who do you know who is living away from the LORD? Who do you know who is living in spiritual trouble? God hears the prayers of His people. He alone can turn a life back to Himself. Be an interceder – pray for someone today!

# # # # #

DAY #129

READ Psalm 106:36-48 (*13 verses*)

***36** And they served their idols: which were a snare unto*
them. ***37** Yea, they sacrificed their sons and their daughters unto*
devils, ***38** And shed innocent blood, even the blood of their sons*
and of their daughters, whom they sacrificed unto the idols of
Canaan: and the land was polluted with blood. ***39** Thus were they*
defiled with their own works, and went a whoring with their own
inventions. ***40** Therefore was the wrath of the LORD kindled*
against his people, insomuch that he abhorred his own
inheritance. ***41** And he gave them into the hand of the heathen;*
and they that hated them ruled over them. ***42** Their enemies also*
oppressed them, and they were brought into subjection under
their hand. ***43** Many times did he deliver them; but they*
provoked him with their counsel, and were brought low for their
iniquity. ***44** Nevertheless he regarded their affliction, when he*
heard their cry: ***45** And he remembered for them his*
covenant, and repented according to the multitude of his
mercies. ***46** He made them also to be pitied of all those that*
carried them captives. ***47** Save us, O LORD our God, and gather*
us from among the heathen, to give thanks unto thy holy name,
and to triumph in thy praise. ***48** Blessed be the LORD God of*
Israel from everlasting to everlasting: and let all the people say,
Amen. Praise ye the LORD.

VERSES OF THE DAY: Psalm 106:43-44
'Many times did he deliver them; but they provoked him with their counsel, and were brought low for their iniquity. Nevertheless he regarded their affliction, when he heard their cry.'

The Israelites have a long record of turning their back on God, having Him discipline them, after a time repenting and then having the LORD deliver them. A great sample of this is seen in the book of **Judges**. The Israelites forsook their God and were handed over to raiders (**Judges 2:11-14**). The LORD, in His mercy, sent **judges** (*leaders*) to deliver His people. The Israelites again forsook their God and were handed over to King Cushan-Rishathaim (**Judges 3:7-11**). After 8 years the LORD sent them a deliverer: ***Othniel.*** The Israelites again forsook their God and were handed over to King Eglon (**Judges 3:12-15, 28-30**). After 18 years the LORD sent them a deliverer: ***Ehud***. The Israelites again forsook their God and were handed over to King Jabin (**Judges 4:1-4, 14-15; 5:31**). After 20 years the LORD sent them a deliverer: ***Deborah***. The Israelites again forsook their God and were handed over to the Midianites (**Judges 6:1-8, 12**). After 7 years the LORD sent them a deliverer: ***Gideon***. The Israelites again forsook their God and were handed over to the Philistines and the Ammonites (**Judges 10:6-8, 32; 11:32**). After 18 years the LORD sent them a deliverer: ***Jephthah***. The Israelites again forsook their God and were handed over to the Philistines (**Judges 13:1**). After 40 years the LORD sent them a deliverer: ***Samson***.

You might think, '*how foolish of the Israelites to completely forsake their God time and time again,*' yet we forsake God repeatedly with our sin (**Romans 5:6-8**). In the fullness of time the LORD sent us a deliverer: **JESUS CHRIST** (**Galatians 4:4-5**). No matter how many times we forsake Him, God desires us to be delivered back to fellowship with Him (**I John 1:9**). When we cry out to Him our God hears our prayer. May we keep short sin accounts with Him!

# # # # #

DAY #130

READ Psalm 107:1-12 (*12 verses*)

1 *O give thanks unto the LORD, for he is good: for his*
mercy endureth for ever. ***2*** *Let the redeemed of the LORD*
say so, whom he hath redeemed from the hand of the
enemy; ***3*** *And gathered them out of the lands, from the east,*
and from the west, from the north, and from the south.
4 *They wandered in the wilderness in a solitary way; they found*
no city to dwell in. ***5*** *Hungry and thirsty, their soul fainted in*
them. ***6*** *Then they cried unto the LORD in their trouble, and he*
delivered them out of their distresses. ***7*** *And he led them*
forth by the right way, that they might go to a city of
habitation. ***8*** *Oh that men would praise the LORD for his*
goodness, and for his wonderful works to the children of men!
9 *For he satisfieth the longing soul, and filleth the hungry soul*
with goodness. ***10*** *Such as sit in darkness and in the shadow of*
death, being bound in affliction and iron; ***11*** *Because they*
rebelled against the words of God, and contemned the counsel of
the most High: ***12*** *Therefore he brought down their heart with*
labour; they fell down, and there was none to help.

VERSE OF THE DAY: Psalm 107:2

'Let the redeemed of the LORD say so, whom he hath redeemed from the hand of the enemy.'

The word *'redeemed'* seen twice in this verse is the Hebrew word **ga'al**. It pictures a purchase of something that was originally your own. Since the fall of Adam we have needed a redeemer. That redeemer is the Lord Jesus Christ! In His death, burial and resurrection He has purchased our redemption.

Fanny Crosby, the great 19th century blind hymnist wrote more than 8,000 hymns, many of which are still sung today. They include *Blessed Assurance*, *Christ the Lord is Risen Today*, *To God Be the Glory*, *I Am Thine O Lord* and *He Hideth My Soul*. In 1882 she published *Redeemed How I Love To Proclaim It*. I could not help but think that today's verse might have been the inspiration for this hymn. When I looked up this hymn in my hymnbook, below the title was listed today's verse.

REDEEMED HOW I LOVE TO PROCLAIM IT

Redeemed, how I love to proclaim it!
Redeemed by the blood of the Lamb;
Redeemed through His infinite mercy,
His child and forever I am.

Redeemed, and so happy in Jesus,
No language my rapture can tell;
I know that the light of His presence
With me doth continually dwell.

I think of my blessèd Redeemer,
I think of Him all the day long:
I sing, for I cannot be silent;
His love is the theme of my song.

I know I shall see in His beauty
The King in whose law I delight;
Who lovingly guardeth my footsteps,

And giveth me songs in the night.
I know there's a crown that is waiting,
In yonder bright mansion for me,
And soon, with the spirits made perfect,
At home with the Lord I shall be.

CHORUS:
Redeemed, redeemed, redeemed by the blood of the Lamb;
Redeemed, redeemed, His child and forever I am.

We have been redeemed! We have been purchased with the precious blood of Christ (**Acts 20:28**)! May we be bold to proclaim it!

# # # # #

DAY #131

READ Psalm 107:13-29 (*17 verses*)

13 *Then they cried unto the LORD in their trouble, and he saved*
them out of their distresses. **14** *He brought them out of*
darkness and the shadow of death, and brake their bands in
sunder. **15** *Oh that men would praise the LORD for his*
goodness, and for his wonderful works to the children of
men! **16** *For he hath broken the gates of brass, and cut the bars*
of iron in sunder. **17** *Fools because of their transgression, and*
because of their iniquities, are afflicted. **18** *Their soul abhorreth*
all manner of meat; and they draw near unto the gates of
death. **19** *Then they cry unto the LORD in their trouble, and he*
saveth them out of their distresses. **20** *He sent his word,*
and healed them, and delivered them from their
destructions. **21** *Oh that men would praise the LORD for his*
goodness, and for his wonderful works to the children of men!
22 *And let them sacrifice the sacrifices of thanksgiving, and*
declare his works with rejoicing. **23** *They that go down to the sea*
in ships, that do business in great waters; **24** *These see the works*
of the LORD, and his wonders in the deep. **25** *For he*
commandeth, and raiseth the stormy wind, which lifteth up the
waves thereof. **26** *They mount up to the heaven, they go down*
again to the depths: their soul is melted because of trouble.
27 *They reel to and fro, and stagger like a drunken man, and are*
at their wits' end. **28** *Then they cry unto the LORD*
in their trouble, and he bringeth them out of their

distresses. 29 *He maketh the storm a calm, so that the waves thereof are still.*

VERSE OF THE DAY: Psalm 107:22

'And let them sacrifice the sacrifices of thanksgiving, and declare his works with rejoicing.'

We read of the sacrifice of thanksgiving in **Leviticus 7**. This sacrifice was a peace offering. Our inner peace of mind is connected to our practice of thanksgiving. It is important as a forgiven child of God that our lives reflect three things: that we are sacrificial, thankful and people who rejoice.

Ask yourself: Are you sacrificial toward the Lord and those around you? Do you have anything to be thankful for? Do you have cause to rejoice in the Lord? May these three attributes be evident in our lives!

'And let the peace of God rule in your hearts, to the which also ye are called in one body; and be ye thankful' (**Colossians 3:15**).

# # # # #

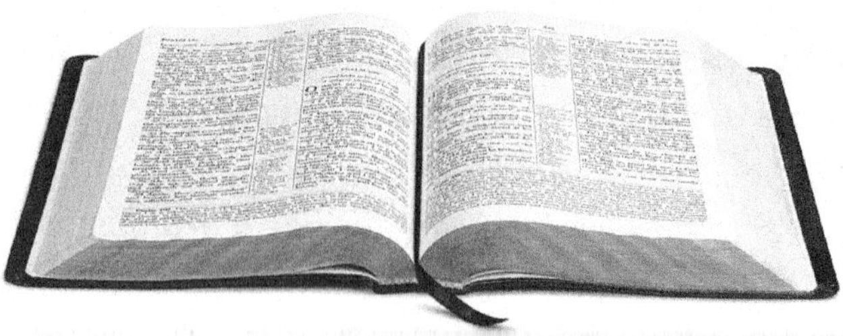

DAY #132

READ Psalm 107:30-43 (*14 verses*)

*30 Then are they glad because they be quiet; so he bringeth them
unto their desired haven. 31 Oh that men would praise the
LORD for his goodness, and for his wonderful works to the
children of men! 32 Let them exalt him also in the
congregation of the people, and praise him in the assembly of the
elders. 33 He turneth rivers into a wilderness, and the
watersprings into dry ground; 34 A fruitful land into barrenness,
for the wickedness of them that dwell therein. 35 He turneth the
wilderness into a standing water, and dry ground into
watersprings. 36 And there he maketh the hungry to dwell,
that they may prepare a city for habitation; 37 And sow the fields,
and plant vineyards, which may yield fruits of
increase. 38 He blesseth them also, so that they are multiplied
greatly; and suffereth not their cattle to decrease. 39 Again, they
are minished and brought low through oppression, affliction, and
sorrow. 40 He poureth contempt upon princes, and causeth them
to wander in the wilderness, where there is no way. 41 Yet setteth
he the poor on high from affliction, and maketh him families like
a flock. 42 The righteous shall see it, and rejoice: and all iniquity
shall stop her mouth. 43 Whoso is wise, and will observe
these things, even they shall understand the lovingkindness of the
LORD.*

VERSE OF THE DAY: Psalm 107:43
'Whoso is wise, and will observe these things, even they shall understand the lovingkindness of the LORD.'

Scripture has much to say about the difference between the wise and the foolish. Consider the following verses:

- *'A wise son maketh a glad father: but a foolish son is the heaviness of his mother.'* **(Proverbs 10:1)**
- *'Wise men lay up knowledge: but the mouth of the foolish is near destruction.'* **(Proverbs 10:14)**
- *'Every wise woman buildeth her house: but the foolish plucketh it down with her hands.'* **(Proverbs 14:1)**
- *'In the mouth of the foolish is a rod of pride: but the lips of the wise shall preserve them.'* **(Proverbs 14:3)**
- *'The crown of the wise is their riches: but the foolishness of fools is folly.'* **(Proverbs 14:24)**
- *'The tongue of the wise useth knowledge aright: but the mouth of fools poureth out foolishness.'* **(Proverbs 15:2)**
- *'The lips of the wise disperse knowledge: but the heart of the foolish doeth not so.'* **(Proverbs 15:7)**
- *'A wise son maketh a glad father: but a foolish man despiseth his mother.'* **(Proverbs 15:20)**
- *'If a wise man contendeth with a foolish man, whether he rage or laugh, there is no rest.'* **(Proverbs 29:9)**

Scripture makes it clear: The wise observes the things of God. The wise live lives pleasing to God. The foolish denies the existence of God (**Psalm 14:1, Psalm 53:1**). Dear friends, be ye wise!

'And they that be wise shall shine as the brightness of the firmament; and they that turn many to righteousness as the stars for ever and ever.' **(Daniel 12:3)**

# # # # #

DAY #133

READ Psalm 108 (*13 verses*)

1 *O God, my heart is fixed; I will sing and give praise, even with*
my glory. **2** *Awake, psaltery and harp: I myself will awake*
early. **3** *I will praise thee, O LORD, among the people: and I will*
sing praises unto thee among the nations. **4** *For thy*
mercy is great above the heavens: and thy truth reacheth unto the
clouds. **5** *Be thou exalted, O God, above the heavens: and thy*
glory above all the earth; **6** *That thy beloved may be delivered:*
save with thy right hand, and answer me. **7** *God hath spoken in*
his holiness; I will rejoice, I will divide Shechem, and mete out
the valley of Succoth. **8** *Gilead is mine; Manasseh is mine;*
Ephraim also is the strength of mine head; Judah is my lawgiver;
9 *Moab is my washpot; over Edom will I cast out my shoe; over*
Philistia will I triumph. **10** *Who will bring me into the strong*
city? who will lead me into Edom? **11** *Wilt not thou,*
O God, who hast cast us off? and wilt not thou, O God, go forth
with our hosts? **12** *Give us help from trouble: for vain is the help*
of man. **13** *Through God we shall do valiantly: for he it is*
that shall tread down our enemies.

VERSE OF THE DAY: Psalm 108:12
'Give us help from trouble: for vain is the help of man.'

When I think of help from man I think of our first responders. Firemen and Policemen can bring help in certain situations. But who can help in the matters of the heart? Who can help the troubled soul? All the counsel of man cannot cure the human condition: we are sinful by birth and by practice. The definition of **help** is '*to save, to rescue.*' I was led to think of two great hymns of the church: *Jesus Saves* written by Priscilla J. Owens in 1882 and *Rescue the Perishing* penned by Fanny Crosby in 1869. These are two great hymns of the faith declaring that Jesus is our help! We have found the only help for the sin-sick soul. We must share this help with a lost world!

JESUS SAVES

We have heard the joyful sound
Jesus saves! Jesus saves!
Spread the tidings all around
Jesus saves! Jesus saves!
Bear the news to every land
Climb the steeps and cross the waves
Onward! 'tis the Lord's command
Jesus saves! Jesus saves!

RESCUE THE PERISHING

Rescue the perishing, care for the dying
Snatch them in pity from sin and the grave
Weep o'er the erring one, lift up the fallen
Tell them of Jesus, the mighty to save
Rescue the perishing, care for the dying
Jesus is merciful, Jesus will save

'God is our refuge and strength, a very present help in trouble.' **(Psalm 46:1)**

# # # # #

DAY #134

READ Psalm 109:1-18 (*18 verses*)

*1 Hold not thy peace, O God of my praise; 2 For the mouth of the
wicked and the mouth of the deceitful are opened against me: they
have spoken against me with a lying tongue. 3 They compassed
me about also with words of hatred; and fought against me
without a cause. 4 For my love they are my adversaries: but
I give myself unto prayer. 5 And they have rewarded me evil for
good, and hatred for my love. 6 Set thou a wicked man over him:
and let Satan stand at his right hand. 7 When he shall be judged,
let him be condemned: and let his prayer become sin. 8 Let his
days be few; and let another take his office. 9 Let his children be
fatherless, and his wife a widow. 10 Let his children be
continually vagabonds, and beg: let them seek their bread also
out of their desolate places. 11 Let the extortioner catch all that
he hath; and let the strangers spoil his labour. 12 Let there be
none to extend mercy unto him: neither let there be any to favour
his fatherless children. 13 Let his posterity be cut off; and in the
generation following let their name be blotted out. 14 Let the
iniquity of his fathers be remembered with the LORD; and let not
the sin of his mother be blotted out. 15 Let them be before the
LORD continually, that he may cut off the memory of them from
the earth. 16 Because that he remembered not to shew mercy, but
persecuted the poor and needy man, that he might even slay the
broken in heart. 17 As he loved cursing, so let it come unto him:
as he delighted not in blessing, so let it be far from him. 18 As he
clothed himself with cursing like as with his garment, so let it*

come into his bowels like water, and like oil into his bones.

VERSE OF THE DAY: Psalm 109:4
'For my love they are my adversaries: but I give myself unto prayer.'

I am reminded of the account of Daniel in **Daniel 6**. They sought to make his faithfulness to the LORD a crime, having a decree signed that allowed the people to pray only to King Darius lest they be thrown into the den of lions. Although they sought to do him in, Daniel was faithful to pray three times a day. In a real crisis Daniel spent time in prayer. What is your response to difficulties and trials in your life? Do you go to the LORD in prayer? We are not persecuted in the United States because of our faith in Jesus but we may be some day. May we be bold to stand for Christ regardless of the circumstances. Go to Him in prayer when life is good and when time is difficult. Remember as we saw yesterday: God is our help! (**Psalm 108:12**).

# # # # #

DAY #135

READ Psalm 109:19-31 (*13 verses*)

19 *Let it be unto him as the garment which covereth him, and for*
a girdle wherewith he is girded continually. **20** *Let this be the*
reward of mine adversaries from the LORD, and of them that
speak evil against my soul. **21** *But do thou for me, O GOD the*
Lord, for thy name's sake: because thy mercy is good, deliver
thou me. **22** *For I am poor and needy, and my heart is wounded*
within me. **23** *I am gone like the shadow when it declineth:*
I am tossed up and down as the locust. **24** *My knees are weak*
through fasting; and my flesh faileth of fatness. **25** *I became also*
a reproach unto them: when they looked upon me they shaked
their heads. **26** *Help me, O LORD my God: O save me according*
to thy mercy: **27** *That they may know that this is thy*
hand; that thou, LORD, hast done it. **28** *Let them curse, but bless*
thou: when they arise, let them be ashamed; but let thy servant
rejoice. **29** *Let mine adversaries be clothed with shame, and let*
them cover themselves with their own confusion, as with a
mantle. **30** *I will greatly praise the LORD with my mouth;*
yea, I will praise him among the multitude. **31** *For he shall stand*
at the right hand of the poor, to save him from those that condemn
his soul.

VERSE OF THE DAY: Psalm 109:30

'I will greatly praise the LORD with my mouth; yea, I will praise him among the multitude.'

Much is said in Scripture about what comes out of our mouth. Our mouths can be used to bless or curse. It can be used to confess Jesus and bring salvation (**Romans 10:9-10**). We are told that was is abundant in our hearts, whether good or bad, will flow out of our mouths (**Matthew 12:34**). We must be careful what comes out of our mouths. In today's verse the Psalmist declares that he will praise the LORD greatly with his mouth. He will be quick to praise the LORD with his mouth among the people. Do you praise the LORD greatly during corporate worship? Do you praise the LORD with your daily conversation? May our mouths be used to exalt the name of Jesus!

'Let the words of my mouth, and the meditation of my heart, be acceptable in thy sight, O LORD, my strength, and my redeemer.' **(Psalm 19:14)**

'I will bless the LORD at all times: His praise shall continually be in my mouth.' **(Psalm 34:1)**

# # # # #

DAY #136

READ Psalm 110 (*7 verses*)

*1 The LORD said unto my Lord, Sit thou at my right hand, until I
make thine enemies thy footstool. 2 The LORD shall send the rod
of thy strength out of Zion: rule thou in the midst of thine
enemies. 3 Thy people shall be willing in the day of thy power, in
the beauties of holiness from the womb of the morning: thou hast
the dew of thy youth. 4 The LORD hath sworn, and will not
repent, Thou art a priest for ever after the order of Melchizedek.
5 The Lord at thy right hand shall strike through kings in the day
of his wrath. 6 He shall judge among the heathen, he shall fill the
places with the dead bodies; he shall wound the heads over many
countries. 7 He shall drink of the brook in the way: therefore
shall he lift up the head.*

VERSE OF THE DAY: Psalm 110:2
'The LORD shall send the rod of thy strength out of Zion: rule thou in the midst of thine enemies.'

The LORD's rod of strength, the sceptre of righteousness **(Psalm 45:6)**, is the gospel, the power of God unto salvation to everyone who believes (**Romans 1:16**). His great salvation was first preached in Jerusalem and then to all parts of the world. He shall rule over all, even those who were once enemies of God. Never forget: '*while we were yet sinners Christ died for us*' (**Romans 5:8**). What a mighty God we serve! What a loving God we serve! May we be diligent to share His great salvation in a world that needs it so!

# # # # #

DAY #137

READAD Psalm 111 (*10 verses*)

*1 Praise ye the LORD. I will praise the LORD with my whole
heart, in the assembly of the upright, and in the
congregation. 2 The works of the LORD are great, sought out of
all them that have pleasure therein. 3 His work is honourable
and glorious: and his righteousness endureth for ever. 4 He hath
made his wonderful works to be remembered: the
LORD is gracious and full of compassion. 5 He hath given meat
unto them that fear him: he will ever be mindful of his
covenant. 6 He hath shewed his people the power of his works,
that he may give them the heritage of the heathen. 7 The works of
his hands are verity and judgment; all his
commandments are sure. 8 They stand fast for ever and ever, and
are done in truth and uprightness. 9 He sent redemption unto his
people: he hath commanded his covenant for ever: holy and
reverend is his name. 10 The fear of the LORD is the beginning
of wisdom: a good understanding have all they that do his
commandments: his praise endureth for ever.*

VERSE OF THE DAY: Psalm 111:10
'The fear of the LORD is the beginning of wisdom: a good understanding have all they that do his commandments: his praise endureth for ever.'

As we have been studying through the **Psalms**, one of the books of Wisdom in Scripture, we are reminded here again where the beginning of wisdom begins: the fear of the LORD. If we do not have a holy reverence for the LORD we will not have a reverence for His Word. It all begins with recognizing who we serve: the one, true, living God! He is the one who created all things by the power of His voice (**Genesis 1**). He is the one who wrote the Scriptures through His Holy Spirit – His Word is God breathed (**II Timothy 3:16 NIV**). When we see Him for who He is and realize His Word is written for us to obey, we will understand that His commandments are to be followed. Jesus said: '*If ye love me, keep my commandments*' (**John 14:15**). May we live lives that show that we have a holy reverence for Jesus! His praise will endure forever!

'*The fear of the LORD is the beginning of knowledge: but fools despise wisdom and instruction*' (**Proverbs 1:7**).

# # # # #

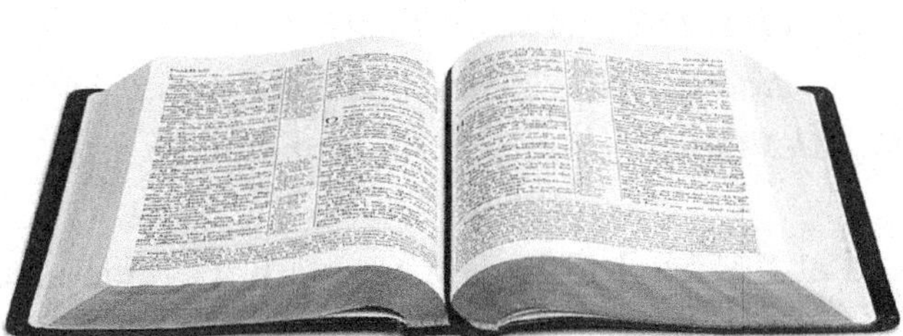

DAY #138

READ Psalm 112 (*10 verses*)

1 Praise ye the LORD. Blessed is the man that feareth the
LORD, that delighteth greatly in his commandments. 2 His seed
shall be mighty upon earth: the generation of the upright shall be
blessed. 3 Wealth and riches shall be in his house: and his
righteousness endureth for ever. 4 Unto the upright there ariseth
light in the darkness: he is gracious, and full of compassion, and
righteous. 5 A good man sheweth favour, and lendeth: he will
guide his affairs with discretion. 6 Surely he shall not be
moved for ever: the righteous shall be in everlasting
remembrance. 7 He shall not be afraid of evil tidings: his heart
is fixed, trusting in the LORD. 8 His heart is established, he shall
not be afraid, until he see his desire upon his enemies. 9 He hath
dispersed, he hath given to the poor; his righteousness endureth
for ever; his horn shall be exalted with honour. 10 The wicked
shall see it, and be grieved; he shall gnash with his teeth, and
melt away: the desire of the wicked shall perish.

VERSE OF THE DAY: Psalm 112:1
'Praise ye the LORD. Blessed is the man that feareth the LORD, that delighteth greatly in his commandments.'

We looked at the need to have a fear, a holy reverence, for the LORD yesterday. Today we see that this man is blessed. The Prosperity Gospel in some portions of today's church see blessing only as financial gain. And although we see wealth and riches mentioned in **verse 3**, spiritual riches are much greater than financial gain. **Psalm 112** listed many characteristics of a blessed man: he is upright (**verse 2**); gracious (**verse 4**); compassionate (**verse 4**); discrete (**verse 5**); unafraid (**verse 7**); trusting (**verse 7**) and charitable (**verse 9**). A person with these attributes is the same person who delights in God's Word! The word '*delighteth*' is the Hebrew word **chaphets**, meaning to '*be pleased, find pleasure.*' May it be said of us that we possess these traits! May we find pleasure in reading, studying, memorizing and obeying His Word!

'But his delight is in the law of the LORD; and in His law doth he meditate day and night' **(Psalm 1:2)**

'Delight thyself also in the LORD; and He shall give thee the desires of thine heart' **(Psalm 37:4)**

'I delight to do thy will, O my God: yea, thy law is within my heart' **(Psalm 40:8)**

# # # # #

DAY #139

READ Psalm 113 (*9 verses*)

*1 Praise ye the LORD. Praise, O ye servants of the LORD, praise
the name of the LORD. 2 Blessed be the name of the LORD from
this time forth and for evermore. 3 From the rising of the sun unto
the going down of the same the LORD'S name is to be
praised. 4 The LORD is high above all nations, and his glory
above the heavens. 5 Who is like unto the LORD our God, who
dwelleth on high, 6 Who humbleth himself to behold the things
that are in heaven, and in the earth! 7 He raiseth up the poor out
of the dust, and lifteth the needy out of the dunghill; 8 That he
may set him with princes, even with the princes of his
people. 9 He maketh the barren woman to keep house, and to
be a joyful mother of children. Praise ye the LORD.*

VERSE OF THE DAY: Psalm 113:3
'From the rising of the sun unto the going down of the same the LORD'S name is to be praised.'

We see the sunrise in the east and the sunset in the west. At least that what it appears to us. We know that the sun does not move but rather the earth rotates around it. Likewise the Son of God is unchanging. He is the same yesterday, today and forever (**Hebrews 13:8**). We saw in **Psalm 1** that the blessed man meditates on the law of the Lord during the day and the night (**Psalm 1:2**). It is to show us that we should never cease to meditate on His Word. In the same fashion we must never cease to praise His name. From the earliest part of our day (*sunrise*) until the end of our day (*sunset*) we must give Him praise. What a great way to start your day and end your day - praising the LORD!

# # # # #

DAY #140

READ Psalm 114 (*8 verses*)

1 When Israel went out of Egypt, the house of Jacob from a
people of strange language; 2 Judah was his
sanctuary, and Israel his dominion. 3 The sea saw it, and fled:
Jordan was driven back. 4 The mountains skipped like
rams, and the little hills like lambs. 5 What ailed thee, O thou
sea, that thou fleddest? thou Jordan, that thou wast driven
back? 6 Ye mountains, that ye skipped like rams; and ye little
hills, like lambs? 7 Tremble, thou earth, at the presence of the
Lord, at the presence of the God of Jacob; 8 Which turned the
rock into a standing water, the flint into a fountain of waters.

VERSE OF THE DAY: Psalm 114:7
'Tremble, thou earth, at the presence of the Lord, at the presence of the God of Jacob.'

In today's verse we see an exhortation to fear God in His church. The Hebrew word **chuwl** for '*tremble*' is found only four times in the Old Testament, here and in **Psalm 97:4**, **Jeremiah 5:22** and **Habakkuk 3:10**. In each occurrence it is in relation to His creation. His creation stands in awe of Him and so should we! He is the Almighty Creator God, the God of Jacob.

'His lightnings enlightened the world: the earth saw, and trembled.' **(Psalm 97:4)**

'Do you have no respect for me? Why do you not tremble in my presence? I, the LORD, am the one who defines the ocean's sandy shoreline, an everlasting boundary that the waters cannot cross. The waves may toss and roar, but they can never pass the bounds I set.' **(Jeremiah 5:22 NLT)**

'The mountains saw thee, and they trembled: the overflowing of the water passed by: the deep uttered his voice, and lifted up his hands on high.' **(Habakkuk 3:10)**

# # # # #

DAY #141

READ Psalm 115 (*18 verses*)

*1 Not unto us, O LORD, not unto us, but unto thy name give glory,
for thy mercy, and for thy truth's sake. 2 Wherefore should the
heathen say, Where is now their God? 3 But our God is in the
heavens: he hath done whatsoever he hath pleased. 4 Their idols
are silver and gold, the work of men's hands. 5 They have mouths,
but they speak not: eyes have they, but they see not: 6 They have
ears, but they hear not: noses have they, but they smell
not: 7 They have hands, but they handle not: feet have they,
but they walk not: neither speak they through their
throat. 8 They that make them are like unto them; so is every one
that trusteth in them. 9 O Israel, trust thou in the LORD:
he is their help and their shield. 10 O house of Aaron, trust in the
LORD: he is their help and their shield. 11 Ye that fear the
LORD, trust in the LORD: he is their help and their shield.
12 The LORD hath been mindful of us: he will bless us;
he will bless the house of Israel; he will bless the house of
Aaron. 13 He will bless them that fear the LORD, both small and
great. 14 The LORD shall increase you more and more, you and
your children. 15 Ye are blessed of the LORD which made
heaven and earth. 16 The haven, even the heavens, are the
LORD'S: but the earth hath he given to the children of
men. 17 The dead praise not the LORD, neither any that go down
into silence. 18 But we will bless the LORD from this time forth
and for evermore. Praise the LORD.*

VERSE OF THE DAY: Psalm 115:13
'He will bless them that fear the LORD, both small and great.'

The concept of '*fearing the LORD*' is seen in no less than 33 of the **Psalms**. We see that those who fear the LORD are honoured (**Psalm 15:4**), enjoy the LORD's presence (**Psalm 25:14**), receive salvation (**Psalm 85:9**), find mercy (**Psalm 103:11**) and are glad (**Psalm 119:74**), just to name a few of the benefits. In today's verse we see that he is simply blessed. This pertains to the small and the great, from the lowliest servant to the highest of royalty. God is no respecter of persons (**Romans 2:11**). He loves all (**John 3:16**). The LORD is not impressed with social status or wealth. He does not choose favorites based on your bank account, your level of education, where you live, what you have, your job or anything else. Those who are popular in today's culture have no advantage over anyone else when it comes to receiving God's blessing. It all starts with fearing the LORD, having a holy reverence for our God (**Psalm 111:10**).

'Behold, that thus shall the man be blessed that feareth the LORD.' (**Psalm 128:4**)

'Let us hear the conclusion of the whole matter: Fear God, and keep His commandments: for this is the whole duty of man.' **(Ecclesiastes 12:13)**

# # # # #

DAY #142

READ Psalm 116 (*19 verses*)

1 *I love the LORD, because he hath heard my voice and my*
supplications. **2** *Because he hath inclined his ear unto me,*
therefore will I call upon him as long as I live. **3** *The sorrows of*
death compassed me, and the pains of hell gat hold upon me:
I found trouble and sorrow. **4** *Then called I upon the name of the*
LORD; O LORD, I beseech thee, deliver my
soul. **5** *Gracious is the LORD, and righteous; yea, our*
God is merciful. **6** *The LORD preserveth the simple: I was*
brought low, and he helped me. **7** *Return unto thy rest, O my soul;*
for the LORD hath dealt bountifully with thee. **8** *For thou hast*
delivered my soul from death, mine eyes from tears, and my feet
from falling. **9** *I will walk before the LORD in the land of the*
living. **10** *I believed, therefore have I spoken: I was greatly*
afflicted: **11** *I said in my haste, All men are liars.* **12** *What shall I*
render unto the LORD for all his benefits toward me? **13** *I will*
take the cup of salvation, and call upon the name of the
LORD. **14** *I will pay my vows unto the LORD now in the presence*
of all his people. **15** *Precious in the sight of the LORD is the*
death of his saints. **16** *O LORD, truly I am thy servant; I am thy*
servant, and the son of thine handmaid: thou hast loosed my
bonds. **17** *I will offer to thee the sacrifice of thanksgiving,*
and will call upon the name of the LORD. **18** *I will pay my vows*
unto the LORD now in the presence of all his people, **19** *In the*
courts of the LORD'S house, in the midst of thee, O Jerusalem.
Praise ye the LORD.

VERSE OF THE DAY: Psalm 116:15
'Precious in the sight of the LORD is the death of his saints.'

We have all experienced the loss of a loved one. From our perspective there is great pain and sorrow, and it is natural to mourn. From God's perspective the promotion of one of His saints to heaven is called '*precious*.' The Hebrew word **yaqar** is used here for '*precious*.' It means costly and excellent. We see this word referring to beautiful and valuable stones (**II Samuel 12:30; I Kings 10:2, 10-11; I Chronicles 20:2; I Chronicles 29:2; II Chronicles 3:6; II Chronicles 9:1, 9-10; II Chronicles 32:27; Job 28:16; Isaiah 28:16; Ezekiel 27:22; Ezekiel 28:13; Daniel 11:38**). How ironic that we are told that he changes cold hearts of stone into hearts of flesh, those receptive to the salvation provided through our Lord Jesus Christ: '*A new heart also will I give you, a new spirit will I put within you: and I will take away the stony heart out of your flesh and I will give you an heart of flesh*' (**Ezekiel 36:26**). This change of a heart was costly, for it took the death of God's Son to make it happen (**Matthew 20:28, Mark 10:45**). The result: a new creation in Christ (**II Corinthians 5:17**). Faith in Christ brings about something that is excellent, something that is precious in the sight of God. What joy the Father must have to welcome a faithful believer to their eternal reward!

# # # # #

DAY #143

READ Psalm 117 (*2 verses*)

1 O praise the LORD, all ye nations: praise him, all ye
people. 2 For his merciful kindness is great toward us: and the
truth of the LORD endureth for ever. Praise ye the LORD.

VERSES OF THE DAY: Psalm 117:1-2
'O praise the LORD, all ye nations: praise him, all ye people. For his merciful kindness is great toward us: and the truth of the LORD endureth for ever. Praise ye the LORD.'

Today we will look at the entire chapter, then again this is the only Psalm with only two verses. We are exhorted to be people of praise. Scripture tells us that every knee shall bow to our great God (**Isaiah 45:23, Romans 14:11, Philippians 2:10**). Those who bow now enjoy the joy of the LORD in this life and the next. Those who bow after this life will bow but will face everlasting damnation. I choose to bow now. I pray you do too.

Verse 1 tells us to praise the LORD. **Verse 2** tells us two reasons why. First His merciful kindness is great toward us. The **NLT** translates this as '*For He loves us with unfailing love.*' He will never let us down. He cannot fail us. Secondly His truth shall never end. His truth is revealed to us in His Word – Thy Word is truth! (**John 17:17**).

What are you going through today? What trials and difficulties do you face on a daily basis? Take heart believer. We have a God who is unfailing and truthful who is always with us (**Hebrews 13:5**). What should our response be day to day? Praise ye the LORD! Lord, may it be so it our lives. Praise You Lord JESUS!

'So if you are suffering according to God's will, keep on doing what is right, and trust yourself to the God who made you, for He will never fail you.' (**I Peter 4:19 NLT**)

# # # # #

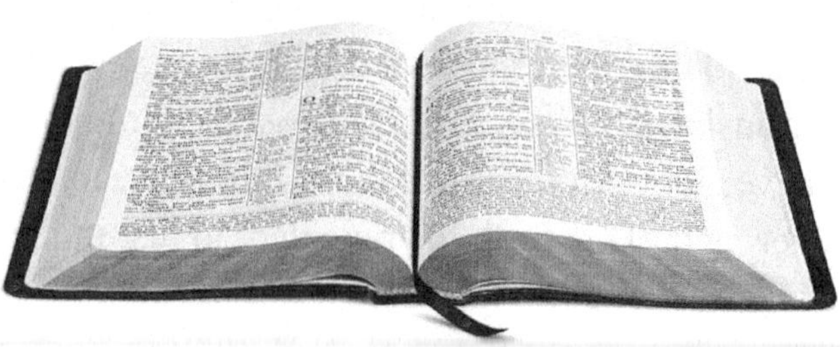

DAY #144

READ Psalm 118:1-16 (*16 verses*)

*1 O give thanks unto the LORD; for he is good: because his
mercy endureth for ever. 2 Let Israel now say, that his
mercy endureth for ever. 3 Let the house of Aaron now say, that
his mercy endureth for ever. 4 Let them now that fear the LORD
say, that his mercy endureth for ever. 5 I called upon the LORD
in distress: the LORD answered me, and set me in a large
place. 6 The LORD is on my side; I will not fear: what can
man do unto me? 7 The LORD taketh my part with them that
help me: therefore shall I see my desire upon them that hate
me. 8 It is better to trust in the LORD than to put confidence in
man. 9 It is better to trust in the LORD than to put confidence in
princes. 10 All nations compassed me about: but in the name of
the LORD will I destroy them. 11 They compassed me about; yea,
they compassed me about: but in the name of the LORD I will
destroy them. 12 They compassed me about like bees; they are
quenched as the fire of thorns: for in the name of the LORD I will
destroy them. 13 Thou hast thrust sore at me that I might fall:
but the LORD helped me. 14 The LORD is my strength and song,
and is become my salvation. 15 The voice of rejoicing and
salvation is in the tabernacles of the righteous: the right hand of
the LORD doeth valiantly. 16 The right hand of the LORD is
exalted: the right hand of the LORD doeth valiantly.*

VERSES OF THE DAY: Psalm 118:8-9

'It is better to trust in the LORD than to put confidence in man. It is better to trust in the LORD than to put confidence in princes.'

This study was originally done during the 2020Presidential election. In the midst of a Presidential election we saw millions passionate about their candidate, either President Trump or former Vice President Biden. The issues of the day were the coronavirus, the economy and healthcare just to name a few. They believed that their candidate would make changes that would be beneficial to the country. So many put their faith and trust in a man. Regardless of who won the election, our trust must be placed in the LORD. He alone can solve the biggest problem that man faces: curing the sin-filled soul.

Where are you putting your trust today? In man or in God? Trust the LORD!

'But it is good for me to draw near to God: I have put my trust in the Lord GOD, that I may declare all Thy works.' **(Psalm 73:28)**

'Trust in the LORD with all thine heart; and lean not unto thine own understanding. In all thy ways acknowledge Him, and He shall direct thy paths.' **(Proverbs 3:5-6)**

\# # # # #

DAY #145

READ Psalm 118:17-29 (*13 verses*)

17 I shall not die, but live, and declare the works of the
LORD. 18 The LORD hath chastened me sore: but he hath not
given me over unto death. 19 Open to me the gates of
righteousness: I will go into them, and I will praise the
LORD: 20 This gate of the LORD, into which the righteous shall
enter. 21 I will praise thee: for thou hast heard me, and art
become my salvation. 22 The stone which the builders refused is
become the head stone of the corner. 23 This is the LORD'S
doing; it is marvellous in our eyes. 24 This is the day which the
LORD hath made; we will rejoice and be glad in it. 25 Save now,
I beseech thee, O LORD: O LORD, I beseech thee, send now
prosperity. 26 Blessed be he that cometh in the name of the
LORD: we have blessed you out of the house of the
LORD. 27 God is the LORD, which hath shewed us light: bind
the sacrifice with cords, even unto the horns of the
altar. 28 Thou art my God, and I will praise thee: thou art my
God, I will exalt thee. 29 O give thanks unto the LORD;
for he is good: for his mercy endureth for ever.

VERSE OF THE DAY: Psalm 118:29
'O give thanks unto the LORD; for he is good: for his mercy endureth for ever.'

The account of the rich young ruler coming to Jesus is recorded in each of the three Synoptic gospels. In each case he calls Jesus

'*Good Master*' (**Matthew 19:16, Mark, 10:17, Luke 18:18**). Jesus response: Only God is good. We are also reminded in **Romans 3:10** that none are righteous – not one. The truth here is that God is far above all. He is over all, He is righteous and there is nothing that compares to Him. He alone is good. He forever will be the only one that is good. Thank the LORD today that we serve a good and merciful God!

# # # # #

DAY #146

READ Psalm 119:1-16 (*16 verses*)

Today we start an 11 day study of **Psalm 119**, the longest of the **Psalms**, containing 176 verses. As a Youth Pastor I once told my kids that I would buy them a bike if they memorized just one chapter in the Bible: **Psalm 119**. I was asked by a parent if I would really do that. Indeed I would have. If a young person would memorize 176 verses that told about the greatness of God and His Word their life would be radically changed! The cost of a bike would be a small price to change a young life toward following God and His Word! It will change our life as well!

The **Psalm** is arranged in an acrostic pattern. There are 22 letters in the Hebrew alphabet, and this Psalm contains 22 units of 8 verses each. We will look at 2 units each day. Each of the 22 sections is given to a letter of the Hebrew alphabet, and each line in that section begins with that letter. The closest parallel to this pattern in Scripture is found in **Lamentations 3**, which is also divided into 22 sections, and there are a few other passages in the Hebrew Scriptures which use an acrostic pattern.

This **Psalm** glorifies God and His Word which is referred to in all but a few verses and a total of 173 times. We will see 8 basic words used to describe the Scriptures, God's written revelation to us:

- **Law** (*torah*, used 25 times in **Psalm 119**): Its parent verb means teach or direct; therefore coming from God it means both law and revelation.
- **Word** (*dabar*, used 24 times): The idea is of the spoken word, God's revealed word to man.
- **Judgments** (*mispatim*, used 23 times): From *shaphat*, to *judge, determine, regulate, order*, and *discern*, because they *judge* concerning our words and works; show the *rules* by which they should be *regulated*; and cause us to *discern* what is *right* and *wrong*, and decide accordingly.
- **Testimonies** (*edut / edot*, used 23 times): This word is related to the word for *witness*. To obey His testimonies signifies loyalty to the terms of the covenant made between the Lord and Israel.
- **Commandments** (*miswah / miswot*, used 22 times): This word emphasizes the straight authority of what is said . . . God's right to give orders.
- **Statutes** (*huqqim*, used 21 times): The noun is derived from the root verb engrave or inscribe, giving the idea is of the written word of God and the authority of His written word to declare His authority and power of giving us laws.
- **Precepts** (*piqqudim*, used 21 times): This is a word drawn from the sphere of an officer or overseer, and man who is responsible to look closely into a situation and take action. This word points to the particular instructions of the Lord, as of one who cares about detail.
- **Word** (*imrah*, used 19 times): Similar in meaning to *dabar*, yet a different term. The word may denote anything God has spoken, commanded, or promised.

In every instance where we see one of these words in our study the words have been ***BOLDED*** intentionally to make it easier for us to see them throughout this chapter.

ALEPH

1 Blessed are the undefiled in the way, who walk in the ***law of the***
LORD. *2 Blessed are they that keep* ***his testimonies****, and*
that seek him with the whole heart. 3 They also do no iniquity:
they walk in ***his ways****. 4 Thou hast commanded us to keep* ***thy***
precepts *diligently. 5 O that my ways were directed to keep* ***thy***
statutes*! 6 Then shall I not be ashamed, when I have respect*
unto all ***thy commandments.*** *7 I will praise thee with uprightness*
of heart, when I shall have learned ***thy righteous***
judgments*. 8 I will keep* ***thy statutes****: O forsake me not utterly.*

BETH

9 Wherewithal shall a young man cleanse his way? by taking
heed thereto according to ***thy word****. 10 With my whole heart*
have I sought thee: O let me not wander from ***thy***
commandments. *11* ***Thy word*** *have I hid in mine heart, that I*
might not sin against thee. 12 Blessed art thou, O LORD: teach
me ***thy statutes****. 13 With my lips have I declared all the*
judgments of thy mouth*. 14 I have rejoiced in the way of* ***thy***
testimonies*, as much as in all riches. 15 I will meditate in* ***thy***
precepts*, and have respect unto thy ways. 16 I will delight myself*
in ***thy statutes****: I will not forget thy word.*

VERSE OF THE DAY: Psalm 119:11
*'**Thy word** have I hid in mine heart, that I might not sin against thee.'*

I learned at an early age the importance of memorizing Scripture. My Pastor would quote passage after passage after passage. As a young child it seemed to me that he had apparently memorized the entire Bible. He was known all over the country as a Bible teacher, a man who had memorized an amazing amount of God's Word. I'm sure today's verse was an important verse he memorized as a new believer that began his desire to memorize. Why is it important to memorize God's Word? The Holy Spirit will bring it to us and keep us from temptation. Knowing God's principles will help us to keep them and not violate them.

What verses have you memorized? I challenge you to memorize Scripture. A verse a week is a good start. May our Lord help you in hiding His Word in your heart!

# # # # #

DAY #147

READ Psalm 119:17-32 (*16 verses*)

GIMEL

17 *Deal bountifully with thy servant, that I may live, and keep*
thy word. 18 *Open thou mine eyes, that I may behold wondrous*
things out of ***thy law***. 19 *I am a stranger in the earth: hide not*
thy commandments *from me.* 20 *My soul breaketh for the*
longing that it hath unto ***thy judgments*** *at all times.* 21 *Thou hast*
rebuked the proud that are cursed, which do err from
thy commandents. 22 *Remove from me reproach and contempt;*
for I have kept ***thy testimonies.*** 23 *Princes also did*
sit and speak against me: but thy servant did meditate in
thy statutes. 24 ***Thy testimonies*** *also are my delight and my*
counsellors.

DALETH

25 *My soul cleaveth unto the dust: quicken thou me according to*
thy word. 26 *I have declared my ways, and thou heardest me:*
teach me ***thy statutes***. 27 *Make me to understand the way of*
thy precepts: *so shall I talk of thy wondrous works.* 28 *My soul*
melteth for heaviness: strengthen thou me according unto
thy word. 29 *Remove from me the way of lying: and grant me*
thy law *graciously.* 30 *I have chosen the way of truth:*
thy judgments *have I laid before me.* 31 *I have stuck unto*

thy testimonies: O LORD, put me not to shame. 32 *I will run the way of **thy commandents,** when thou shalt enlarge my heart.*

VERSE OF THE DAY: Psalm 119:24
*'**Thy testimonies** also are my delight and my counsellors.'*

As was mentioned in the introduction to this Psalm last week the word **testimonies** is related to the word for *witness*. To obey His testimonies signifies loyalty to the terms of the covenant made between the Lord and Israel. To obey is to find joy and wise counsel.

Psalm 1 warned about unwise counsel for the ungodly. We can find advice from many different counsellors. We must seek godly advice. When we do that we will find delight in God's Word!

'Blessed is the man that walketh not in the counsel of the ungodly, nor standeth in the way of sinners, nor sitteth in the seat of the scornful. But his delight is in the law of the LORD; and in his law doth he meditate day and night.' (**Psalm 1:1-2**)

# # # # #

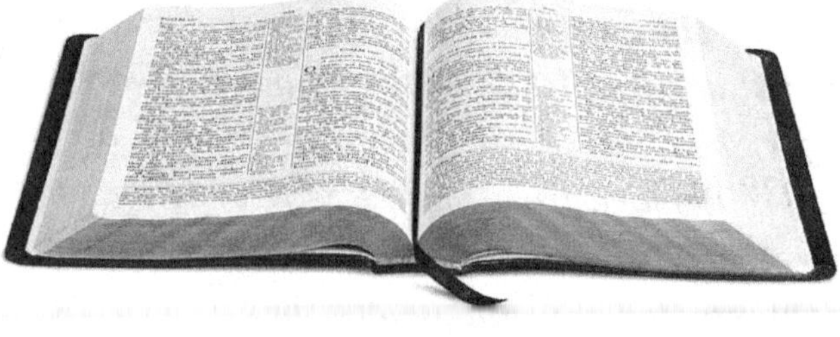

DAY #148

READ Psalm 119:33-48 (*16 verses*)

HE

*33 Teach me, O LORD, the way of **thy statutes**; and I shall keep
it unto the end. 34 Give me understanding, and I shall keep **thy
law**; yea, I shall observe it with my whole heart. 35 Make me to
go in the path of **thy commandments**; for therein do I
delight. 36 Incline my heart unto **thy testimonies**, and not to
covetousness. 37 Turn away mine eyes from beholding
vanity; and quicken thou me in **thy way**. 38 Stablish **thy word**
unto thy servant, who is devoted to thy fear. 39 Turn away my
reproach which I fear: for **thy judgments** are good. 40 Behold,
I have longed after **thy precepts**: quicken me in thy righteousness.*

VAU

*41 Let thy mercies come also unto me, O LORD, even thy
salvation, according to **thy word**. 42 So shall I have wherewith
to answer him that reproacheth me: for I trust in **thy
word**. 43 And take not the word of truth utterly out of my mouth;
for I have hoped in **thy judgments**. 44 So shall I keep **thy law**
continually for ever and ever. 45 And I will walk at liberty:
for I seek **thy precepts**. 46 I will speak of **thy testimonies** also
before kings, and will not be ashamed. 47 And I will delight
myself in **thy commandments**, which I have loved. 48 My hands*

also will I lift up unto **thy commandments**, *which I have loved; and I will meditate in thy statutes.*

VERSE OF THE DAY: Psalm 119:46
'I will speak of **thy testimonies** *also before kings, and will not be ashamed.'*

It is important that we share the gospel with those that our LORD has put into our path. There may be someone that you know who does not know another Christian. We may not talk to kings, but we may talk to business owners, executives and others who the world might put on a pedestal. We must speak with our lips and live our lives to share the gospel. Do not be ashamed! You have been entrusted with the power of God. Seek to share it. He will go with you and give you the words to say. May we be faithful in our witness for Christ.

'For I am not ashamed of the gospel of Christ: for it is the power of God unto salvation to every one that believeth; to the Jew first, and also to the Greek.' **(Romans 1:16)**

# # # # #

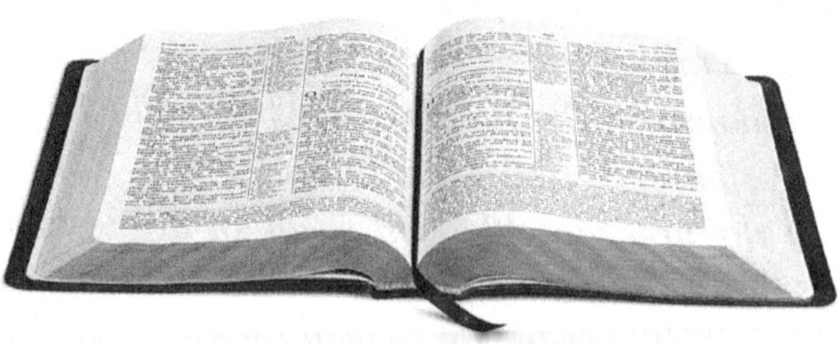

DAY #149

READ Psalm 119:49-64 (*16 verses*)

ZAIN

49 *Remember* ***the word*** *unto thy servant, upon which thou hast*
caused me to hope. 50 *This is my comfort in my affliction: for* ***thy***
word *hath quickened me.* 51 *The proud have had me greatly in*
derision: yet have I not declined from ***thy law***. 52 *I remembered*
thy judgments *of old, O LORD; and have comforted*
myself. 53 *Horror hath taken hold upon me because of the wicked*
that forsake ***thy law***. 54 ***Thy statutes*** *have been my songs in the*
house of my pilgrimage. 55 *I have remembered thy name,*
O LORD, in the night, and have kept ***thy law***. 56 *This I had,*
because I kept ***thy precepts***.

CHETH

57 *Thou art my portion, O LORD: I have said that I would keep*
thy words. 58 *I intreated thy favour with my whole heart:*
be merciful unto me according to ***thy word.*** 59 *I thought on my*
ways, and turned my feet unto ***thy testimonies***. 60 *I made haste,*
and delayed not to keep ***thy commandments***. 61 *The bands of*
the wicked have robbed me: but I have not forgotten ***thy***
law. 62 *At midnight I will rise to give thanks unto thee because of*
thy righteous judgments. 63 *I am a companion of all them that*
fear thee, and of them that keep ***thy precepts.*** 64 *The earth,*
O LORD, is full of thy mercy: teach me ***thy statutes***.

VERSE OF THE DAY: Psalm 119:50

'This is my comfort in my affliction: for **thy word** *hath quickened me.'*

Life is full of affliction. Where do you go for some comfort? The Hebrew word **chayah** is here translated '*quickened*' meaning '*to bring life.*' The worst **affliction** in the human life is the ravages of sin. God's Word is alive and active (**Hebrews 4:12 NASB**). In His Word we learn of the salvation available in Jesus Christ that brings eternal life (**John 3:16, 36; John 4:14; John 5:24; John 6:27, 40, 47**). Take comfort in Jesus. Through simple repentance and faith in Him you will have eternal life! There is nothing more comforting than knowing that!

# # # # #

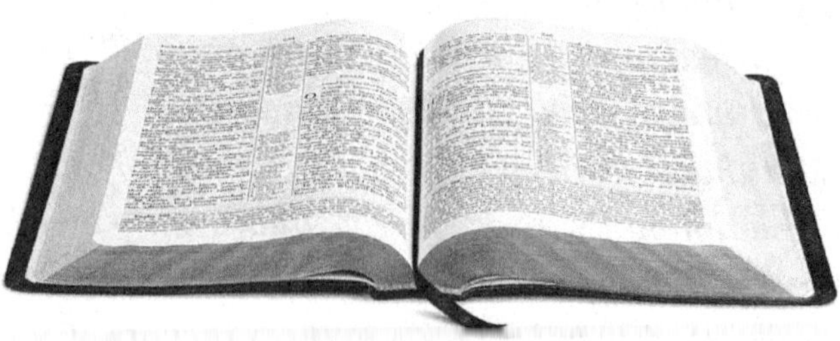

DAY #150

READ Psalm 119:65-80 (*16 verses*)

TETH

65 *Thou hast dealt well with thy servant, O LORD, according
unto* ***thy word****.* 66 *Teach me good judgment and knowledge: for I
have believed* ***thy commandments****.* 67 *Before I was afflicted I
went astray: but now have I kept* ***thy word.*** 68 *Thou art good, and
doest good; teach me* ***thy statutes****.* 69 *The proud have forged a lie
against me: but I will keep* ***thy precepts*** *with my whole
heart.* 70 *Their heart is as fat as grease; but I delight in* ***thy
law****.* 71 *It is good for me that I have been afflicted; that I might
learn* ***thy statutes.*** 72 ***The law of thy mouth*** *is better unto me
than thousands of gold and silver.*

JOD

73 *Thy hands have made me and fashioned me:
give me understanding, that I may learn* ***thy
commandments****.* 74 *They that fear thee will be glad when they
see me; because I have hoped in* ***thy word****.* 75 *I know, O LORD,
that* ***thy judgments*** *are right, and that thou in faithfulness hast
afflicted me.* 76 *Let, I pray thee, thy merciful kindness be for my
comfort, according to* ***thy word*** *unto thy servant.* 77 *Let thy
tender mercies come unto me, that I may live: for* ***thy law*** *is my
delight.* 78 *Let the proud be ashamed; for they dealt perversely
with me without a cause: but I will meditate in* ***thy precepts.***

*79 Let those that fear thee turn unto me, and those that have
known **thy testimonies**. 80 Let my heart be sound in **thy statutes**;
that I be not ashamed.*

VERSE OF THE DAY: Psalm 119:71
*'It is good for me that I have been afflicted; that I might learn **thy statutes**.'*

Sometimes the LORD puts trials in our lives to teach us lessons. This week's study hits me where I am: last Friday I lost my job due to the effects of the COVID virus on our business. Problems in life do not mean we are in sin. Remember Job? He was afflicted even though he was a man who was '*perfect and upright, and one that feareth God, and eschewed evil.*'(**Job 1:1**). The disciples asked Jesus in **John 9:2** who had sinned to make a man born blind: the blind man or his parents. Jesus answered them: '*Neither hath this man sinned, nor his parents: but that the works of God should be made manifest in him*' (**John 9:3**).

Maybe your current affliction is meant to bring glory to Christ. Many times we learn to get closer to God during troubled times. It is easy to get bitter when trouble comes. Run to God and His Word. When we face difficulty may we be driven to His Word. He is there for you!

'Many are the afflictions of the righteous: but the LORD delivereth him out of them all.' (**Psalm 34:19**)

# # # # #

DAY #151

READ Psalm 119:81-96 (*16 verses*)

CAPH

81 *My soul fainteth for thy salvation: but I hope in*
thy word. ***82*** *Mine eyes fail for* ***thy word***, *saying, When wilt thou*
comfort me? ***83*** *For I am become like a bottle in the*
smoke; yet do I not forget ***thy statutes***. ***84*** *How many are the*
days of thy servant? when wilt thou execute judgment
on them that persecute me? ***85*** *The proud have digged*
pits for me, which are not after ***thy law***. ***86*** *All* ***thy***
commandments *are faithful: they persecute me wrongfully; help*
thou me. ***87*** *They had almost consumed me upon earth;*
but I forsook not ***thy precepts***. ***88*** *Quicken me after thy*
lovingkindness; so shall I keep the ***testimony of thy mouth***.

LAMED

89 *For ever, O LORD,* ***thy word*** *is settled in*
heaven. ***90*** *Thy faithfulness is unto all generations: thou hast*
established the earth, and it abideth. ***91*** *They continue this day*
according to ***thine ordinances***: *for all are thy servants.*
92 *Unless* ***thy law*** *had been my delights, I should then have*
perished in mine affliction. ***93*** *I will never forget* ***thy precepts***:
for with them thou hast quickened me. ***94*** *I am thine, save me;*
for I have sought ***thy precepts***. ***95*** *The wicked have waited for me*
to destroy me: but I will consider ***thy testimonies***. ***96*** *I have seen*

*an end of all perfection: but **thy commandment** is exceeding broad.*

VERSE OF THE DAY: Psalm 119:89
*'For ever, O LORD, **thy word** is settled in heaven.'*

Benjamin Franklin once said that the only things certain in life are death and taxes. Well there are two things on earth that will certainly be in heaven: God's Word and the souls of men. Forever God's Word will be settled in heaven. How blessed we are to have the full, complete revelation of the Almighty Creator God in our own language in our own hands.

Do you treasure God's eternal Word? It is my prayer that our time in **Psalms** has given you a love for His Word.

'But the word of the Lord endureth for ever. And this is the word which by the gospel is preached unto you.' **(I Peter 1:25)**

# # # # #

DAY #152

READ Psalm 119:97-112 (*16 verses*)

MEM

97 *O how love I* ***thy law****! It is my meditation all the*
day. **98** *Thou through* ***thy commandments*** *hast made me wiser*
than mine enemies: for they are ever with me. **99** *I have more*
understanding than all my teachers: for ***thy testimonies*** *are my*
meditation. **100** *I understand more than the ancients, because I*
keep ***thy precepts.*** **101** *I have refrained my feet from every evil*
way, that I might keep ***thy word****.* **102** *I have not departed from* ***thy***
judgments*: for thou hast taught me.* **103** *How sweet are* ***thy***
words *unto my taste! yea, sweeter than honey to my*
mouth! **104** *Through* ***thy precepts*** *I get understanding:*
therefore I hate every false way.

NUN

105 ***Thy word*** *is a lamp unto my feet, and a light unto my*
path. **106** *I have sworn, and I will perform it, that I will keep*
thy righteous judgments*.* **107** *I am afflicted very much: quicken*
me, O LORD, according unto ***thy word****.* **108** *Accept, I beseech*
thee, the freewill offerings of my mouth, O LORD, and teach me
thy judgments*.* **109** *My soul is continually in my hand: yet do I*
not forget ***thy law****.* **110** *The wicked have laid a snare for me:*
yet I erred not from ***thy precepts****.* **111** ***Thy testimonies*** *have I*
taken as an heritage for ever: for they are the rejoicing of my

heart. ***112*** *I have inclined mine heart to perform* ***thy statutes*** *alway, even unto the end.*

VERSE OF THE DAY: Psalm 119:105
'Thy word *is a lamp unto my feet, and a light unto my path.'*

We see throughout Scripture that light and darkness are opposites. Starting in **Genesis 1:4** we see that '*God saw the light, that it was good: and God divided the light from the darkness.*' Jesus, the light of the world (**John 9:5**) shined in the darkness of this world and the darkness knew Him not (**John 1:5**). Jesus said in **John 8:12** that if we followed Him we would not walk in darkness but have the light of life. We see in today's verse that God's Word has been given to us to light our path. When we allow God's Word to penetrate our heart it will transform us. People will see a difference in us. We will be able to follow Jesus' command give to us in **Matthew 5:16**: '*Let your light so shine before men, that they may see your good works, and glorify your Father which is in heaven.*'

Michael W. Smith wrote a song entitled THY WORD based on today's verse. The lyrics are below:

<u>THY WORD</u>
Thy word is a lamp unto my feet
And a light unto my path
Thy word is a lamp unto my feet
And a light unto my path

When I feel afraid and I think I've lost my way
Still, you're right there beside me
Nothing will I fear as long as you are near
Please be near me to the end

Thy word is a lamp unto my feet and a light unto my path
Thy word is a lamp unto my feet and a light unto my path

I will not forget
Your love for me and yet
My heart forever is wandering
Jesus be my guide and hold me to your side
And I will love you to the end

One of the benefits of our daily **Psalms** study is to get into the habit of spending time daily in the light of God's Word. We will be better witnesses for Christ because of it! As we sang as children: '*this little light of mine, I'm gonna let it shine.*' My friend, shine your light! May Jesus be praised and exalted in our lives!

# # # # #

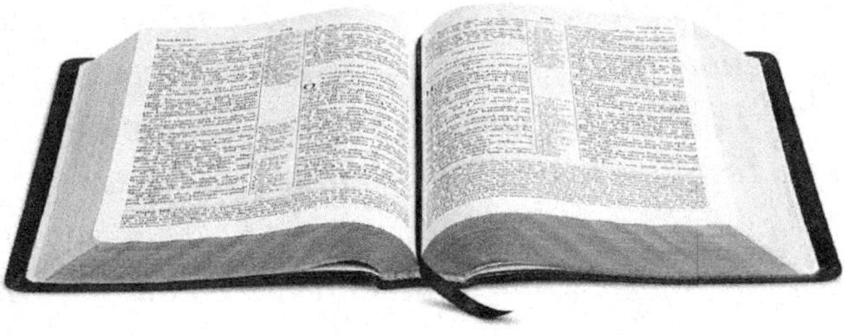

DAY #153

READ Psalm 119:113-128 (*16 verses*)

SAMECH

*113 I hate vain thoughts: but **thy law** do I love. 114 Thou art my
hiding place and my shield: I hope in **thy word**. 115 Depart from
me, ye evildoers: for I will keep the **commandments of my
God**. 116 Uphold me according unto **thy word**, that I may live:
and let me not be ashamed of my hope. 117 Hold thou me up, and
I shall be safe: and I will have respect unto **thy statutes**
continually. 118 Thou hast trodden down all them that err from
thy statutes: for their deceit is falsehood. 119 Thou puttest away
all the wicked of the earth like dross: therefore I love **thy
testimonies**. 120 My flesh trembleth for fear of thee; and I am
afraid of **thy judgments**.*

AIN

*121 I have done judgment and justice: leave me not to mine
oppressors. 122 Be surety for thy servant for good: let not the
proud oppress me. 123 Mine eyes fail for thy salvation, and for
the **word of thy righteousness**. 124 Deal with thy servant
according unto thy mercy, and teach me **thy
statutes**. 125 I am thy servant; give me understanding, that I may
know **thy testimonies**. 126 It is time for thee, LORD, to
work: for they have made void **thy law**. 127 Therefore I love **thy
commandments** above gold; yea, above fine gold. 128 Therefore*

*I esteem all **thy precepts** concerning all things to be right; and I hate every false way.*

VERSE OF THE DAY: Psalm 119:127
*'Therefore I love **thy commandments** above gold; yea, above fine gold.'*

This verse is not warning about investing in the precious metal gold, rather a desire to love the things of God above wealth. **Isaiah 56:11**, talking about those who seek their worth in monetary things, states that they are like greedy dogs which can never have enough. If you try to find your worth in money you will never be satisfied. When you look to the LORD and His Word you will find satisfaction and contentment.

In a time where health and wealth are preached as God's reward, we must be reminded that true contentment comes in eternal treasures. We are to be good stewards of the money we have been entrusted with, but we must not look to our finances as our security and strength. Those who seek pleasure in money stray from the faith and cause themselves many sorrows (**I Timothy 6:10**).

Where do you find your contentment? True contentment comes from the LORD, far above gold!

'Lay not up for yourselves treasures upon earth, where moth and rust doth corrupt, and where thieves break through and steal: But lay up for yourselves treasures in heaven, where neither moth nor rust doth corrupt, and where thieves do not break through nor steal.' (**Matthew 6:20-21**)

'But godliness with contentment is great gain.' (**I Timothy 6:6**)

DAY #154

READ Psalm 119:129-144 (*16 verses*)

PE

129 ***Thy testimonies*** *are wonderful: therefore doth my soul keep*
them. 130 The entrance of ***thy words*** *giveth light; it giveth*
understanding unto the simple. 131 I opened my mouth, and
panted: for I longed for ***thy commandments****. 132 Look thou upon*
me, and be merciful unto me, as thou usest to do unto those that
love thy name. 133 Order my steps in ***thy word****: and let not any*
iniquity have dominion over me. 134 Deliver me from the
oppression of man: so will I keep ***thy precepts****. 135 Make thy face*
to shine upon thy servant; and teach me ***thy statutes****. 136 Rivers*
of waters run down mine eyes, because they keep not ***thy law****.*

TZADDI

137 Righteous art thou, O LORD, and upright are ***thy***
judgments*. 138* ***Thy testimonies*** *that thou hast*
commanded are righteous and very faithful. 139 My zeal hath
consumed me, because mine enemies have forgotten ***thy***
words*. 140* ***Thy word*** *is very pure: therefore thy servant loveth*
it. 141 I am small and despised: yet do not I forget ***thy***
precepts*. 142 Thy righteousness is an everlasting righteousness,*
and ***thy law*** *is the truth. 143 Trouble and anguish*
have taken hold on me: yet ***thy commandments*** *are my*
delights. 144 The righteousness of ***thy testimonies*** *is everlasting:*
give me understanding, and I shall live.

VERSE OF THE DAY: Psalm 119:142
'Thy righteousness is an everlasting righteousness, and ***thy law*** *is the truth.'*

Righteousness is defined as '*the quality or state of being just or rightful.*' Since God never changes (**Hebrews 13:8**) He is forever righteous, forever just. We are told in **I John 1:9** that '*if we confess our sins, He is faithful and just to forgive us our sins and cleanse us from all unrighteousness.*' Because He is just He can make the unjust just. That includes you and me. Praise the LORD!

His Word is truth (**John 17:17**). Jesus said that He was the way, the truth and the life (**John 14:6**). How can we tell the truth from a lie? We must read, study, learn and apply God's Word to our daily lives. God's Word is the truth standard. Everything contrary is untrue. How important it is to seek God's truth by the study of His Word, the Word of truth!

'I have chosen the way of truth: thy judgments have I laid before me.' (**Psalm 119:30**)

'Thy righteousness is an everlasting righteousness, and thy law is the truth.' (**Psalm 119:142**)

'Thou art near, O LORD; and all thy commandments are truth.' (**Psalm 119:151**)

'Thy word is true from the beginning: and every one of thy righteous judgments endureth for ever' (**Psalm 119:160**)

# # # # #

DAY #155

READ Psalm 119:145-160 (*16 verses*)

KOPH

145 I cried with my whole heart; hear me, O LORD: I will keep
***thy statutes**. 146 I cried unto thee; save me, and I shall keep*
***thy testimonies**. 147 I prevented the dawning of the morning,*
*and cried: I hoped in **thy word**. 148 Mine eyes*
*prevent the night watches, that I might meditate in **thy***
***word**. 149 Hear my voice according unto thy lovingkindness:*
*O LORD, quicken me according to **thy judgment**. 150 They draw*
*nigh that follow after mischief: they are far from **thy***
law**. 151 Thou art near, O LORD; and all **thy
***commandments** are truth. 152 Concerning **thy testimonies**,*
I have known of old that thou hast founded them for ever.

RESH

153 Consider mine affliction, and deliver me: for I do not forget
***thy law**. 154 Plead my cause, and deliver me: quicken me*
*according to **thy word.** 155 Salvation is far from the wicked:*
*for they seek not **thy statutes**. 156 Great are thy tender*
*mercies, O LORD: quicken me according to **thy***
***judgments**. 157 Many are my persecutors and mine*
*enemies; yet do I not decline from **thy testimonies**. 158 I beheld*
the transgressors, and was grieved; because they kept
*not **thy word**. 159 Consider how I love **thy precepts**:*

quicken me, LORD, according to thy lovingkindness. ***160 Thy word*** *is true from the beginning: and every one of thy righteous judgments endureth for ever.*

VERSE OF THE DAY: Psalm 119:158
'I beheld the transgressors, and was grieved; because they kept not ***thy word****.'*

We see in today's verse the Psalmist's compassion and concern for the lost. He is grieved for those who would not keep God's law. The Hebrew word used here for '*grieved*' is **quwt**, meaning '*to detest, to dislike greatly*.' Do you have a great displeasure to see family and friends living in opposition to God's commandments?

As we saw last week, God's Word is the truth (**Psalm 119:142**). We must be diligent to share God's good news, the gospel. Who can you share Christ with today? Pray and ask the LORD to give you a deep desire to reach out to those that are not following Jesus. May He put people in our path who need to hear of a loving God's plan of redemption. May we be bold to share the gospel, the power of God unto salvation to all who believe (**Romans 1:16**).

# # # # #

DAY #156

READ Psalm 119:160-176 (*16 verses*)

SCHIN

161 *Princes have persecuted me without a cause: but my heart standeth in awe of* ***thy word****.* ***162*** *I rejoice at* ***thy word****, as one that findeth great spoil.* ***163*** *I hate and abhor lying: but* ***thy law*** *do I love.* ***164*** *Seven times a day do I praise thee because of* ***thy righteous judgments****.* ***165*** *Great peace have they which love* ***thy law****: and nothing shall offend them.* ***166*** *LORD, I have hoped for thy salvation, and done* ***thy commandments****.* ***167*** *My soul hath kept* ***thy testimonies****; and I love them exceedingly.* ***168*** *I have kept* ***thy precepts*** *and* ***thy testimonies****: for all my ways are before thee.*

TAU

169 *Let my cry come near before thee, O LORD: give me understanding according to* ***thy word****.* ***170*** *Let my supplication come before thee: deliver me according to* ***thy word****.* ***171*** *My lips shall utter praise, when thou hast taught me* ***thy statutes****.* ***172*** *My tongue shall speak of* ***thy word****: for all* ***thy commandments*** *are righteousness.* ***173*** *Let thine hand help me; for I have chosen* ***thy precepts****.* ***174*** *I have longed for thy salvation, O LORD; and* ***thy law*** *is my delight.* ***175*** *Let my soul live, and it shall praise thee; and let* ***thy judgments*** *help me.* ***176*** *I have gone astray like a lost sheep; seek thy servant; for I do not forget* ***thy commandments****.*

VERSE OF THE DAY: Psalm 120:163
'I hate and abhor lying: but ***thy law*** *do I love.'*

We see in this verse two things that are complete opposites: hate and love. In **Psalm 119** the Psalmist shares things that he hates: every false way (**verses 104 & 128**), vain thoughts (**verse 113**) and lying (**verse 163**). These are all godless things. He also states how he loves God's Word: '*I will delight myself in thy commandments, which I have loved*' (**verse 47**), '*My hands also will I lift up unto thy commandments, which I have loved*' (**verse 48**), '*O how love I thy law!*' (**verse 97**), '*Thy law do I love*' (**verse 113**), '*I love Thy testimonies*' (**verse 119**), '*I love Thy commandments above gold*' (**verse 127**), '*I love Thy precepts*' (**verse 159**), '*Thy law do I love*' (**verse 163**), '*My soul hath kept Thy testimonies; and I love them exceedingly*' (**verse 167**).

We must abstain from every appearance of evil (**I Thessalonians 5:22**). We must love the things of God. Like the Psalmist, do you love God's Word? Do you love it exceedingly? May we love and cling to God's truth!

' . . . Abhor that which is evil; cleave to that which is good.' **(Romans 12:9)**

# # # # #

DAY #157

READ Psalm 120 (*7 verses*)

1 In my distress I cried unto the LORD, and he heard
me. 2 Deliver my soul, O LORD, from lying lips, and from a
deceitful tongue. 3 What shall be given unto thee? or what shall
be done unto thee, thou false tongue? 4 Sharp arrows of the
mighty, with coals of juniper. 5 Woe is me, that I sojourn in
Mesech, that I dwell in the tents of Kedar! 6 My soul hath long
dwelt with him that hateth peace. 7 I am for peace: but when I
speak, they are for war.

VERSE OF THE DAY: Psalm 120:1
'In my distress I cried unto the LORD, and he heard me.'

Today's verse has three Hebrew words that give us the focus of this verse. The first word gives us the scenario: **tsarah** is translated '*distress*' meaning '*adversity, affliction, anguish, distress, tribulation, trouble.*' It shows us times of difficulty, times where stress is maximized and answers are hard to find. The next two words show a response. The Psalmist '*cried*' because of the hard times. **Qara** is the Hebrew word for '*cried*' signifying '*one calling out to someone by name.*' Like a small child calling for their parents when they are scared at night in the dark, we see the Psalmist crying out to the LORD by name. He seeks the LORD as his refuge, his strength and his comfort. The third word we see is **anah**, Hebrew for '*heard.*' It means '*to heed, to pay attention.*' There is never a time where a child of

God cries out to their Heavenly Father, their Papa, and He is not there ready to answer.

When life is difficult cry out to the LORD. He will hear. He is there for you. He loves you!

'The righteous cry, and the LORD heareth, and delivereth them out of all their troubles.' **(Psalm 34:17)**

'And call upon me in the day of trouble. I will deliver thee, and thou shalt glorify me.' **(Psalm 50:15)**

'In the day of my trouble I will call upon thee: for thou wilt answer me.' **(Psalm 86:7)**

'Then they cried unto the LORD in their trouble, and he delivered them out of their distresses.' **(Psalm 107:6)**

# # # # #

DAY #158

READ Psalm 121 (*8 verses*)

1 I will lift up mine eyes unto the hills, from whence cometh my
help. 2 My help cometh from the LORD, which made heaven and
earth. 3 He will not suffer thy foot to be moved: he that keepeth
thee will not slumber. 4 Behold, he that keepeth Israel shall
neither slumber nor sleep. 5 The LORD is thy keeper:
the LORD is thy shade upon thy right hand. 6 The sun shall not
smite thee by day, nor the moon by night. 7 The LORD
shall preserve thee from all evil: he shall preserve thy
soul. 8 The LORD shall preserve thy going out and thy coming in
from this time forth, and even for evermore.

VERSE OF THE DAY: Psalm 122:4
'Behold, he that keepeth Israel shall neither slumber nor sleep.'

We serve a God who has no need to take a nap. This verse reminded me of the account of Elijah and the prophets of Baal in **I Kings 18:27**: '*It came to pass at noon, that Elijah mocked them and said, "Cry aloud: for he is a god; either he is talking, or he is pursuing, or he is in a journey, or peradventure he sleepeth, and must be awaked.*"' I like how the **CJB** translates **verse 27**: '*Shout louder! After all, he's a god, isn't he? Maybe he's daydreaming, or he's on the potty, or he's away on a trip. Maybe he's asleep, and you have to wake him up.*' '*He is pursuing*' is translated '*Is he gone aside?*' in the **NASB** meaning '*is he in the bathroom?*' What kind of a god has to use the bathroom? Just when you need your god he has diarrhea!?! What a humorous question that was! Maybe he's on vacation or taking a nap. What god needs to take a vacation or is so tired he has to take a break?

We serve a God who is always there when we call. He is never too busy to hear from us. He is never distracted. He has promised to never leave us or never forsake us **(Hebrews 13:5)**. He is always available to us – and He is always awake!

# # # # #

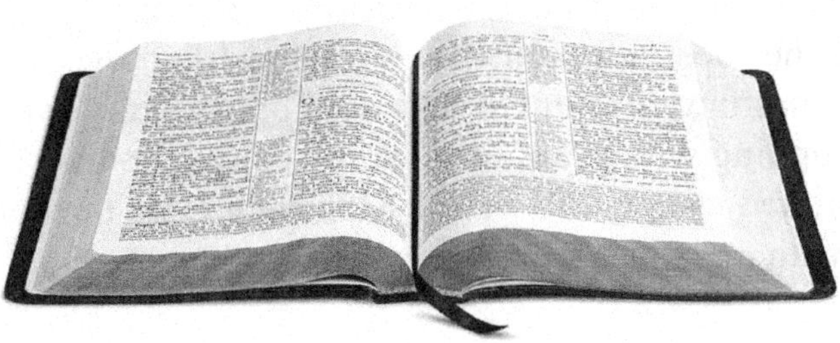

DAY #159

READ Psalm 122 (*9 verses*)

1 I was glad when they said unto me, Let us go into the house of
the LORD. 2 Our feet shall stand within thy gates,
O Jerusalem. 3 Jerusalem is builded as a city that is compact
together: 4 Whither the tribes go up, the tribes of the LORD,
unto the testimony of Israel, to give thanks unto the name of the
LORD. 5 For there are set thrones of judgment, the thrones of the
house of David. 6 Pray for the peace of Jerusalem: they shall
prosper that love thee. 7 Peace be within thy
walls, and prosperity within thy palaces. 8 For my brethren and
companions' sakes, I will now say, Peace be within
thee. 9 Because of the house of the LORD our God I will seek thy
good.

VERSE OF THE DAY: Psalm 123:1
'I was glad when they said unto me, Let us go into the house of the LORD.'

This was one of the first verses I remember memorizing as a child. Does this verse reflect your attitude about Sunday morning? Is going to church whenever the doors are open something that you look forward to? Years ago as a Financial Advisor the most important appointment I had every week was Sunday morning at church. The highlight of my week is still fellowshipping with my church family, singing praise to my God and being fed from God's Word. May we go into the house of the LORD with a glad and thankful heart!

# # # # #

DAY #160

READ Psalm 123 (*4 verses*)

1 Unto thee lift I up mine eyes, O thou that dwellest in the
heavens. 2 Behold, as the eyes of servants look unto the hand of
their masters, and as the eyes of a maiden unto the hand of her
mistress; so our eyes wait upon the LORD our God, until that he
have mercy upon us. 3 Have mercy upon us, O LORD, have
mercy upon us: for we are exceedingly filled with
contempt. 4 Our soul is exceedingly filled with the scorning of
those that are at ease, and with the contempt of the proud.

VERSE OF THE DAY: Psalm 123:3
'Have mercy upon us, O LORD, have mercy upon us: for we are exceedingly filled with contempt.'

The phrase '*have mercy upon us*' is seen only three times in the **Psalms**: twice in this verse and once in the preceding verse (**Psalm 123:2**). The Psalmist knows his own heart: it is filled with '*contempt*' which is translated from the Hebrew **buwz**, meaning '*disrespectful, spiteful, shameful.*' He knows how wicked his heart is. We are all wicked as well. There is no one righteous (**Psalm 14:3, Romans 3:10**). In spite of our sinful hearts, He is merciful toward us! Praise the LORD for His great mercy!

'For His merciful kindness is great toward us: and the truth of the LORD endureth for ever. Praise ye the LORD.'
(Psalm 117:2)

# # # # #

DAY #161

READ Psalm 124 (*8 verses*)

1 If it had not been the LORD who was on our side, now may
Israel say; 2 If it had not been the LORD who was on our side,
when men rose up against us: 3 Then they had swallowed us up
quick, when their wrath was kindled against us: 4 Then the
waters had overwhelmed us, the stream had gone over our
soul: 5 Then the proud waters had gone over our
soul. 6 Blessed be the LORD, who hath not given us as a prey to
their teeth. 7 Our soul is escaped as a bird out of the snare of the
fowlers: the snare is broken, and we are escaped. 8 Our help is in
the name of the LORD, who made heaven and earth.

VERSE OF THE DAY: Psalm 124:2
'If it had not been the LORD who was on our side, when men rose up against us.'

Moses came down from Mt. Sinai after God had given him tablets containing the Ten Commandments. The people, in Moses' absence, had turned from the LORD having built a golden calf. Moses challenged the people: '*Who is on the LORD's side?*' (**Exodus 32:26**).

We live in a culture that places their trust in things other than the Lord God. We are surrounded by many gods that people live for. We must choose to stand with Christ or fall away. Jesus said: '*He that is not with me is against me, and he that gathereth not with me scattereth abroad*' (**Matthew 12:30**). There are only two sides: with Jesus and against Jesus. We must stand boldly with Christ. Like David facing Goliath, with God on our side we cannot fail (**I Samuel 17:50**). Are you on the LORD's side?

'What shall we then say to these things? If God be for us, who can be against us?' (**Romans 8:31**)

# # # # #

DAY #162

READ Psalms 125 & 126 (*11 verses*)

PSALM 125

1 They that trust in the LORD shall be as mount Zion, which cannot be removed, but abideth for ever. 2 As the mountains are round about Jerusalem, so the LORD is round about his people from henceforth even for ever. 3 For the rod of the wicked shall not rest upon the lot of the righteous; lest the righteous put forth their hands unto iniquity. 4 Do good, O LORD, unto those that be good, and to them that are upright in their hearts. 5 As for such as turn aside unto their crooked ways, the LORD shall lead them forth with the workers of iniquity: but peace shall be upon Israel.

PSALM 126

1 When the LORD turned again the captivity of Zion, we were like them that dream. 2 Then was our mouth filled with laughter, and our tongue with singing: then said they among the heathen, The LORD hath done great things for them. 3 The LORD hath done great things for us; whereof we are glad. 4 Turn again our captivity, O LORD, as the streams in the south. 5 They that sow in tears shall reap in joy. 6 He that goeth forth and weepeth, bearing precious seed, shall doubtless come again with rejoicing, bringing his sheaves with him.

VERSE OF THE DAY: Psalm 125:2

'As the mountains are round about Jerusalem, so the LORD is round about his people from henceforth even for ever.'

The city of Jerusalem rests on a limestone plateau 2,500 feet above sea level. On the west side of Jerusalem are the Judean mountains. It is physically impossible to look at Jerusalem without noticing the mountains around the city. Just like that, the LORD surrounds His people. He is an ever present presence around those that He loves. It is impossible to see the believer without sensing the presence of Almighty God around him. The LORD is always near to His children!

'Thou art near, O LORD; and all thy commandments are truth.' **(Psalm 119:151)**

# # # # #

DAY #163

READ Psalms 127 & 128 (*11 verses*)

PSALM 127

1 Except the LORD build the house, they labour in vain that build
it: except the LORD keep the city, the watchman waketh but in
vain. 2 It is vain for you to rise up early, to sit up late,
to eat the bread of sorrows: for so he giveth his beloved
sleep. 3 Lo, children are an heritage of the LORD: and the fruit
of the womb is his reward. 4 As arrows are in the hand of a
mighty man; so are children of the youth. 5 Happy is the man
that hath his quiver full of them: they shall not be ashamed,
but they shall speak with the enemies in the gate.

PSALM 128

1 Blessed is every one that feareth the LORD; that walketh
in his ways. 2 For thou shalt eat the labour of thine
hands: happy shalt thou be, and it shall be well with
thee. 3 Thy wife shall be as a fruitful vine by the sides of thine
house: thy children like olive plants round about thy
table. 4 Behold, that thus shall the man be blessed that feareth
the LORD. 5 The LORD shall bless thee out of Zion: and thou
shalt see the good of Jerusalem all the days of thy life. 6 Yea, thou
shalt see thy children's children, and peace upon Israel.

VERSE OF THE DAY: Psalm 127:1
'Except the LORD build the house, they labour in vain that build it: except the LORD keep the city, the watchman waketh but in vain.'

This is another verse that pertains to the sovereignty of the LORD. He knows all. We must trust His plans fully. To live a life that is contrary to His written Word is futile and in vain. We must search the Scriptures to know the things that are pleasing in His sight. We must pursue His plan for our lives, not necessarily our plan. We labour in vain to do anything contrary to God's plan for us.

In a world that tells us that life is all about us, we must be careful to seek the Lord's guidance. We must live according to His Word. Keith Green wrote a song in 1980 that was inspired by today's verse. May the lyrics be an encouragement to you today.

UNLESS THE LORD BUILDS THE HOUSE
Unless the Lord builds the house
They labor in vain to try at all
Building anything not according to His call
Unless the Lord wants it done
You better not work another day
Building anything that will stand in His way

You love the Lord and it seems like He's been leading
You've asked Him to bless all your plans
But are you so sure you're just doing what you want to
Building your house on the sand, the sand

Working so hard at the things that you believe in
No one can tear you away
But don't you lose sight of the very one who calls you
You may be sorry some day, some day

For wood, hay and stubble, will all burn up in the fire
But to love the Lord with all your heart, should be your one desire

# # # # #

DAY #164

READ Psalm 129 (*8 verses*)

1 Many a time have they afflicted me from my youth, may Israel
now say: 2 Many a time have they afflicted me from my youth:
yet they have not prevailed against me. 3 The plowers
plowed upon my back: they made long their
furrows. 4 The LORD is righteous: he hath cut asunder the cords
of the wicked. 5 Let them all be confounded and turned back that
hate Zion. 6 Let them be as the grass upon the housetops, which
withereth afore it groweth up: 7 Wherewith the mower filleth not
his hand; nor he that bindeth sheaves his bosom. 8 Neither do
they which go by say, The blessing of the LORD be upon you: we
bless you in the name of the LORD.

VERSE OF THE DAY: Psalm 129:4
'The LORD is righteous: he hath cut asunder the cords of the wicked.'

We serve a God who is love but is also righteous. He will judge those who do not accept His salvation. The wicked, those who turn their back on God, will be judged. In today's verse we see that their cords are cut asunder, alluding to the cutting of the cords attached to the oxen as one is ploughing. Their ploughing will be stopped immediately. Their ungodly ways will be stopped in their tracks. There will come a day of accountability as we will all give account of ourselves before God (**Romans 14:12**).

Does knowing that God will judge the ungodly drive you to share Christ with those you know who are without Christ? Our righteous LORD will accept all those who come to Him in faith with a repentant heart. May we realized the fate of those without Jesus and be moved to share His great gospel!

DAY #165

READ Psalm 130 (*8 verses*)

1 Out of the depths have I cried unto thee, O LORD. 2 Lord, hear
my voice: let thine ears be attentive to the voice of my
supplications. 3 If thou, LORD, shouldest mark iniquities,
O Lord, who shall stand? 4 But there is forgiveness with thee,
that thou mayest be feared. 5 I wait for the LORD, my soul doth
wait, and in his word do I hope. 6 My soul waiteth for the Lord
more than they that watch for the morning: I say, more than they
that watch for the morning. 7 Let Israel hope in the LORD:
for with the LORD there is mercy, and with him is plenteous
redemption. 8 And he shall redeem Israel from all his iniquities.

VERSE OF THE DAY: Psalm 130:4
'But there is forgiveness with thee, that thou mayest be feared.'

We saw yesterday that the ungodly will be judged. That does not have to be. We serve a God who is ready and willing to forgive (**I John 1:9**). We must reverence our LORD who forgives us. We receive God's forgiveness; how dare we not desire His forgiveness for those truly in need of it! May the LORD burden our hearts for the lost. May they see Jesus in us and may we be bold to share the gospel!

'For thou, Lord, art good, and ready to forgive; and plenteous in mercy unto all them that call upon thee.' (**Psalm 86:5**)

# # # # #

DAY #166

READ Psalm 131 (*3 verses*)

1 LORD, my heart is not haughty, nor mine eyes lofty: neither do
I exercise myself in great matters, or in things too high for
me. 2 Surely I have behaved and quieted myself, as a child that is
weaned of his mother: my soul is even as a weaned child. 3 Let
Israel hope in the LORD from henceforth and for ever.

VERSE OF THE DAY: Psalm 131:3
'Let Israel hope in the LORD from henceforth and for ever.'

Hope is defined as '*to look forward to with desire and reasonable confidence.*' Israel had their hope in the LORD. Their hope rested in Him henceforth (*from this point forward*) and forever (*without end*). The word HOPE is seen 27 times in the **Psalms** as hope is put in the LORD, His salvation and His Word.

We as believers find our hope in these three things as well. We are reminded in **I Thessalonians 1:3** that our hope is in our Lord Jesus Christ. When we realize our hope is in Christ we must seek to share that hope: '*But sanctify the Lord God in your hearts: and be ready always to give an answer to every man that asketh you a reason of the hope that is in you with meekness and fear*' (**I Peter 3:15**). May we always be ready to share hope we have in Jesus!

'Blessed is the man that trusteth in the LORD, and whose hope the LORD is.' (**Jeremiah 17:7**)

'The LORD is my portion, saith my soul; therefore will I hope in him.' (**Lamentations 3:24**)

# # # # #

DAY #167

READ Psalm 132 (*18 verses*)

1 *A Song of degrees. LORD, remember David, and all his*
afflictions: **2** *How he sware unto the LORD, and vowed unto the*
mighty God of Jacob; **3** *Surely I will not come into the tabernacle*
of my house, nor go up into my bed; **4** *I will not give sleep to mine*
eyes, or slumber to mine eyelids, **5** *Until I find out a place for the*
LORD, an habitation for the mighty God of Jacob. **6** *Lo, we*
heard of it at Ephratah: we found it in the fields of the wood. **7** *We*
will go into his tabernacles: we will worship at his
footstool. **8** *Arise, O LORD, into thy rest; thou, and the ark of thy*
strength. **9** *Let thy priests be clothed with righteousness; and let*
thy saints shout for joy. **10** *For thy servant David's sake turn not*
away the face of thine anointed. **11** *The LORD hath*
sworn in truth unto David; he will not turn from it; Of the fruit of
thy body will I set upon thy throne. **12** *If thy children will keep my*
covenant and my testimony that I shall teach them, their children
shall also sit upon thy throne for evermore. **13** *For the LORD*
hath chosen Zion; he hath desired it for his
habitation. **14** *This is my rest for ever: here will I dwell; for I*
have desired it. **15** *I will abundantly bless her provision: I will*
satisfy her poor with bread. **16** *I will also clothe her priests with*
salvation: and her saints shall shout aloud for joy. **17** *There will*
I make the horn of David to bud: I have ordained a lamp for mine
anointed. **18** *His enemies will I clothe with shame: but upon*
himself shall his crown flourish.

VERSE OF THE DAY: Psalm 132:12

'If thy children will keep my covenant and my testimony that I shall teach them, their children shall also sit upon thy throne for evermore.'

Today's verse reminds us of the great responsibility of every parent and grandparent who believe in the LORD and His Word. We live in a world where God's standards laid out in the Bible are considered antiquated. Some people would even endorse negotiating with a small child instead of instilling discipline and basic rules to live by. How important it is to share God's truth with little ones! We all can have a hand in sharing with our children, grandchildren, nieces and nephews. I am not sure if there is a more rewarding ministry in the local church than working with young people. We all can have a godly influence in the life of a child.

Pray for God's guiding hand in raising up a generation for Christ that will raise up a generation for Christ!

'Train up a child in the way he should go: and when he is old, he will not depart from it.' **(Proverbs 22:6)**

# # # # #

DAY #168

READ Psalms 133 & 134 (*6 verses*)

PSALM 133

*1 Behold, how good and how pleasant it is for brethren to dwell
together in unity! 2 It is like the precious ointment upon the head,
that ran down upon the beard, even Aaron's beard: that went
down to the skirts of his garments; 3 As the dew of Hermon, and
as the dew that descended upon the mountains of Zion: for there
the LORD commanded the blessing, even life for evermore.*

PSALM 134

*1 Behold, bless ye the LORD, all ye servants of the LORD, which
by night stand in the house of the LORD. 2 Lift up your
hands in the sanctuary, and bless the LORD. 3 The LORD that
made heaven and earth bless thee out of Zion.*

VERSE OF THE DAY: Psalm 133:1
'Behold, how good and how pleasant it is for brethren to dwell together in unity!'

What a joy to be in a church that has unity! It is most definitely good and pleasant. We are admonished to '*keep the unity of the Spirit in the bond of peace*' (**Ephesians 4:3**). We see unity within the early church. The phrase '*one accord*' is use throughout the book of **Acts**.

- *'These all continued with one accord in prayer and supplication . . .'* **(Acts 1:14)**

- *'And when the day of Pentecost was fully come, they were all with one accord in one place'* **(Acts 2:1)**

- *'And they, continuing daily with one accord in the temple, and breaking bread from house to house, did eat their meat with gladness and singleness of heart'* **(Acts 2:46)**

- *'. . . they lifted up their voice to God with one accord, and said, Lord, thou art God, which hast made heaven, and earth, and the sea . . .'* **(Acts 4:24)**

Unity brings joy and blessing. On the contrary, there may be nothing more discouraging in the body of Christ than bickering and complaining within the local church. We are directed to '*do all things without murmurings and disputings*' **(Philippians 2:14)**. The **NLT** puts it this way: '*In everything you do, stay away from complaining and arguing.*' We are sternly warned that God hates those '*who soweth discord among brethren*' **(Proverbs 6:19)**. Stay away from idle talk that would cause division. If you have a church gossip, avoid them. Do all you can to contribute to the unity of the saints.

If you are a member of a local church that lives in unity – and I am! - thank the LORD for that today!

'Fulfil ye my joy, that ye be likeminded, having the same love, being of one accord, of one mind.' **(Philippians 2:2)**

# # # # #

DAY #169

READ Psalm 135 (*21 verses*)

1 Praise ye the LORD. Praise ye the name of the LORD;
praise him, O ye servants of the LORD. 2 Ye that stand in the
house of the LORD, in the courts of the house of our
God, 3 Praise the LORD; for the LORD is good: sing praises
unto his name; for it is pleasant. 4 For the LORD hath
chosen Jacob unto himself, and Israel for his peculiar treasure.
5 For I know that the LORD is great, and that our Lord is above
all gods. 6 Whatsoever the LORD pleased, that did he in heaven,
and in earth, in the seas, and all deep places. 7 He causeth the
vapours to ascend from the ends of the earth; he maketh
lightnings for the rain; he bringeth the wind out of his
treasuries. 8 Who smote the firstborn of Egypt, both of man and
beast. 9 Who sent tokens and wonders into the midst of thee,
O Egypt, upon Pharaoh, and upon all his servants. 10 Who smote
great nations, and slew mighty kings; 11 Sihon king of the
Amorites, and Og king of Bashan, and all the kingdoms of
Canaan: 12 And gave their land for an heritage, an heritage unto
Israel his people. 13 Thy name, O LORD, endureth for
ever; and thy memorial, O LORD, throughout all
generations. 14 For the LORD will judge his people, and he will
repent himself concerning his servants. 15 The idols
of the heathen are silver and gold, the work of men's
hands. 16 They have mouths, but they speak not; eyes have they,
but they see not; 17 They have ears, but they hear not; neither is
there any breath in their mouths. 18 They that make them are like

unto them: so is every one that trusteth in them. **19** *Bless the*
LORD, O house of Israel: bless the LORD, O house of Aaron:
20 *Bless the LORD, O house of Levi: ye that fear the LORD,*
bless the LORD. **21** *Blessed be the LORD out of Zion,*
which dwelleth at Jerusalem. Praise ye the LORD.

VERSE OF THE DAY: Psalm 135:3
'Praise the LORD; for the LORD is good: sing praises unto his name; for it is pleasant.'

We see the word '*pleasant*' six times in the **Psalms**. It is the Hebrew word **naiym** meaning '*delightful.*' Three of those six times it pertains to music. Today's verse has to do with pleasant singing. **Psalm 147:1** also has to do with pleasant singing; **Psalm 81:2** mentions a pleasant harp. I believe that the LORD finds pleasure in our singing when it comes from a thankful and worship-filled heart. You may not have the greatest voice, then again, who does? If you sing out of thanksgiving it will sound pleasant to God!

You may not play the harp, but you might play the piano, the guitar, or any of a number of instruments. Do you use that talent to praise the LORD? Do you take pleasure in corporate praise and worship? May our musical abilities be focused on bringing praise to our great God!

# # # # #

DAY #170

READ Psalm 136:1-15 (*15 verses*)

***1** O give thanks unto the LORD; for he is good: for his*
*mercy endureth for ever. **2** O give thanks unto the God of gods:*
*for his mercy endureth for ever. **3** O give thanks to the Lord of*
*lords: for his mercy endureth for ever. **4** To him who alone*
*doeth great wonders: for his mercy endureth for ever. **5** To him*
that by wisdom made the heavens: for his mercy endureth for
*ever. **6** To him that stretched out the earth above the waters:*
*for his mercy endureth for ever. **7** To him that made great lights:*
*for his mercy endureth for ever: **8** The sun to rule by day: for his*
*mercy endureth for ever: **9** The moon and stars to rule by night:*
*for his mercy endureth for ever. **10** To him that smote Egypt in*
*their firstborn: for his mercy endureth for ever: **11** And brought*
out Israel from among them: for his mercy endureth for
*ever: **12** With a strong hand, and with a stretched out arm:*
*for his mercy endureth for ever. **13** To him which divided the Red*
*sea into parts: for his mercy endureth for ever: **14** And made*
Israel to pass through the midst of it: for his mercy endureth for
*ever: **15** But overthrew Pharaoh and his host in the Red sea:*
for his mercy endureth for ever.

VERSES OF THE DAY: Psalm 136:1-3

'O give thanks unto the LORD; for he is good: for his mercy endureth for ever. O give thanks unto the God of gods: for his mercy endureth for ever. O give thanks to the Lord of lords: for his mercy endureth for ever.'

Today and next week we will read **Psalm 136**. To end each verse in this Psalm, the Psalmist uses the same phrase: '*for his mercy endureth for ever.*' That's 26 times! The first three verses tells us what our response to His mercy should be: to give thanks. When we know the LORD as good, as the God of gods and as the Lord of lords, we will give thanks. Since President Abraham Lincoln declared the last Thursday in November as Thanksgiving Day in 1863, it has been a national holiday where families and friends gather to give thanks. As Christians, every day should be Thanksgiving Day. Tomorrow we celebrate a risen Savior: Are you thankful?

# # # # #

DAY #171

READ Psalm 136:16-26 (*11 verses*)

16 *To him which led his people through the wilderness: for his*
mercy endureth for ever. **17** *To him which smote great kings:*
for his mercy endureth for ever: **18** *And slew famous kings:*
for his mercy endureth for ever: **19** *Sihon king of the Amorites:*
for his mercy endureth for ever: **20** *And Og the king of Bashan:*
for his mercy endureth for ever: **21** *And gave their land for an*
heritage: for his mercy endureth for ever: **22** *Even an*
heritage unto Israel his servant: for his mercy endureth for
ever. **23** *Who remembered us in our low estate: for his*
mercy endureth for ever: **24** *And hath redeemed us from our*
enemies: for his mercy endureth for ever. **25** *Who giveth food to*
all flesh: for his mercy endureth for ever. **26** *O give thanks unto*
the God of heaven: for his mercy endureth for ever.

VERSE OF THE DAY: Psalm 136:26
'O give thanks unto the God of heaven: for his mercy endureth for ever.'

Throughout this **Psalm** we are given the mighty deeds of God:

- *He made the heavens* **(v. 5)**
- *He stretched out the earth above the waters* **(v. 6)**
- *He made great lights* **(v. 7)**
- *He made the sun to rule by day* **(v. 8)**
- *He made the moon and stars to rule by night* **(v. 9)**
- *He smote Egypt in their firstborn* **(v. 10)**

- *He delivered Israel* **(v. 11)**
- *He divided the Red Sea for Israel to pass through* **(v. 13-14)**
- *He overthrew Pharaoh and his host in the Red sea* **(v. 15)**
- *He led Israel through the wilderness* **(v. 16)**
- *He defeated great and famous kings* **(v. 17-20)**
- *He provided land for His people* **(v. 21-22)**
- *He remembered them* **(v. 23)**
- *He redeemed them* **(v. 24)**
- *He provided for them* **(v. 25)**

Today's verse is an exclamation point on this **Psalm**. The God of heaven did great things for His people. He has done great things for us as well. May we not take it for granted. May we remember His goodness. He deserves our thanks. He has been so good and merciful to us: Praise the LORD today!

# # # # #

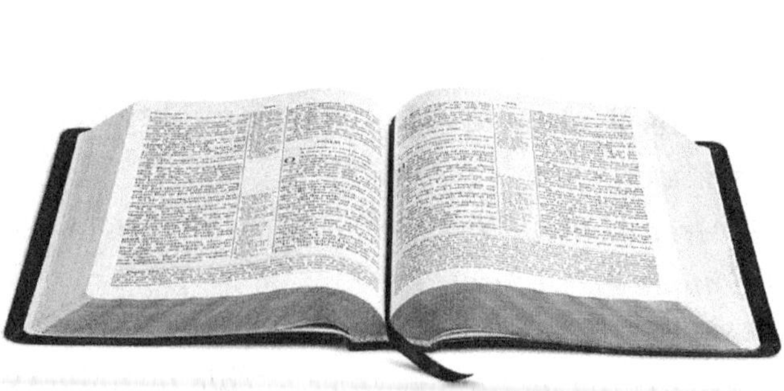

DAY #172

READ Psalm 137 (*9 verses*)

*1 By the rivers of Babylon, there we sat down, yea, we wept,
when we remembered Zion. 2 We hanged our harps upon the
willows in the midst thereof. 3 For there they that carried us
away captive required of us a song; and they that wasted
us required of us mirth, saying, Sing us one of the songs of
Zion. 4 How shall we sing the LORD'S song in a strange
land? 5 If I forget thee, O Jerusalem, let my right hand forget her
cunning. 6 If I do not remember thee, let my tongue cleave to the
roof of my mouth; if I prefer not Jerusalem above my chief joy.
7 Remember, O LORD, the children of Edom in the day of
Jerusalem; who said, Rase it, rase it, even to the foundation
thereof. 8 O daughter of Babylon, who art to be destroyed;
happy shall he be, that rewardeth thee as thou hast served
us. 9 Happy shall he be, that taketh and dasheth thy little ones
against the stones.*

VERSE OF THE DAY: Psalm 137:4
'How shall we sing the LORD'S song in a strange land?'

Today's verse reminds me to sing praise to the LORD regardless of my circumstances. Some days life is difficult, some days life just seems unfair. In the midst of what we might call disaster there is always a calm God who is in control. One of the most difficult verses to obey for me is **I Thessalonians 5:18**: '*In everything give thanks: for this is the will of God in Christ Jesus concerning* *you.*' Some days I just don't feel thankful, although I always should be. This negative attitude is always when I take my eyes off of Jesus and look at my own circumstances from my perspective. Like Peter who stepped out of the boat to walk on the water, as soon as he took His eyes off of Jesus he immediately began to sink (**Matthew 14:29**). Jesus lovingly reached out and saved Peter. What a great reminder that Jesus needs to be my daily focus regardless of where I am or what is going on.

When you find yourself in a difficult situation look to Jesus. Keep your eyes on Him. Should you stumble He will lift you up. He is your refuge and strength (**Psalm 46:1**). Do your best to give thanks in all situations and with all circumstances. That is God's will for you!

'Giving thanks always for all things unto God and the Father in the name of our Lord Jesus Christ.' (**Ephesians 5:20**)

# # # # #

DAY #173

READ Psalm 138 (*8 verses*)

1 *I will praise thee with my whole heart: before the gods will I*
sing praise unto thee. 2 *I will worship toward thy holy temple,*
and praise thy name for thy lovingkindness and for thy truth:
for thou hast magnified thy word above all thy name. 3 *In the day*
when I cried thou answeredst me, and strengthenedst
me with strength in my soul. 4 *All the kings of the earth shall*
praise thee, O LORD, when they hear the words of thy
mouth. 5 *Yea, they shall sing in the ways of the LORD:*
for great is the glory of the LORD. 6 *Though the LORD be high,*
yet hath he respect unto the lowly: but the proud he knoweth afar
off. 7 *Though I walk in the midst of trouble, thou wilt revive me:*
thou shalt stretch forth thine hand against the wrath of mine
enemies, and thy right hand shall save me. 8 *The LORD will*
perfect that which concerneth me: thy mercy, O LORD,
endureth for ever: forsake not the works of thine own hands.

VERSE OF THE DAY: Psalm 138:6
'Though the LORD be high, yet hath he respect unto the lowly: but the proud he knoweth afar off.'

We cannot comprehend the greatness of God. There are no words in the English language to completely and accurately describe the greatness of God. We see here the Hebrew word **ruwm** translated '*high*' meaning '*raised up, exalted.*' The more we recognize how low we are the more clear it becomes that we cannot understand how high He is. Even though He is above all, the most exalted in the universe, He loves the lowly, the humble. As much as He cares for the humble, He rejects the proud in heart. It is important that we understand our standing with the LORD. '*He must increase, but I must decrease*' (**John 3:30**).

May we live humbly before our great God and focus our lives on Him, not ourselves.

'*By humility and the fear of the LORD are riches, and honour, and life.*' (**Proverbs 22:4**)

'. . . *all of you be subject one to another, and be clothes in humility: for God resisteth the proud, and giveth grace to the humble.*' (**I Peter 5:5**)

# # # # #

DAY #174

READ Psalm 139:1-13 (*13 verses*)

*1 O LORD, thou hast searched me, and known me. 2 Thou
knowest my downsitting and mine uprising, thou understandest
my thought afar off. 3 Thou compassest my path and my lying
down, and art acquainted with all my ways. 4 For there is not a
word in my tongue, but, lo, O LORD, thou knowest it
altogether. 5 Thou hast beset me behind and before, and laid
thine hand upon me. 6 Such knowledge is too wonderful for me;
it is high, I cannot attain unto it. 7 Whither shall I go from thy
spirit? or whither shall I flee from thy presence? 8 If I ascend up
into heaven, thou art there: if I make my bed in hell, behold,
thou art there. 9 If I take the wings of the morning, and dwell in
the uttermost parts of the sea; 10 Even there shall thy hand lead
me, and thy right hand shall hold me. 11 If I say, Surely the
darkness shall cover me; even the night shall be light about
me. 12 Yea, the darkness hideth not from thee; but the night
shineth as the day: the darkness and the light are both alike to
thee. 13 For thou hast possessed my reins: thou hast covered me
in my mother's womb.*

VERSE OF THE DAY: Psalm 139:1
'O LORD, thou hast searched me, and known me.'

We serve a God that knows everything about us. One of the major differences between the God of Israel and the other gods of the other nations was that Yahweh was a personal God. He desired to have a covenant relationship with His people. He knows us so intimately that we are told that the very hairs of our head are numbered (**Luke 12:7**). That is numbered, not counted. He knows every hair on your head individually. You are valuable to God! You are worth enough that He sent His Son to redeem you (**I John 4:14**). The Creator God knows you; He loves you; He desires to hear from you; He desires to bless you. He blesses those who obey and live for Him.

He know us; how well do we know Him? We learn of Him through the study of His Word. Seek Him today above everything else. May you be encouraged as you desire to live for Him!

'*But seek ye first the kingdom of God, and his righteousness; and all these things shall be added unto you.*' (**Matthew 6:33**)

# # # # #

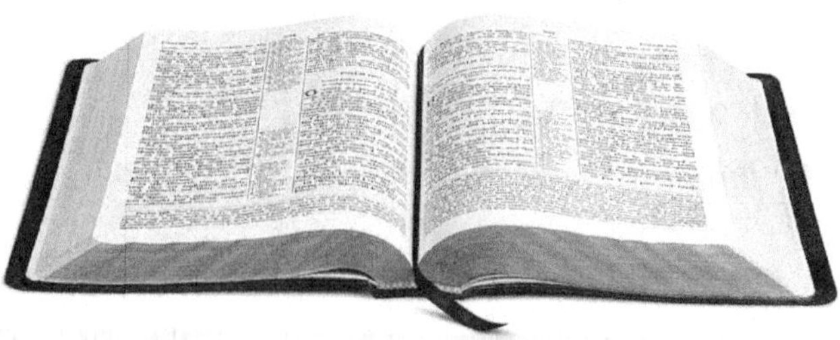

DAY #175

READ Psalm 139:14-24 (*11 verses*)

14 *I will praise thee; for I am fearfully and wonderfully made:*
marvellous are thy works; and that my soul knoweth right
well. **15** *My substance was not hid from thee, when I was made*
in secret, and curiously wrought in the lowest parts of the
earth. **16** *Thine eyes did see my substance, yet being unperfect;*
and in thy book all my members were written, which in
continuance were fashioned, when as yet there was none of them.
17 *How precious also are thy thoughts unto me, O God!*
how great is the sum of them! **18** *If I should count them, they are*
more in number than the sand: when I awake, I am still with
thee. **19** *Surely thou wilt slay the wicked, O God: depart from me*
therefore, ye bloody men. **20** *For they speak against thee*
wickedly, and thine enemies take thy name in vain. **21** *Do not I*
hate them, O LORD, that hate thee? and am not I grieved with
those that rise up against thee? **22** *I hate them with perfect*
hatred: I count them mine enemies. **23** *Search me, O God,*
and know my heart: try me, and know my thoughts: **24** *And see*
if there be any wicked way in me, and lead me in the way
everlasting.

VERSE OF THE DAY: Psalm 139:14
'I will praise thee; for I am fearfully and wonderfully made: marvellous are thy works; and that my soul knoweth right well.'

The first half of this verse is often quoted to support the pro-life movement. And it is true: we are great proof of an awesome Creator. The **NLT** translates it this way: '*Thank you for making me so wonderfully complex!*' In fact, all of His creation – His works – are incredible. The Psalmist closes the verse with the recognition of God's mighty work in Creation. How wonderful to know our Creator, yet sadly many today would deny that such a mighty and incredible Creator exists.

Verses that speak of His Creation are found throughout the Old and New Testaments. And why did He create all things? **Revelation 4:11** tells us: '*Thou art worthy, O Lord, to receive glory and honour and power: for thou has created all things, and for thy pleasure they are and were created.*' The vast excellence of His Creation shows us that He alone is worthy of receiving all glory and all honour. He deserves all of our worship! When we truly see Him for who He is we have no other response than to bow before Him. We should also be compelled to share Him with a lost world who needs Him so. We are fearfully and wonderfully made. He is wonderful and worthy to be feared and reverenced. May you be drawn closer to Him today and led to reach out to those in your world of influence.

'*. . . Fear God, and give glory to him; for the hour of his judgment is come: and worship him that made heaven, and earth, and the sea, and the fountains of waters.*' (**Revelation 14:7**)

# # # # #

DAY #176

READ Psalm 140 (*13 verses*)

*1 Deliver me, O LORD, from the evil man: preserve me from the
violent man; 2 Which imagine mischiefs in their heart;
continually are they gathered together for war. 3 They have
sharpened their tongues like a serpent; adders' poison is under
their lips. Selah. 4 Keep me, O LORD, from the hands of the
wicked; preserve me from the violent man; who have purposed to
overthrow my goings. 5 The proud have hid a snare for me, and
cords; they have spread a net by the wayside; they have set gins
for me. Selah. 6 I said unto the LORD, Thou art my God: hear
the voice of my supplications, O LORD. 7 O GOD the Lord, the
strength of my salvation, thou hast covered my head in the day of
battle. 8 Grant not, O LORD, the desires of the wicked:
further not his wicked device; lest they exalt themselves.
Selah. 12 As for the head of those that compass me about, let the
mischief of their own lips cover them. 10 Let burning coals fall
upon them: let them be cast into the fire; into deep pits, that they
rise not up again. 11 Let not an evil speaker be established in the
earth: evil shall hunt the violent man to overthrow him. 12 I know
that the LORD will maintain the cause of the afflicted, and the
right of the poor. 13 Surely the righteous shall give thanks unto
thy name: the upright shall dwell in thy presence.*

VERSE OF THE DAY: Psalm 140:7
'O GOD the Lord, the strength of my salvation, thou hast covered my head in the day of battle.'

We must realize that we are in a spiritual battle every day. We are instructed in **Ephesians 6** to '*put on the whole armor of God.*' (**v. 11**). This armor includes the belt of truth (**v. 14**), the body armor of God's righteousness (**v. 14**), peace as protection for our feet (**v. 15**), the shield of faith (**v. 16**), salvation as a helmet (**v. 17**) and God's Word, the sword of the LORD (**v. 17**).This is all to be covered by prayer as we are to '*Pray always with all prayer and supplication in the Spirit*' (**v. 18**). We are to go into battle prepared and protected.

Today's verse focused on the helmet of salvation which is also pictured in **Ephesians 6:17**. One commentator writing on **Ephesians 6** stated the following:

> *'In the ancient world this (the helmet) usually was a leather cap studded with metal for extra strength. Often some kind of plume or decoration was added perhaps to identify the soldier to his regiment. Salvation is pictured as this kind of helmet, protecting an essential part of the body. A soldier would be foolish to go into battle without his helmet. The helmet of salvation protects us against discouragement, against the desire to give up, giving us hope not only in knowing that we are saved, but that we will be saved. It is the assurance that God will triumph.'*

The helmet of salvation identifies to the world that we belong to Christ. Have you received His great salvation? It is yours for the taking: it has already been paid for. It is a free gift (**Ephesians 2:8-9**). It will protect you and can never be taken away.

Believer, are you ready for the battle? Do you have your armor on? Be careful: the enemy is fully prepared to fight you! Be assured: '*. . . greater is he that is in you than he that is in the world.*' (**I John 4:4**). We can be confidently run to the battle!

DAY #177

READ Psalm 141 (*10 verses*)

1 LORD, I cry unto thee: make haste unto me; give ear unto my
voice, when I cry unto thee. 2 Let my prayer be set forth before
thee as incense; and the lifting up of my hands as the evening
sacrifice. 3 Set a watch, O LORD, before my mouth; keep the
door of my lips. 4 Incline not my heart to any evil thing,
to practise wicked works with men that work iniquity: and let me
not eat of their dainties. 5 Let the righteous smite me; it shall be a
kindness: and let him reprove me; it shall be an excellent oil,
which shall not break my head: for yet my prayer also shall be in
their calamities. 6 When their judges are overthrown in stony
places, they shall hear my words; for they are sweet. 7 Our bones
are scattered at the grave's mouth, as when one cutteth and
cleaveth wood upon the earth. 8 But mine eyes are unto thee,
O GOD the Lord: in thee is my trust; leave not my soul
destitute. 9 Keep me from the snares which they have laid for me,
and the gins of the workers of iniquity. 10 Let the wicked fall into
their own nets, whilst that I withal escape.

VERSE OF THE DAY: Psalm 141:3
'Set a watch, O LORD, before my mouth; keep the door of my lips.'

We must be careful what comes out of our mouths. It is so serious that the Psalmist is asking the LORD for help. With our mouths we can bless or curse. We can encourage or discourage.

We can share the gospel or destroy our testimony. We must place a watch over our lips and seek the LORD's help in doing so. Our speech is actually a matter of the heart. '*A good man out of the good treasure of his heart bringeth forth that which is good; and an evil man out of the evil treasure of his heart bringeth forth that which is evil: for of the abundance of the heart his mouth speaketh*' (**Luke 6:45**). We must be careful what we say: our testimony can be destroyed in a matter of sentences. To place a watch over our lips will help us keep our Christian testimony intact. '*A good name is rather to be chosen than great riches, and loving favour rather than silver and gold*' (**Proverbs 22:1**).

The Christian must pause before speaking, as the unrighteous blurt out their words without pause. '*The heart of the righteous studieth to answer: but the mouth of the wicked poureth out evil things*' (**Proverbs 15:28**). Studying God's Word will cause us to be slow to speak as we learn God's ways. '*My lips shall utter praise, when thou hast taught me thy statutes*' (**Psalm 119:171**). May we be careful not to condemn, quick to encourage and constant in our praise. Lord, guard our lips. May our speech reflect the love of Christ!

'*Let the words of my mouth, and the meditations of my heart, be acceptable in thy sight, O LORD, my strength, and my redeemer.*' (**Psalm 19:14**)

'*Wherefore, my beloved brethren, let every man be swift to hear, slow to speak, slow to wrath.*' (**James 1:19**)

# # # # #

DAY #178

READ Psalm 142 (*7 verses*)

1 I cried unto the LORD with my voice; with my voice unto the
LORD did I make my supplication. 2 I poured out my complaint
before him; I shewed before him my trouble. 3 When my spirit
was overwhelmed within me, then thou knewest my path.
In the way wherein I walked have they privily laid a snare for me.
4 I looked on my right hand, and beheld, but there was no man
that would know me: refuge failed me; no man cared for my
soul. 5 I cried unto thee, O LORD: I said, Thou art my
refuge and my portion in the land of the living. 6 Attend unto my
cry; for I am brought very low: deliver me from my persecutors;
for they are stronger than I. 7 Bring my soul out of prison,
that I may praise thy name: the righteous shall compass me
about; for thou shalt deal bountifully with me.

VERSE OF THE DAY: Psalm 142:2
'I poured out my complaint before him; I shewed before him my trouble.'

I think it is important to note the word translated here '*complaint*' is not a complaint toward the Lord and His providence, but rather the Psalmist's sin and his unbelief. Out of the abundance of his heart and the bitterness of his soul he lays out his confession before a holy God. '*Complaint*' here is the Hebrew word **siyach**, meaning '*to speak aloud, to publicly declare.*' In his repentance he bore his soul before His God. Like us the Psalmist was a man who struggled with sin. We may not all struggle with the same sin but we all have some issue of sin in our lives that we wrestle with in an ongoing fashion.

He took his '*trouble*' to the LORD. This is the Hebrew word **tsarah** meaning '*affliction.*' What do you struggle with in your life? What is your affliction in your spiritual walk? Take it to the LORD. He already knows yet He desires for you to confess it to Him. He is there to guide you, to strengthen you and to bring you through triumphantly. Be quick to run to the LORD!

'Look upon mine affliction and my pain; and forgive all my sins.' **(Psalm 25:18)**

'Many are the afflictions of the righteous: but the LORD delivereth him out of them all.' **(Psalm 34:19)**

'Mine eye mourneth by reason of affliction: LORD, I have called daily upon thee, I have stretched out my hands unto thee.'
(Psalm 88:9)

# # # # #

DAY #179

READ Psalm 143 (*12 verses*)

1 *Hear my prayer, O LORD, give ear to my supplications: in thy*
faithfulness answer me, and in thy righteousness. **2** *And enter not*
into judgment with thy servant: for in thy sight shall no man living
be justified. **3** *For the enemy hath persecuted my soul; he hath*
smitten my life down to the ground; he hath made me to dwell in
darkness, as those that have been long dead. **4** *Therefore is*
my spirit overwhelmed within me; my heart within me is
desolate. **5** *I remember the days of old; I meditate on all thy*
works; I muse on the work of thy hands. **6** *I stretch forth my hands*
unto thee: my soul thirsteth after thee, as a thirsty land. Selah.
7 *Hear me speedily, O LORD: my spirit faileth: hide not thy face*
from me, lest I be like unto them that go down into the
pit. **8** *Cause me to hear thy lovingkindness in the morning; for in*
thee do I trust: cause me to know the way wherein I should walk;
for I lift up my soul unto thee. **9** *Deliver me, O LORD, from mine*
enemies: I flee unto thee to hide me. **10** *Teach me to do thy will;*
for thou art my God: thy spirit is good; lead me into the land of
uprightness. **11** *Quicken me, O LORD, for thy name's sake: for*
thy righteousness' sake bring my soul out of trouble. **12** *And of*
thy mercy cut off mine enemies, and destroy all them that afflict
my soul: for I am thy servant.

VERSE OF THE DAY: Psalm 143:5
'I remember the days of old; I meditate on all thy works; I muse on the work of thy hands.'

It is so important for us at times to just stop and look around. As some would say, be sure to smell the roses. We see in today's verse a reminder to reflect on the goodness of God. It is good for us to stop and think. If you take the time to think about it you will find that He has been so good to us. If we meditate (*to engage in thought or contemplation*) on all His works we should be drawn to thank and praise our LORD! To '*muse*' means to meditate in silence. One of my favorite verses in the **Psalms** is **Psalm 46:10** which reminds us to '*be still and know that I am is God.*' We looked at that verse on Day #53 of our study. We need to stop everything and give attention to meditating on His works in your life.

When is the last time you just took some time away from your busy schedule and just reflected on God's wonderful hand in your life? Every good and perfect gift in your life is handed down directly from the Father. I will occasionally go for a long walk and just spend time with my LORD. In the center of conflict and distress He is the calming, loving, providing JESUS! In spite of life's trials, He is good. He is there. He is the sovereign LORD.

I would encourage you today to spend a few moments in silence with Him. Reflect on His goodness. Be thankful. Live a life of thankfulness. Praise His mighty name! Amen and amen . . .

'Every good gift and every perfect gift is from above, and cometh down from the Father of lights, with whom is no variableness, neither shadow of turning.' **(James 1:17)**

'For the LORD God is a sun and shield: the LORD will give grace and glory: no good think will he withhold from them that walk uprightly.' **(Psalm 84:11)**

'Praise ye the LORD. O give thanks unto the LORD; for he is good: for his mercy endureth for ever.' **(Psalm 106:1)**

# # # # #

DAY #180

READ Psalm 144 (*15 verses*)

*1 Blessed be the LORD my strength, which teacheth my hands to
war, and my fingers to fight: 2 My goodness, and my fortress; my
high tower, and my deliverer; my shield, and he in whom I trust;
who subdueth my people under me. 3 LORD, what is man,
that thou takest knowledge of him! or the son of man, that thou
makest account of him! 4 Man is like to vanity: his
days are as a shadow that passeth away. 5 Bow thy
heavens, O LORD, and come down: touch the mountains, and
they shall smoke. 6 Cast forth lightning, and scatter them: shoot
out thine arrows, and destroy them. 7 Send thine hand from
above; rid me, and deliver me out of great waters, from the hand
of strange children; 8 Whose mouth speaketh vanity, and their
right hand is a right hand of falsehood. 9 I will sing a new song
unto thee, O God: upon a psaltery and an instrument of ten
strings will I sing praises unto thee. 10 It is he that giveth
salvation unto kings: who delivereth David his servant from the
hurtful sword. 11 Rid me, and deliver me from the hand of
strange children, whose mouth speaketh vanity, and their right
hand is a right hand of falsehood: 12 That our sons may be as
plants grown up in their youth; that our daughters may be as
corner stones, polished after the similitude of a palace:
13 That our garners may be full, affording all manner of
store: that our sheep may bring forth thousands and ten
thousands in our streets: 14 That our oxen may be strong to
labour; that there be no breaking in, nor going out; that there be*

no complaining in our streets. **15** *Happy is that people, that is in such a case: yea, happy is that people, whose God is the LORD.*

VERSE OF THE DAY: Psalm 144:15
'Happy is that people, that is in such a case: yea, happy is that people, whose God is the LORD.'

What makes you happy? For some it is their family, for others it is their job or their possessions. Many people look for happiness in worldly pleasures. They eventually find that these things are fleeting. But what brings true happiness? True happiness and real joy and peace only comes from the LORD. We see the Hebrew word **esher** in today's verse translated twice as '*happy*' meaning '*blessed.*'

Do you consider yourself blessed? Does the world see that you are happy because you are a follower of Jesus? We are truly blessed to be called a child of Almighty God. May the world see the happiness that only comes from Jesus in our lives!

'Blessed is the man that trusteth in the LORD, and whose hope the LORD is.' (**Jeremiah 17:7**)

# # # # #

DAY #181

READ Psalm 145 (*21 verses*)

1 *I will extol thee, my God, O king; and I will bless thy name for*
ever and ever. **2** *Every day will I bless thee; and I will praise thy*
name for ever and ever. **3** *Great is the LORD, and greatly to be*
praised; and his greatness is unsearchable. **4** *One generation*
shall praise thy works to another, and shall declare thy mighty
acts. **5** *I will speak of the glorious honour of thy majesty, and of*
thy wondrous works. **6** *And men shall speak of the might of thy*
terrible acts: and I will declare thy greatness. **7** *They shall*
abundantly utter the memory of thy great goodness, and shall
sing of thy righteousness. **8** *The LORD is gracious,*
and full of compassion; slow to anger, and of great
mercy. **9** *The LORD is good to all: and his tender*
mercies are over all his works. **10** *All thy works shall praise thee,*
O LORD; and thy saints shall bless thee. **11** *They shall speak of*
the glory of thy kingdom, and talk of thy power; **12** *To make*
known to the sons of men his mighty acts, and the glorious
majesty of his kingdom. **13** *Thy kingdom is an everlasting*
kingdom, and thy dominion endureth throughout all
generations. **14** *The LORD upholdeth all that fall, and raiseth up*
all those that be bowed down. **15** *The eyes of all wait upon thee;*
and thou givest them their meat in due season. **16** *Thou openest*
thine hand, and satisfies the desire of every living
thing. **17** *The LORD is righteous in all his ways, and holy in all*
his works. **18** *The LORD is nigh unto all them that call upon him,*
to all that call upon him in truth. **19** *He will fulfil the desire of*
them that fear him: he also will hear their cry, and will save

them. **20** *The LORD preserveth all them that love him: but all the
wicked will he destroy.* **21** *My mouth shall speak the praise of the
LORD: and let all flesh bless his holy name for ever and ever.*

VERSE OF THE DAY: Psalm 145:8
'The LORD is gracious, and full of compassion; slow to anger, and of great mercy.'

I believe that God's greatest attribute is love: He IS love! (**I John 4:8**). Here we have a great list of four of the LORD's wonderful attributes: grace, compassion, patience and mercy. If we were to put together a Mt. Rushmore of God's attributes, four of His greatest attributes, behind love these might top the list. To get a grasp on these let's define these terms:

- **GRACE** – *unmerited favor*
- **COMPASSION** – *deep sympathy for another who is stricken with the strong desire to alleviate the suffering*
- **PATIENCE** – *the bearing of provocation, annoyance, misfortune or pain without complaint, loss of temper or irritation*
- **MERCY** – *kindly forbearance shown to an offender or an enemy*

I cannot help but be grateful for God's grace, compassion, patience and mercy toward a sinner like me. It would be impossible to decide which one of these four is most needed in my life. He constantly displays them all! It's sad to say that far too often I live in a way where all these attributes are needed. Praise God that He loves me enough to shower His blessings upon me day after day after day!

'But thou, O Lord, art a God full of compassion, and gracious, longsuffering, and plenteous in mercy and truth.' **(Psalm 86:15)**

# # # # #

DAY #182

READ Psalm 146 (*10 verses*)

1 Praise ye the LORD. Praise the LORD, O my soul. 2 While I
live will I praise the LORD: I will sing praises unto my God while
I have any being. 3 Put not your trust in princes, nor in the son
of man, in whom there is no help. 4 His breath goeth forth, he
returneth to his earth; in that very day his thoughts perish.
5 Happy is he that hath the God of Jacob for his help, whose
hope is in the LORD his God: 6 Which made heaven, and earth,
the sea, and all that therein is: which keepeth truth for
ever: 7 Which executeth judgment for the oppressed:
which giveth food to the hungry. The LORD looseth the
prisoners: 8 The LORD openeth the eyes of the blind: the LORD
raiseth them that are bowed down: the LORD loveth the
righteous: 9 The LORD preserveth the strangers; he relieveth the
fatherless and widow: but the way of the wicked he turneth upside
down. 10 The LORD shall reign for ever, even thy God, O Zion,
unto all generations. Praise ye the LORD.

VERSE OF THE DAY: Psalm 146:8
'The LORD openeth the eyes of the blind: the LORD raiseth them that are bowed down: the LORD loveth the righteous.'

We see in the New Testament accounts of Jesus healing the blind in **Matthew 9, Matthew 12, Matthew 20, Mark 8, Mark 10, Luke 18** and **John 9**. We also see general references that Jesus gave sight to the blind in **Matthew 11, Matthew 15,**

Matthew 21, Luke 4, Luke 7, John 10 and **John 11**. We also see a different kind of blindness, spiritual blindness, mentioned in **Matthew 23, John 12, Romans 2, Romans 11, II Corinthians 3, II Corinthians 4, Ephesians 4, II Peter 1** and **I John 2**. It's one thing to have blindness in your eyes, but some have blinded minds **(II Corinthians 4:4)** and blinded hearts **(Ephesians 4:18)**.

Jesus is still in the miracle business! Today He takes those who are spiritually blind and gives them spiritual sight! He takes hearts of stone and changes them into hearts of flesh **(Ezekiel 36:26)**.He makes the unrighteous righteous **(I John 1:9)**. Do you remember the day when you received your spiritual sight? Who do you know who is spiritually blind? Jesus is their only hope to receive spiritual sight!

# # # # #

DAY #183

READ Psalm 147 (*20 verses*)

1 Praise ye the LORD: for it is good to sing praises unto our
God; for it is pleasant; and praise is comely. **2** *The LORD doth*
build up Jerusalem: he gathereth together the outcasts of
Israel. **3** *He healeth the broken in heart, and bindeth up their*
wounds. **4** *He telleth the number of the stars; he calleth them all*
by their names. **5** *Great is our Lord, and of great power:*
his understanding is infinite. **6** *The LORD lifteth up the meek:*
he casteth the wicked down to the ground. **7** *Sing unto the LORD*
with thanksgiving; sing praise upon the harp unto our
God: **8** *Who covereth the heaven with clouds, who prepareth rain*
for the earth, who maketh grass to grow upon the
mountains. **9** *He giveth to the beast his food, and to the young*
ravens which cry. **10** *He delighteth not in the strength of the*
horse: he taketh not pleasure in the legs of a man. **11** *The LORD*
taketh pleasure in them that fear him, in those that hope in his
mercy. **12** *Praise the LORD, O Jerusalem; praise thy God,*
O Zion. **13** *For he hath strengthened the bars of thy gates;*
he hath blessed thy children within thee. **14** *He maketh*
peace in thy borders, and filleth thee with the finest of the
wheat. **15** *He sendeth forth his commandment upon earth:*
his word runneth very swiftly. **16** *He giveth snow like wool:*
he scattereth the hoarfrost like ashes. **17** *He casteth forth his ice*
like morsels: who can stand before his cold? **18** *He sendeth out*
his word, and melteth them: he causeth his wind to blow, and the
waters flow. **19** *He sheweth his word unto Jacob, his statutes and*

his judgments unto Israel. **20** *He hath not dealt so with any nation: and as for his judgments, they have not known them. Praise ye the LORD.*

VERSE OF THE DAY: Psalm 147:3
'He healeth the broken in heart, and bindeth up their wounds.'

We mentioned yesterday how God changes the cold and hard human heart (**Ezekiel 36:26**). Even though we have a new heart in Christ, we sometimes can have a heavy heart. Have you ever had a broken heart? A broken heart, along with today's verse, is mentioned in **Psalm 34**, **Psalm 51** and **Psalm 69**. The word translated '*broken*' is the Hebrew word **shabar** meaning '*broken into pieces, crushed.*' What a comfort to know that God can heal our broken heart and put all the pieces back together.

What troubles your heart? What has happened that has wounded you? Know that you can take all our cares to Him (**I Peter 5:7**). He is the great healer!

'The LORD is nigh unto them that are of a broken heart, and saveth such as be of a contrite spirit.' (**Psalm 34:18**)

# # # # #

DAY #184

READ Psalm 148 (*14 verses*)

*1 Praise ye the LORD. Praise ye the LORD from the heavens:
praise him in the heights. 2 Praise ye him, all his angels: praise
ye him, all his hosts. 3 Praise ye him, sun and moon: praise him,
all ye stars of light. 4 Praise him, ye heavens of heavens, and ye
waters that be above the heavens. 5 Let them praise the name of
the LORD: for he commanded, and they were created. 6 He hath
also stablished them for ever and ever: he hath made a decree
which shall not pass. 7 Praise the LORD from the earth, ye
dragons, and all deeps: 8 Fire, and hail; snow, and vapour;
stormy wind fulfilling his word: 9 Mountains, and all hills;
fruitful trees, and all cedars: 10 Beasts, and all cattle; creeping
things, and flying fowl: 11 Kings of the earth, and all people;
princes, and all judges of the earth: 12 Both young men, and
maidens; old men, and children: 13 Let them praise the name of
the LORD: for his name alone is excellent; his glory is above the
earth and heaven. 14 He also exalteth the horn of his people, the
praise of all his saints; even of the children of Israel, a people
near unto him. Praise ye the LORD.*

VERSE OF THE DAY: Psalm 148:2
'Praise ye him, all his angels: praise ye him, all his hosts.'

Angels are mentioned throughout Scripture. They are mentioned in 17 Old Testament books **(Genesis, Exodus, Numbers, Judges, I Samuel, II Samuel, I Kings, II Kings, I Chronicles, II Chronicles, Job, Psalms, Ecclesiastes, Isaiah, Daniel,**

Hosea, Zechariah) and in 16 New Testament books (**Matthew, Mark, Luke, John, Acts, Romans, I Corinthians, Galatians, Colossians, II Thessalonians, I Timothy, Hebrews, I Peter, II Peter, Jude, Revelation**). We are given a wonderful example of the heavenly hosts praising God in **Luke 2:8-14**:

> *'And there were in the same country shepherds abiding in the field, keeping watch over their flock by night. And, lo, the angel of the Lord came upon them, and the glory of the Lord shone round about them: and they were sore afraid. And the angel said unto them, Fear not: for, behold, I bring you good tidings of great joy, which shall be to all people. For unto you is born this day in the city of David a Saviour, which is Christ the Lord. And this shall be a sign unto you; Ye shall find the babe wrapped in swaddling clothes, lying in a manger. And suddenly there was with the angel a multitude of the heavenly host praising God, and saying, Glory to God in the highest, and on earth peace, good will toward men.'*

One angel arrives to share the news of the birth of the Messiah, Jesus Christ. I can picture the scene in heaven. The heaven is full of angels watching on. I can imagine their amazement as they say to the Father, '*Can we go rejoice too!?!*' I can see the Father smiling, then saying, '. . . *Go ahead!*' What an awesome sight that must have been for the shepherds!

As the army of angels praised the coming King so many years ago, may we have the same joy to shout our praise to our Savior and King, the Lord Jesus Christ!

'O praise the LORD, all ye nations: praise him, all ye people.' **(Psalm 117:1)**

# # # # #

DAY #185

READ Psalm 149 (*9 verses*)

1 *Praise ye the LORD. Sing unto the LORD a new song, and his*
praise in the congregation of saints. **2** *Let Israel rejoice in him*
that made him: let the children of Zion be joyful in their
King. **3** *Let them praise his name in the dance: let them sing*
praises unto him with the timbrel and harp. **4** *For the LORD*
taketh pleasure in his people: he will beautify the meek with
salvation. **5** *Let the saints be joyful in glory: let them sing aloud*
upon their beds. **6** *Let the high praises of God be in their*
mouth, and a two-edged sword in their hand; **7** *To execute*
vengeance upon the heathen, and punishments upon the
people; **8** *To bind their kings with chains, and their nobles with*
fetters of iron; **9** *To execute upon them the judgment written: this*
honour have all his saints. Praise ye the LORD.

VERSE OF THE DAY: Psalm 149:1
'*Praise ye the LORD. Sing unto the LORD a new song, and his praise in the congregation of saints.*'

23 times in the Psalms we see the phrase '*Praise ye the LORD.*' **Praise** is '*to offer grateful homage in words or song as an act of worship.*' We should live a life that praises the LORD, but what a blessing to come together in the congregation of saints within the local church and corporately offer praise to our God. As we are nearing the end of our study of the book of **Psalms** I pray that you not only have a newfound desire to read and study

God's Word but also a reenergized spirit toward corporate worship. May the melody of your heart praise the LORD!

'Praise ye the LORD. I will praise the LORD with my whole heart, in the assembly of the upright, and in the congregation.' **(Psalm 111:1)**

# # # # #

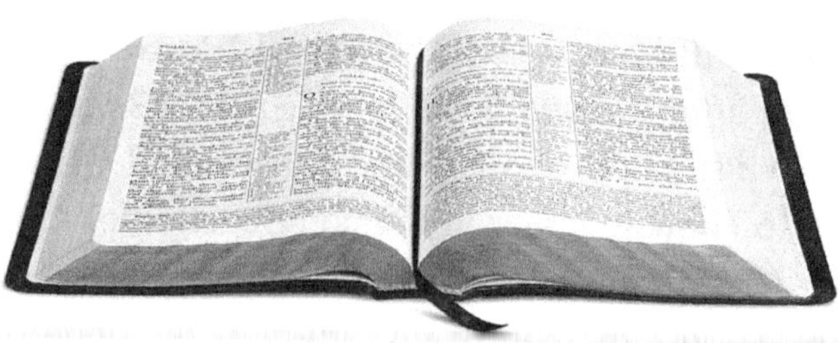

DAY #186

READ Psalm 150 (*6 verses*)

1 Praise ye the LORD. Praise God in his sanctuary: praise him
in the firmament of his power. 2 Praise him for his mighty acts:
praise him according to his excellent greatness. 3 Praise him
with the sound of the trumpet: praise him with the psaltery and
harp. 4 Praise him with the timbrel and dance: praise him with
stringed instruments and organs. 5 Praise him upon the loud
cymbals: praise him upon the high sounding cymbals. 6 Let every
thing that hath breath praise the LORD. Praise ye the LORD.

VERSE OF THE DAY: Psalm 150:6
'Let every thing that hath breath praise the LORD. Praise ye the LORD.'

What a fitting verse to finish our study. The last verse of the last **Psalm** says it all: **Let everything that hath breath praise the LORD!** I pray that you have been encouraged by the greatness of our God and His goodness to us through the study of **Psalms**. May we have a new appreciation for all that He has done for us. He is worthy to receive all our praise.

Dear friends - **PRAISE YE THE LORD!**

'I will call upon the LORD, who is worthy to be praised . . .' **(Psalm 18:3)**

# # # # #

CONCLUSION

We have arrived at the end of our study! I pray that you have been blessed during your time reading through the **Psalms**. I would encourage you to continue your study of God's Word. It will be a blessing to you day by day.

It would be an encouragement to me to hear from you. Please drop me a message at **matteckel44@yahoo.com** and let me know how the LORD blessed you through these studies.

Be blessed in **JESUS!**

# # # # #

THE GOSPEL

A study through the Psalms shares the story of a great God who loves His people. Nothing shows His love more than the gospel, the good news, the sending of His Son, Jesus, to redeem His people. The gospel is simply:

God loves you:

> '*For God so loved the world that he gave his only Son, so that everyone who believes in him will not perish but have eternal life.*' **(John 3:16 NLT)**

Jesus came for all mankind, for we all have fallen short:

> '*For all have sinned; all fall short of God's glorious standard.*' **(Romans 3:23 NLT)**

We cannot pay for the forgiveness of our sins. We cannot earn forgiveness of our sins by doing any works, living righteously or by saying penance. It is only through faith in Christ Jesus:

> '*God saved you by his special favor when you believed. And you can't take credit for this; it is a gift from God. Salvation is not a reward for the good things we have done, so none of us can boast about it.*'
> **(Ephesians 2:8-9 NLT)**

The sentence put upon us for our sin is death. We will all die physically because of our sinful flesh, but we will all die spiritually as well unless we accept the free gift of salvation provided for us through the death, burial and resurrection of Jesus Christ:

> '*For the wages of sin is death, but the free gift of God is eternal life through Christ Jesus our Lord.*'
> **(Romans 6:23 NLT)**

Even while we were lost sinners, Jesus loved us enough to provide a way of escape from our sins:

> '*But God showed his great love for us by sending Christ to die for us while we were still sinners.*'
> **(Romans 5:8 NLT)**

It's simple. If we come as a repentant sinner, understanding that Jesus was sent to pay the penalty for your sins on the cross of Calvary through His shed blood and accept Him into your life as Lord and Savior, we can be saved from God's wrath:

> '*For "Anyone who calls on the name of the Lord will be saved."*'' **(Romans 10:13 NLT)**

We do not have to work for God's favor. We cannot earn God's favor. We do not have to wonder what will happen to us after this life. We can KNOW as well as we know our name that we have God's assurance that He will guide us in this life and give us eternal life in Heaven:

'I write this to you who believe in the Son of God, so that you may know you have eternal life.' **(I John 5:13 NLT)**

If you have not already, you need to accept Jesus as your personal Savior. It will transform your life! God desires that all come to Him with a repentant and humble heart. There is no magic prayer that you have to pray to call out to God for salvation. A simple prayer recognizing yourself as a sinner and the desire to receive God's forgiveness through His Son Jesus alone and His finished work on the cross will save you. Call out to Him today!

If you have accepted Jesus as your Lord and personal Savior, find a good Bible-believing, Bible-teaching church and get involved. There you will find, through the teaching of the Word, the offering of praise and worship in song and the fellowship of the saints the tools needed to grow in your faith. Get a Bible and read it, study it, memorize it and treasure it. If you find the right church you will feel uncomfortable without it.

For those who have been in the faith for some time, I pray that this study has been an encouragement and blessing to you. May we keep the focus of our lives not on our careers, our possessions, our families or anything else, but on obeying and honoring our loving, Lord Jesus, seeking His wisdom every day of our lives. He is worthy of all our worship, all our praise and all our life. May we be recommitted to giving our lives as a living sacrifice for the cause of our great God and Savior the Lord Jesus Christ. After all, it is reasonable, an act of service and an act of worship. When we consider what He has done for us, is it too much to ask?:

'And so, dear brothers and sisters, I plead with you to give your bodies to God. Let them be a living and holy sacrifice -- the kind he will accept. When you think of what he has done for you, is this too much to ask?'
(Romans 12:1 NLT)

ABOUT THE AUTHOR

Matthew Eckel has a Master of Arts in Theological Studies from Liberty Baptist Theological Seminary, Lynchburg, VA. He is currently the Associate Pastor of the Central Bible Church, Clinton Township, MI. He currently resides in Sterling Heights, MI with my wife Jackie. Together they have four children: Amanda, Brett (*married to Gina*), Luke and Kami. Matt is Papa to their six grandchildren: Avery, Victor, Anthony, Calvin, Ezekiel and Elise.

Other paperbacks available through Amazon:

SATURDAYS IN PSALMS

Made in the USA
Middletown, DE
29 December 2023

46968473R00195